Reading and Writing Short Essays

Second Edition

Reading and Writing Short Essays

Second Edition

MORTON A. MILLER

Advisory Editor

Richard L. Larson
Herbert H. Lehman College,
City University of New York

RANDOM HOUSE
New York

In Memoriam
Jonathan Farrington Miller
1946–1972

Second Edition

9 8 7 6 5 4 3

Copyright © 1980, 1983 by Random House, Inc.

Library of Congress Cataloging in Publication Data

Main entry under title:

Reading and writing short essays.

Includes index.
1. College readers.   2. English language—
Rhetoric.   I. Miller, Morton A., 1914–
PE1417.R37 1982   808'.0427   82–13220
ISBN 0-394-33009-9

Manufactured in the United States of America

Cover design by Sirow Design.

Preface

THE second edition of *Reading and Writing Short Essays*, like its predecessor, attempts to help college students become more proficient readers and more accomplished writers. It retains those components that teachers using the first edition found successful in their classes: a broad range of material rhetorically organized; comprehensive introductions; short nonfiction prose chosen for ease of reading and comprehension; and exercises containing questions on reading and writing that encourage students to ascertain precisely what writers say as well as how they put their ideas into words. But the book has been changed to incorporate as many as practicable of the welcome recommendations of its users and to make it more effective as a teaching tool:

1. The mix of authors has been changed to increase the ratio of contemporary to classic essayists.

2. The subject matter of the essays has been updated by incorporating a greater proportion of present-day authors writing on current topics.

3. In the questions that follow each selection, more space has been assigned to methods of encouraging students to read more perceptively, most notably in the third group, "For Discussion, Reading, and Writing."

4. Greater emphasis has been placed, in questions and writing suggestions, on writing as process.

5. The space formerly assigned to a part on style has been given to a section on division and classification.

Although the arrangement in the first edition of the book's parts and of the sections within them seemed to me a good one, teachers reported that they rearranged the book's contents in different ways. Since its six parts and eighteen sections are self-contained units and there are ample selections in each, *Reading and Writing Short Essays* remains adaptable to the tastes and preferences of the teachers who use it and to the needs of their students.

I am grateful to the many persons whose useful suggestions helped shape this new edition, among them Santi Buscemi, Middlesex County College; Paul Cioe, Western Illinois University; John Dick, University of Texas, El Paso; Alice Heim, Bowling Green University; Robert Logan, University of Hartford; Marilyn Maxwell, Massasoit Community College; Fred Moramurco, San Diego State University; Hilda Norton, Jacksonville State University; Amy Richards, Wayne State University; William Stuhl, University of Hartford; and James Tee, North Texas State University.

I acknowledge, too, the recommendations of Richard L. Larson; the cooperation of the College Department of Random House, especially that of Steve Pensinger and Fred Burns, and of Sean Devlin, who copyedited the manuscript for this edition; and also the faith and support of Anne E. Miller.

MORTON A. MILLER

Contents

Sentences   *50*

Words   *74*

3. Sources of Material   *103*

Personal Experiences   *104*

Observation   *116*

Diaries and Journals   *134*

Reading and Interviews   *145*

4. Types of Essays 167

Narration 168

Description 193

Exposition 213

5. Patterns of Organization 235

Illustration 236

Comparison and Contrast 258

Definition   276

Division and Classification   301

Process   323

Causal Analysis   342

Argumentation   366

Glossary   385

Index of Terms, Authors, and Titles   391

Thematic Table of Contents

Growing Up

The Human Condition

Nature and the Outdoors

People

Social Issues

Sports

Values

Women in America

Work

Writing

1

The Essay: Thesis

AN essay is a short composition in prose that discusses a subject limited in scope. The degree of limitation will depend on the length of the essay. In an essay of from five hundred to one thousand words —such as you are likely to be called upon to write in your course in composition—you would not be able to treat adequately a broad subject such as weather, sailing, or architecture. But you could, in a short essay, do justice to limited or specific parts of those subjects:

The Cause of Hail; or, What Is a Thunderstorm?

The Difference Between a Catboat and a Sloop; or, How to Sail Against the Wind

The Purpose of the Flying Buttress; or, Why the Leaning Tower of Pisa Leans

To a subject sufficiently restricted for you to be able to explain it to your reader in a short essay we will apply the term *topic*.

When it is up to you to choose a topic, first choose a subject that appeals to you—for example, the energy crisis. Then, since the subject is vast, too large to be covered adequately in a short composition, limit it progressively, as follows:

Energy

Sources of Energy

Wind as a Source of Energy

How a Windmill Works

The Windmill on My Grandfather's Farm

This list of possible topics ranges from the most general to the most specific. Unless you have done so at the outset, your aim will be to pick a topic that is sufficiently limited for you to be able to discuss it in a short essay to the extent necessary to explain it to your reader. A diagram of the process of limiting a subject would resemble a triangle balancing on one of its points.

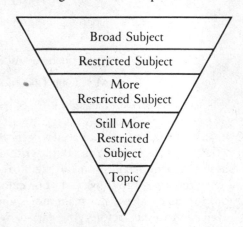

Broad Subject

Restricted Subject

More Restricted Subject

Still More Restricted Subject

Topic

Preferable, among the subjects you might select, are ones that you already know something about. In your personal experiences and observations, as well as in your reading, you will find ample material for intelligible short essays on a variety of topics. (I will discuss these and other sources of the writer's materials in Part Three.) If your broad subject is education, you might already know enough to write a short essay on topics such as

The Advantages of a Small College

The Importance of Learning a Foreign Language

A Proposal for Greater Freedom in Choosing Courses in
   College

Why I Chose to Attend a Two- Instead of a Four-Year
   College

Professor Jones, the Best Teacher I Ever Had

If necessary, you can supplement your knowledge of your topic
with, for example, research in a library.
   Here are other examples of broad and restricted subjects:

Broad Subject	*Restricted Subject*
Vacations	My Trip to Aruba and Back on an Oil Tanker
College Sports	Coaching an Intramural Softball Team
Television	The Humor of *All in the Family*
Hobbies	My Stamp Collection
Cooking	Baking a Pie

Whereas the subjects in the first column are too general for a short
essay, those in the second are not. You could write about any of
them briefly but in sufficient detail to explain them to your readers.
   After you have restricted the subject of your composition, gather information, formulate ideas, and make notes about the relevant material available to you—before you start to write the first
draft of your essay. Your notes might be complete sentences or
merely phrases or single words. On the topic "My Trip to Aruba
and back on an Oil Tanker," you might jot down

> Harbor pilot. Navigational aids. Steering a big ship. Changes in the
> weather between New York and Aruba. A storm at sea. Thoughts
> on sighting land (Hispaniola) after five days at sea. Dolphins. Fly-
> ing fish. The first mate lets me take the wheel of the ship in Mona
> Passage (between Hispaniola and Puerto Rico). Arrival in Aruba.
> Water ballast pumped out. Oil pumped in. Vessel turned around
> and on way back north (to Boston) with full tanks. Hull low in

the sea; decks barely above water. The ship's crew: friendly; make me feel at home.

When you have finished your jottings, you might find that you have more than enough material for a short essay. Your next steps would be to mull over and evaluate your ideas and then to restrict your subject still more by deciding on what part of your jottings you will focus. Let's assume that the essay about the trip to Aruba will flesh out the idea in the last note: "The ship's crew: friendly; make me feel at home." You would then jot down specific details relating to this idea, for example:

All-Italian crew. Only the captain and second mate speak English. We communicate with the help of an Italian-English dictionary. Also hand signs. Body communication? I'm invited to eat in the officers' mess. Entire crew considerate of me, the only woman on board. Played checkers with Aldo Barzolo, a Florentine, chief engineer; chess with Luigi Covici, steward, who is from Lerici on the Gulf of La Spezia. He tells me Shelley's last home still stands there. On its façade is a plaque with his words (in Italian): "Oh, bless the beaches where love, liberty, and dreams have not chains." Romanticism. Shades of Lit. 134. Exchanged addresses with crew members. Will we ever write to one another? Meet again? I have the run of the wheelhouse. First mate Enzo Finardi shows me how radar works; how to use loran to locate our position; how to read charts. Helmsman Alfredo Bettolucci lets me take a turn at the wheel.

These specific details will need to be winnowed until you find among them an idea you can focus on, relate other information to, and make the main idea of your essay.

Sometimes the main idea that you ultimately focus on will not be evident at the outset, but will become clear to you as you write the first draft of your essay. Generally, but not always, you will be able to express that idea explicitly in a single sentence. Such a statement is called a *thesis*. Often, but not always, it sums up an essay's content. A thesis for an essay about the trip to Aruba might be: "The best part of my trip to Aruba on an oil tanker was making friends with the ship's crew."

Sometimes you will find when you read your first draft that parts of what you have written do not relate to your thesis or that what appeared to be the expression of your main idea is not so. You could correct these defects in a second draft by cutting out the irrelevant material or by writing a new thesis statement that does express what you discover the main idea of your essay to be.

Jottings about the other topics just presented might yield thesis statements such as these:

> Coaching an intramural softball team last term taught me that teamwork is more important to winning than is individual athletic ability.

> Much of the humor in *All in the Family* stems from Archie Bunker's misuse of language.

> Buying commemorative issues is an easy way to start a stamp collection.

> The key element of a pie is the pie crust.

A thesis may be stated anywhere in an essay: its beginning, middle, or end. A writer may want to delay stating it because its meaning might be clearer to the reader after other material has been presented. Or a writer may choose to place the thesis in the middle or, to give it greater emphasis, at the end. But, more often than not, you will find that the best place to state a thesis is in the first paragraph, as in the first of the following examples, or soon thereafter, as in the second (the thesis statements are in italics):

> Next to Gerald Ford and Leonid Brezhnev, the most powerful man in the world is not Mao Tse-tung or the head of any other government. *The third most powerful man in the world is a commander of a* Trident *submarine* [Norman Cousins, "The Third Most Powerful Man in the World"].

> How many women do you know who can take home seventy thousand dollars a year? A psychiatrist might take home half of that. A Congresswoman? Shirley Chisholm's salary is forty-two-five.
> *No, the quickest way for a woman to get ahead in this country is to*

take up the oldest profession: prostitution [Gail Sheehy, "$70,000 a Year, Tax Free"].

The reason for placing a thesis in the first paragraph of an essay or as soon after it as possible is that the sooner you state it the more likely you are to remain aware of your main idea and the less likely you are to wander from that idea as you write.

Sometimes the main idea of an essay is not stated. Instead of making the thesis *explicit*, expressed in so many words, a writer may leave it *implied*, that is, suggested by the essay's contents. Whether explicit or implied, the thesis will help you to keep in mind your restriction of the broad subject, to avoid digressive information and ideas, and to focus on relevant material to explain and develop your essay's main idea.

There are three requirements for a good thesis:

1. *The thesis must be restricted.* It must limit the range of a subject to what the writer can discuss in adequate detail in an essay of a given length. Thus "restricted" is a relative term. For a short essay to be written in your composition course, this thesis would not be sufficiently restricted:

Learning how to write well is essential for success.

But this thesis would be:

Learning how to write clearly is essential for achieving high grades in college courses in the humanities.

2. *The thesis must be unified.* It must state a single main idea:

Learning how to write well, to think clearly, and to study efficiently are essential for success in college.

This statement, although in three parts, enumerates the ingredients for "success in college," the one main idea of a proposed essay. Thus it is a unified thesis. Nonetheless, a student writing a short essay would do well to consider limiting it to a discussion of just one of the three ingredients because an essay of about five hundred words, for example, might not permit adequate explanation of all three.

The difference between unity and restriction is this: *unity* limits the number of main ideas—in a short essay, to one; *restriction* limits the scope of that single idea.

3. *The thesis must be precise.* The thesis

> Learning how to write well is a wonderful idea for success in college.

is not precise because "wonderful idea," being vague, can have more than one meaning. (For a discussion of vague words, see "Ambiguous and Vague Words," pages 75–76.)

Now let's apply these criteria to this thesis:

> Ronald Reagan's choice of cabinet members, his legislative programs, and his handling of foreign affairs show that he is a terrific President.

This statement is unified because it has a single main idea, Mr. Reagan's achievements. Nevertheless, it does not sufficiently restrict the subject of his accomplishments as President to a topic that could be discussed in adequate detail in a short essay. It commits the writer to discuss many, perhaps all, of Mr. Reagan's cabinet appointees; to write about some, if not many, of his legislative proposals; and to evaluate his dealings with two or more nations or groups of nations. Moreover, since "terrific" is vague, the thesis is not precise.

Compare it with this thesis:

> Ronald Reagan's choice of George Bush as his vice-president is sound.

This statement fulfills the requirements of a good thesis for a short essay: It is unified; it is restricted; and it is precise because there are criteria for evaluating Mr. Reagan's choice of vice-president. The thesis could be improved, however, by adding "because" and the reason for the writer's judgment of Mr. Bush:

Ronald Reagan's choice of George Bush as his vice-president is
sound because Mr. Bush is well trained in government.

This statement, in addition to being a good thesis, clearly establishes the single direction its essay must take: a discussion of Mr.
Bush's training in government.

A good thesis is to the writer what a compass is to a navigator:
It establishes and helps maintain direction. In addition, by stating
the limits of a topic it helps the writer to keep in mind the essay's
main idea.

If, in an essay on highway safety, you were to include material
on rural roads, jaywalking in cities, and riding a bicycle with no
hands, you would end up with an essay lacking unity. To include
this material would be to stray from your essay's main idea: *highway* safety. A good thesis, by pointing to the direction your essay
should take—and maintain—will help you to avoid this defect.

TEENAGER'S PRIVACY
Haim G. Ginott

Haim G. Ginott (1922–1973) wrote the definitive
Group Psychotherapy for Children (1961) and popular
books such as **Between Parent and Teenager** (1969),
which is based on his extensive experience in child psychotherapy
and parental guidance. It is the source of this passage.

1   Teenagers need privacy; it allows them to have a life of their
own. By providing privacy, we demonstrate respect. We help them
disengage themselves from us and grow up. Some parents pry too
much. They read their teenagers' mail and listen in on their tele-

From "Don't Violate His Privacy," in *Between Parent and Teenager* by Haim G.
Ginott (New York: Macmillan, 1969), pp. 39–41. Reprinted by permission of Dr.
Alice Ginott.

phone calls. Such violations may cause permanent resentment. Teenagers feel cheated and enraged. In their eyes, invasion of privacy is a dishonorable offense. As one girl said: "I am going to sue my mother for malpractice of parenthood. She unlocked my desk and read my diary."

₂   One sixteen-year-old boy complained: "My mother has no respect for me. She invades my privacy and violates my civil rights. She comes into my room and rearranges my drawers. She can't stand disorder, she says. I wish she'd tidy up her own room and leave mine alone. I deliberately mess up my desk as soon as she cleans it up. But mother never learns."

₃   Some teenagers complain that their parents participate too eagerly in their social life.

₄   Bernice, age seventeen, speaks with bitterness: "My mother dresses up before my date arrives. She gossips with him while I'm getting ready. She even walks down with us to the car. When I return, I find her waiting for me, bursting with curiosity. She wants to know everything. What did he say? What did I answer? How did I feel? How much money did he spend? What are my future plans? My life is an open book; every page is a public announcement. My mother tries to be a pal. I don't want to hurt her feelings but I don't need a forty-year-old pal. I'd rather have some privacy."

₅   Respect for privacy requires distance which parents find hard to maintain. They want closeness and fraternization. For all their good will, they intrude and invade. Such familiarity does not breed mutual esteem. For respect to flourish, parents and teenagers must keep some distance. They can "Stand together yet not too near together." Respect encompasses an awareness of our teenager as a distinct and unique individual, a person apart from us. In the last analysis, neither parent nor teenager "belongs" to the other. Each belongs to himself.

Questions About "The Essay: Thesis"

1. Where does Ginott express the main idea of this essay?

2. Explain whether in his thesis he states precisely one restricted idea.

3. How does his thesis determine the content of the essay?

4. Does Ginott, at any time, digress from his subject? Explain.

Questions on Diction and Writing Techniques

1. Reporting in the third person instead of using dialogue, rewrite the last sentence of paragraph 1. Which version of the sentence do you prefer? Why? What is the writer's purpose in quoting the teenagers directly?

2. Ginott introduces the first quotation with "said" (par. 1). What is his purpose in introducing the second with "complained" (par. 2) and the third with "speaks with bitterness" (par. 4)?

3. Explain whether he cites sufficient evidence of "invasion of privacy" to convince you that "Some parents pry too much" (par. 1).

4. Whom did Ginott have in mind as his readers when he wrote this essay—child psychologists or the general public? What clues do you find in the essay to help you arrive at your conclusion? What changes might Ginott have made had he written for a different audience?

For Discussion, Reading, and Writing

1. Which of these statements, according to Ginott, is true (T), which false (F)?

   A. _____ By providing privacy for teenagers, parents demonstrate their own maturity.

   B. _____ Teenagers should have an equal right to open parents' mail and to listen in on telephone calls.

   C. _____ One sixteen-year-old boy complained that his mother rewrote his homework.

   D. _____ For all their good will, parents intrude and invade.

   E. _____ Neither parent nor teenager belongs to the other.

2. The media have reported instances of children suing parents for malpractice. Should the courts permit such lawsuits?

3. Write a short essay about teenagers, using as much material as possible from your own experience and that of friends. In limiting the subject, you may find it useful to focus on and perhaps to further restrict one of the points in this passage from John E. Horrocks' *The Psychology of Adolescence* (2nd ed.):

> In Western culture there are five points of reference from which to view adolescent growth and development:
> 1. It is a time of physical development and growth.
> 2. It is a time when group relations become of major importance.
> 3. Adolescence is a time of seeking status as an individual.
> 4. It is a time of intellectual expansion, development, and academic experience.
> 5. It is a time of development and evaluation of values.

PAINFUL CHOICE
Maeve Brennan

Maeve Brennan is a short-story writer and a frequent contributor of nonfiction prose—such as this succinct one-paragraph essay— to **The New Yorker** magazine, among whose writers have been America's greatest prose stylists, essayists like James Thurber and E. B. White.

I was in a new small supermarket the other evening, waiting to have my things put in a bag, when I saw a shabby tall man with red eyes, who had obviously been drinking heavily since the cradle, trying to decide between a can of beans, a canned whole dinner, a canned soup, and a canned chicken à la king. He had thirty-seven cents or twenty-nine cents or some sum like that, and he was standing there with the four cans, glaring down at them and all around at the stalls of vegetables and fruit and bread and so on. He couldn't make up his mind what to buy to feed himself with, and it was plain that what he really wanted wasn't food at all. I was thinking I wouldn't blame him a bit if he just put the cans back on their shelves, or dropped them on the floor, and dashed into the bar-and-grill next door, where he could simply ask for a beer and drink it. Later on, it occurred to me that, putting it roughly, there is usually only one thing we yearn to do that's bad for us, while if we try to make the effort to do a virtuous or good thing, the choice is so great and wide that we're really worn out before we can settle on what to do. I mean to say that the impulse toward good involves choice, and is complicated, and the impulse toward bad is hideously simple and easy, and I feel sorry for that poor tall red-eyed man.

Questions About "The Essay: Thesis"

1. What is Brennan's purpose in telling the anecdote of the man in the supermarket?

2. What is the thesis of the paragraph?

3. Why did Brennan place the thesis where she did?

4. Comment on whether the writing would be as, more, or less effective if Brennan had placed the thesis elsewhere in her essay.

Questions on Diction and Writing Techniques

1. List the details the writer chooses to portray the man.

2. Explain whether Brennan might properly have divided her essay into two paragraphs, and thus have made it easier to read and to understand.

For Discussion, Reading, and Writing

1. Using Brennan's strategy, write a one-paragraph piece based on your observations of anyone anywhere, concluding it with an appropriate generalization that is your essay's thesis.

2. Observe the behavior of people in a supermarket, making notes as you do. Then write a one-paragraph essay about the behavior of one of them—at the deli counter, the fruit and vegetable section, the check-out counters, or anywhere else—that, with appropriate details, illustrates a thesis reflecting on human beings or their behavior.

KILLING THE THING ONE LOVES
Noel Perrin

Noel Perrin is a professor of English at Dartmouth College and also a writer and sometime farmer.

Each man kills the thing he loves, Oscar Wilde wrote in a poem that later became a popular song. As a general statement, this won't do. Lincoln didn't kill the Union; lots of men don't kill their wives; so far from killing the ERA, Betty Friedan and Kate Millett have worked hard to keep it alive.

But practically all tourists and most people who move to the country do kill the thing they love. They don't mean to—they may not even realize they have done it—but they still kill it.

The tourist does it simply by being a tourist. What he loves is foreignness, difference, the exotic. So he goes in search of it—and, of course, brings himself along. The next thing you know there's a Holiday Inn in Munich.

The case with people who move to the country is more complicated. What they bring along is a series of unconscious assumptions. It might be better for rural America if they brought a few sticks of dynamite, or a can of arsenic.

Take a typical example. Mr. and Mrs. Nice are Bostonians. They live a couple of miles off Route 128 in a four-bedroom house. He's a partner in an ad agency; she has considerable talent as an artist. For some years they've had a second home in northern New Hampshire. The kids love it up there in Grafton County.

For some years, too, both Nices have been feeling they'd like to simplify their lives. They look with increasing envy on their New Hampshire neighbors, who never face a morning traffic jam, or an evening one, either; who don't have a long drive to the country on Friday night and a long drive back on Sunday; who aren't cramped into a suburban lot; who live in harmony with the natural rhythm of the year; who think the rat race is probably some kind of minor event at a country fair.

One Thursday evening Don Nice says to Sue that he's been talking to the other partners, and they've agreed there's no reason he can't do some of his work at home. If he's in the office Wednesday and Thursday every week, why the rest of the time he can stay in touch by telephone. Sue, who has been trapped all year as a Brownie Scout leader and who has recently had the aerial snapped off her car in Boston, is delighted. She reflects happily that in their little mountain village you don't even need to lock your house, and there *is* no Brownie troop. "You're wonderful," she tells Don.

So the move occurs. In most ways Don and Sue are very happy. They raise practically all their own vegetables the first year; Sue takes up cross-country skiing; Don personally splits some of the wood they burn in their new wood stove.

But there are some problems. The first one Sue is conscious of is the school. It's just not very good. It's clear to Sue almost immediately that the town desperately needs a new school building—and also modern playground equipment, new school buses, more and better art instruction at the high school, a different principal. Don is as upset as Sue when they discover that only about forty percent of the kids who graduate from that high school go on to any form of college. The rest do native things, like becoming farmers and mechanics, and joining the Air Force. An appalling number of the girls marry within twelve months after graduation. How are Jeanie and Don, Jr., going to get into good colleges from this school?

Pretty soon Sue and Don join an informal group of newcomers in town who are working to upgrade education. All they want for starters is the new building (2.8 million dollars) and a majority of their kind on the school board.

As for Don, though he really enjoys splitting the wood—in fact, next year he's planning to get a chainsaw and start cutting a few trees of his own—he also does like to play golf. There's no course within twenty miles. Some of the nice people he's met in the education lobby feel just as he does. They begin to discuss the possibility of a nine-hole course. The old native who owns the land they have in mind seems to be keeping only four or five cows on it, anyway. Besides, taxes are going up and the old fellow is going to have to sell, sooner or later. (Which is too bad, of course. Don and Sue both admire the local farmers, and they're sincerely sorry whenever one has to quit.)

Over the next several years, Don and Sue get more and more adjusted to rural living—and they also gradually discover more things that need changing. For example, the area needs a good French restaurant. And it needs a *much* better airport. At present there are only two flights a day to Boston, and because of the lack of sophisticated equipment, even they are quite often canceled. If Don wants to be really sure of getting down for an important meeting, he has to drive. Sue would be glad of more organized activities for the kids. There's even talk of starting a Brownie troop.

In short, if enough upper-middle-class people move to a rural town, they are naturally going to turn it into a suburb of the nearest city. For one generation it will be a very nice and a very rustic suburb, with real farms dotted around it, and real natives speaking their minds at town meeting. Then as the local people are gradually taxed out of existence (or at least out of town), one more piece of rural America has died.

Questions About "The Essay: Thesis"

1. Is Perrin's main idea expressed or implied? If it is expressed, say where. If it is implied, state it in your own words.

2. Does Perrin, anywhere in this essay, digress from its main idea? Explain.

3. Explain whether the essay is unified.

Questions on Diction and Writing Techniques

1. What is the tone of this essay? Where does Perrin first reveal this to you? What other evidence do you find to support your answer?

2. Does Perrin's "typical example," Mr. and Mrs. Nice, support his thesis? Explain.

For Discussion, Reading, and Writing

1. Why did Mr. and Mrs. Nice want to move to the country?

2. What problems do they discover in the country?

3. What things do they gradually discover need changing?

THE STUDENT ATHLETE
Red Smith

Red Smith (1905–1982), an American sports writer, regularly contributed articles on sports to **The New York Times**.

1　　Some edifying words about student athletes were heard on the air over the weekend. Whenever a college football game is on radio

From "The Student Athlete," © 1979 by The New York Times Company. Reprinted by permission.

or television, it is accompanied by edifying words about student
athletes, about the importance of intercollegiate athletics in a
rounded educational program and about the vital role played by the
National Collegiate Athletic Association. The edifying words are
composed by writers for the N.C.A.A.

2   Student athlete is a term susceptible to various definitions. It
can mean a biochemistry major who participates in sports, or a
Heisman Trophy candidate who is not necessarily a candidate for a
bachelor's degree. Some student athletes are more studious than
athletic, and vice versa.

3   There is at hand a piece written by a student athlete in his
senior year at a major university that has been polishing young in-
tellects for more than a century. He is an attractive young man,
short months away from graduation, the best wide receiver in the
school. One of his professors, who happens to be a football buff,
asked him why his teammate, John Doe, never played first string although he was a better passer than Richard Spelvin, the starting
quarterback. The young man said he would write the answer "like
it was a quiz."

4   What follows is an exact copy of the young man's answer.
That is, it is exact except for the names. The quarterbacks are not
really named John Doe and Richard Spelvin and the university's
athletic teams are not known as the Yankees.

5   "People (Some) feel that Doe did not have the ability to run
the type of offense that the yankys ran. He also made some mistakes with the ball like fumbling.

6   "As a wide receiver it didnt make me any different who quarterback. But I feel he has the best arm I ever saw or play with on a team.
Only why I feel the I do about the quarterback position is because I
am a receiver who came from J.C. out of state I caught a lot of pass
over 80 and I did not care a damn thing but about 24 in one year.

7   "Spelvin is my best friend and quarterback at my J.C. school.
Spelvin has an arm but when you don't thrown lot of half the time I
dont care who you are you will not perform as best you can. Spelvin
can run, run the team and most of all he makes little mistakes.

8   "So since they didn't pass Spelvin was our quarterback. But if
we did pass I feel Spelvin still should of start but Doe should have
play a lot. Tell you the truth the yanky's in the pass two years had
the best combintion of receivers in a season that they will ever

have. More—ask to talk about politics alum Doe problems just before the season coaches hate?"

9   The last appears to be a suggestion that alumni politics may have played a part in the coaches' decision on which quarterback would play first string. However, the professor who forwarded this material did so without comment or explanation.

10   The importance of disguising the names of these student athletes and the identity of the university is obvious. It would be unforgivable to hold a kid up to public ridicule because his grip on a flying football was surer than his grasp of the mother tongue. He is only a victim. The culprit is the college, and the system.

11   The young man's prose makes it achingly clear how some institutions of learning use some athletes. Recruiters besiege a high school senior with bulging muscles and sloping neck who can run 40 yards in 4.3 seconds. The fact that he cannot read without facial contortions may be regrettable, but if his presence would help make a team a winner, then they want his body and are not deeply concerned about his mind.

12   Some colleges recruit scholar athletes in the hope that the scholar can spare enough time from the classroom to help the team. Others recruit athletes and permit them to attend class if they can spare the time from the playing field. If the boy was unprepared for college when he arrived, he will be unqualified for a degree four years later, but some culture foundries give him a degree as final payment for his services.

13   One widely accepted definition of the role of a college is "to prepare the student for life after he leaves the campus." If the young man quoted above gets a job as a wide receiver for the Green Bay Packers, then perhaps the university will have fulfilled its purpose. However, only a fraction of college players can make a living in the National Football League. Opportunities are even more limited for college basketball players, for pro basketball employs fewer players.

14   Where outside of pro football can our wide receiver go? He can pump gas. He can drive a truck. He has seen his name in headlines, has heard crowds cheering him, has enjoyed the friendship and admiration of his peers and he has a diploma from a famous university. It is unconscionable.

Questions About "The Essay: Thesis"

1. What is the general subject of this essay?

2. Reread the essay and mark the place where Smith first gave you an inkling of its thesis.

3. What is Smith's thesis? Is it expressed or implied? If expressed, underline it. If implied, express it in your own words.

4. Is the thesis sufficiently restricted for a short essay? Explain.

5. Explain whether Smith digresses anywhere in the essay from its main idea.

Questions on Diction and Writing Techniques

1. Mark in your text all words in this essay that, though new to you, you understood from their context. Define them in your own words. Compare your definitions with those in your dictionary. Look up in your dictionary all other words that are new to you. Use the words in both groups in sentences.

2. How many times, in paragraph 1, does Smith use "edifying"? What is his purpose in repeating the word?

3. What word(s) might Smith have used instead of "polishing" (par. 3)? Why did he choose the verb he did? Find, in paragraph 12, a phrase or phrases that Smith chose for the same reason.

4. What is Smith's purpose in writing, and the effect on you of reading, the student athlete's answer to the professor's question?

5. What is Smith's purpose in asking the question in the last paragraph?

For Discussion, Reading, and Writing

1. This essay is mainly about (circle one):

   A. College athletes who play football well but who write poorly.

B. Colleges that fail to properly prepare student athletes for a degree.

C. The graduation from college of student athletes who are unqualified for a degree.

D. The victimization of students by their colleges.

E. "Where outside of pro football can the wide receiver go?"

2. Who does Smith blame for the state of affairs he writes about? Do you agree with him? Why or why not?

3. Write a short essay in which you explain why preference in college admissions should, or should not, be given to applicants who excel in sports in high school. If your thesis is stated explicitly, underline it. If it is implied, state it in a sentence of not over twenty-five words.

2

Units of Composition

Paragraphs

THE paragraph is the largest unit of composition that you will use to express your ideas when writing. It is a unit designed to divide longer writing into more readily readable and understood sections. Its length, structure, and density—the amount of information it contains—may be varied to suit the intended audience and the function the writer wants it to perform, especially as the beginning, part of the middle portion, or the end of an essay.

The basic paragraph is like an essay, and like an essay, it should be unified. Also, it should be complete and be developed in an orderly manner. And, just as in an essay there should be smooth transitions between paragraphs, so in a paragraph there should be smooth transitions between sentences.

Unity: The Topic Sentence

By unity in a paragraph, teachers of composition mean consistency of content. All the sentences in a paragraph must discuss one topic only—one restricted subject—and they must relate to one another, as they do in this example:

> Spain is the stronghold of the vultures. There are four listed species in Europe, two common and two rare; if they are anywhere, they are in Spain. The bearded vulture and the black survive there, the Egyptian flourishes, and the great griffon swarms. The further south you go the more numerous they become, until you reach the hot grazing plains of Andalusia. There, summer and winter through, they hang in hordes in the roofless sky, for Andalusia is the vulture country [John D. Stewart, "Vulture Country"].

The sentences must, without deviating from this objective, develop the main idea of the paragraph, the idea that the paragraph is all about, the one point that the paragraph makes.

The easiest way to assure the unity of a paragraph is to announce its main idea in a sentence, which, because it states the paragraph's topic, is called a *topic sentence*. In this example the topic sentence is in italics:

> *Each man had, to begin with, the great virtue of utter tenacity and fidelity.* Grant fought his way down the Mississippi Valley in spite of acute personal discouragement and profound military handicaps. Lee hung on in the trenches at Petersburg after hope itself had died. In each man there was an indomitable quality . . . the born fighter's refusal to give up as long as he can still remain on his feet and lift his two fists [Bruce Catton, "Grant and Lee: A Study in Contrasts"].

A topic sentence is to a paragraph what a thesis is to an essay. A topic sentence helps the writer to keep the main idea of the paragraph in mind while writing, to focus on it, to control it. It helps the writer to avoid sentences that would be extraneous—that would stray from the paragraph's main idea and thus destroy its unity.

A topic sentence is like a promise. In it the writer in effect says to the reader, "This is what I promise to explain to you in my paragraph." Readers have the right to expect that you will fulfill your promise. Having taken you at your word, they are sure to be disappointed if you don't. It is thus foolish to promise more than you can deliver. Accordingly, avoid making too broad a statement in a topic sentence if limited knowledge of the subject or the limitation of space will prevent you from giving your reader the information needed to prove it valid.

Like an arrow on the road sign that directs the traveler, a topic sentence points out to the writer the direction a paragraph should take. Thus, the sooner the topic sentence is presented, the sooner will the writer see what information is needed to develop it. This is not an unalterable rule, however. The topic sentence may be put anywhere in a paragraph: at its beginning, end, or in between.

Often it is more effective not to make the topic sentence the paragraph's first sentence. Preliminary information might clarify its meaning, or placement at or near the end of the paragraph may give it greater emphasis, as in this example (topic sentence in italics).

If Man has benefited immeasurably by his association with the dog, what, you may ask, has the dog got out of it? His scroll has, of course, been heavily charged with punishments: he has known the muzzle, the leash, and the tether; he has suffered the indignities of the show bench, the tin can on the tail, the ribbon in the hair; his love life with the other sex of his species has been regulated by the frigid hand of authority, his digestion ruined by the macaroons and marshmallows of doting women. *The list of his woes could be continued indefinitely.* But he has also had his fun, for he has been privileged to live with and study at close range the only creature with reason, the most unreasonable of creatures [James Thurber, *Thurber's Dogs*].

Sometimes an author will not write a topic sentence at all. The main idea will not be expressed in so many words but will, nonetheless, be clear to the reader from the content of the paragraph. In this instance, we say that the paragraph's main idea is *implied.* Such a paragraph — lacking the signpost we mentioned — is more difficult to write than one where the topic sentence explicitly states the paragraph's main idea.

Often, when beginning a paragraph, a writer may not be aware of all that might be said in it and thus may not be able to state its main idea accurately at first. As the writing proceeds, the author may be expressing various unrelated ideas that come to mind. This is not unusual in a first draft. In the course of writing, the writer will realize what the main idea is to be and can then compose a suitable topic sentence and, by rewriting the paragraph, can eliminate the extraneous material.

Finally, there are instances where a single topic sentence may serve more than one paragraph. This will be the case where two or more consecutive paragraphs form a unit with a single main idea.

Coherence: Smooth Sentence Flow

In addition to being unified, a paragraph should be coherent. "To cohere" means to stick together. To be coherent, a paragraph must have a smooth sentence flow. One sentence should lead easily to the next, requiring a minimum of effort from the reader. The function of coherence is to interrelate the ideas in a paragraph or essay; its effect is to make their meaning intelligible.

Here is an example of a coherent paragraph (italics added). A reading of this paragraph with and without the italicized words will demonstrate the function and effect of coherence.

> *When* the grave is finished, the wasp returns to the tarantula to complete her ghastly enterprise. *First* she feels it all over once more with her antennae. *Then* her behavior becomes more aggressive. She bends her abdomen, protruding her sting, and searches for the soft membrane at the point where the spider's leg joins its body—the only spot where she can penetrate the horny skeleton. *From time to time*, as the exasperated spider slowly shifts ground, the wasp turns on her back and slides along with the aid of her wings, trying to get under the tarantula for a shot at the vital spot. *During all this maneuvering*, which can last for several minutes, the tarantula makes no move to save itself. *Finally* the wasp corners it against some obstruction and grasps one of its legs in her powerful jaws. *Now at last* the harassed spider tries a desperate but vain defense. The two contestants roll over and over on the ground. It is a terrifying sight and the outcome is always the same. The wasp *finally* manages to thrust her sting into the soft spot and holds it there *for a few seconds* while she pumps in the

poison. *Almost immediately* the tarantula falls paralyzed on its back. Its legs stop twitching; its heart stops beating. *Yet* it is not dead, as is shown by the fact that if taken from the wasp it can be restored to some sensitivity by being kept in a moist chamber for several months [Alexander Petrunkivitch, "The Spider and the Wasp"].

One way to attain smooth connections between sentences, as this paragraph demonstrates, is to make the order in a sequence of actions or events clear to the reader by using temporal words—words like "before," "now," "after," "when," and "at the same time" (see page 33).

This paragraph illustrates the distinction between unity and coherence. All its sentences deal with a single topic: the wasp's method of attacking the tarantula; thus the paragraph is unified. It would be unified even if the italicized words were omitted. But in that case the sentences would not flow smoothly, and the paragraph would not be coherent. With them, the paragraph is both unified and coherent.

Completeness

In addition to being unified and coherent, a paragraph must be complete. Your response to a person who makes a statement without supporting it is likely to be doubt or disbelief. You are likely to and would have the right to say, "I'm not convinced." Similarly, your reader will be skeptical—and disappointed—if you neglect to develop sufficiently the main idea of a paragraph you write.

How much development is needed depends in part on the topic and in part on your reader. In general, the more complicated the topic and the more specialized is the knowledge required to understand it, the more extensive will the paragraph need to be. But even if the topic is simple, the writer must be sure to develop the topic sentence with sufficiently detailed information and ideas.

Completeness is a relative term. A paragraph is not necessarily complete because it is long. Nor is it necessarily incomplete because it is short. A paragraph is complete when it contains as much information as is needed to explain to its reader its main idea. The criterion of completeness is satisfied if the reader understands the paragraph's topic sentence or its implied central idea and accepts it as valid.

The paragraph just quoted, about the spider and the wasp, is relatively long and satisfies the criterion of completeness with its explanation of the wasp's "ghastly enterprise." From the same essay here is a relatively short paragraph, which is also complete (topic sentence in italics):

> In all this the behavior of the wasp evidently is qualitatively different from that of the spider. *The wasp acts like an intelligent animal.* This is not to say that instinct plays no part or that she reasons as man does. But her actions are to the point; they are not automatic and can be modified to fit the situation. We do not know for certain how she identifies the tarantula—probably it is by some olfactory or chemo-tactile sense—but she does it purposefully and does not blindly tackle a wrong species.

Special Paragraphs: Transitional, Introductory, Concluding

The purpose of the paragraphs discussed so far in this introduction is expository, that is, they explain the essay's subject or some portion of it. There are other kinds of paragraphs with different purposes: to *introduce,* to *conclude,* and to *serve as a transition between the parts of* an essay. We turn to the last of these first.

The *transitional paragraph* is a type that you will have occasion to use, especially in long essays. It is generally short, often only one sentence. A writer uses a transitional paragraph to inform readers that one section of an essay is completed and another is about to begin. Such a paragraph may summarize what has been written:

> In short, the defining characteristic of the valedictory address is its statement of the opposition between the university on one hand and the world on the other [Lionel Trilling, "A Valedictory"].

It may signal a change from general to more specific information:

> I am not talking pure theory. I will just give you two or three illustrations [Clarence Darrow, "Address to the Prisoners in the Cook Street Jail"].

It may hint at what is to come or announce the introduction of new material:

> Before the end of my trial period in the field I made two really exciting discoveries—discoveries that made the previous months of frustration well worth while [Jane van Lawick-Goodall, *In the Shadow of Man*].

> Looking back over my journal, I see that events of my first week in San Jose pretty much foreshadowed the shape of things to come [Jessica Mitford, "My Short and Happy Life as a Distinguished Professor"].

Or it may state explicitly what new material the writer is about to turn to:

> In what follows, the parallels are not always in physical events but rather in the effect on society, and sometimes in both [Barbara Tuchman, "History as Mirror"].

A transitional paragraph is a useful device for achieving coherence between paragraphs and groups of paragraphs:

> Certainly, there are additional liabilities, but those that I have indicated are a representative lot—perhaps the most serious ones. Let us turn now to the assets. What has technology done for the good life? [Stuart Chase, "Two Cheers for Technology"].

Note how, in this paragraph, the writer tries to connect—especially in sentence 2—his preceding paragraphs and the ones that are to follow.

You will be writing two other kinds of paragraph with special purposes: to introduce and to conclude an essay. You have seen examples of the former, by Norman Cousins and Gail Sheehy, on pages 6–7. The *introductory paragraph* has the distinctive purpose of engaging readers' attention.

The purposes of a *concluding paragraph* are to evaluate the rest of the essay, to summarize, or to draw a conclusion. Here are two examples of the third function:

I have written at such length about this problem because any attempt to describe the America of today must take into account the issue of racial equality, around which much of our thinking and our present-day attitudes turn. We will not have overcome the trauma that slavery has left on our society, North and South, until we cannot remember whether the man we just spoke to in the street was Negro or white [John Steinbeck, *America and Americans*].

It is not difficult to make a terrifying indictment of technology. It is not difficult to make a heartening list of benefits. The problem is so complex on one level, and yet, in essence, so simple. Granting the available resources of this planet, how many human beings and their fellow creatures can be supported at a level that makes life worth living? A dependable evaluation is very difficult. We can be sure, however, that nothing is to be gained by following the prophets of doom back to the Stone Age. [Stuart Chase, "Two Cheers for Technology"].

Analysis of the Paragraphs of a Sample Essay

To further illustrate what I have been saying about paragraphs, I will analyze a sample five-paragraph, seven-hundred-word essay, "Menial Jobs Taught Me a Lot," which begins:

1 When I graduated from high school I decided that, having spent fourteen years without interruption in grammar and secondary schools, I would take a year or two, perhaps more, away from school before going on to college. Now, after three years of nondescript jobs, I am convinced that my decision to take a long break between high school and college was wise. *From the menial jobs I had I learned a valuable lesson.*

   Here is an introductory paragraph—relatively short, as such a paragraph very often is—that attempts to engage the reader's attention. The writer, in addition to trying to induce his audience to read on, states the thesis of his essay (in italics).

Here is the second paragraph, the first of three paragraphs in the *body*, or middle section, of the essay:

2   I learned, first of all, that the jobs available to a teenager without special training do not pay well. Mowing lawns, my first job, paid $2.75 an hour. My second job, waiting on tables in a restaurant, paid, tips included, little more. Packaging groceries at the check-out counter of a supermarket paid somewhat less. Work on the production line of a hardware factory paid $3.00 an hour. My best-paying job, my last, was as a laborer on a construction project where my wages were $3.90 an hour.

Notice, first of all, that the second paragraph has a single main idea, expressed in a topic sentence: ". . . the jobs available to a teenager without special training do not pay well." Because the writer does not digress from this idea, the paragraph is unified. It contains ample evidence to convince us that indeed the jobs available to an unskilled worker do not pay well and is thus complete. It is developed in an orderly way, with the writer going from one job to another, beginning with his first and ending with his last. This development helps achieve coherence—smooth sentence flow—as does the repetition of the key word "paid." Finally, the use of "learned" in the first sentence helps to achieve coherence between the second paragraph and the opening paragraph, in whose last sentence the same word appears.

Here is the third paragraph:

3   More important, I found that my jobs, even if they weren't so at the outset, soon became boring. Take my last job, for example. The first thing each morning, I had to drive a truck to a supply depot to pick up odds and ends of building materials. Then, having driven back to the construction site, I had to unload them where they were needed. After that, I had to haul materials from one or another location on the site to others. That done, and for most of the rest of the day, I had to unload by hand from trailers and to stack in orderly piles tons and tons of bulky material such as rough lumber, roofing shingles, and kegs of nails. At the end of the day, I was obliged to clean up rubbish from the outside and inside of buildings under construction, load it on my truck and

then unload it at a refuse dump on the site. As a laborer on a construction site, even though I found some variety in the day's work, the routine of each day was like that of every other. However, in the factory where I worked pulling the levers on the same machine, every day and every hour of each day was like the next. Working there was like being on a treadmill; it was monotonous, unrelieved drudgery.

Here, too, since content is consistent, we have a unified paragraph. Its main idea is expressed at the outset in a topic sentence whose key word is "boring." The writer supports this idea with two examples of boring jobs, one on a construction project, the other in a factory. Since this information is sufficient to explain to the reader the paragraph's main idea, the paragraph is complete.

Notice how in this paragraph the writer establishes order and smooth sentence flow by arranging his sentences chronologically, with words indicating the passage of time: "the first thing each morning"; "then"; "after that"; "that done"; "and for most of the rest of the day"; "at the end of the day." The words "for example" and "however" — sometimes called *transition words* — also help achieve coherence within the paragraph. (A few more examples of transition words, not used here, are "thus," "for instance," "to illustrate," used to introduce an example; "in the second place," "moreover," "likewise," used to add a thought; "but," "on the contrary," "on the other hand," used to signal a qualification or contrast; and "consequently," "therefore," "to sum up," used to indicate a conclusion or result.) And "found," a synonym of "learned," helps achieve coherence between this paragraph and the other two, where "learned" is used.

Let's now take a look at the fourth paragraph:

4 Most important perhaps, I discovered that none of the jobs I had was fulfilling. The best that can be said for my lawn mowing is that it was good exercise and kept me outdoors during the summer months. Waiting on tables, after the newness of the job wore off, was uninteresting. Packaging groceries was unstimulating, to say the least. The same was true for my unchallenging work at a machine in the factory. Even my last job — which was the most satisfying because I was curious about how buildings were put together and because I had to make some decisions on my own even

if they were as insignificant as directing a newly arrived trailer to stop here or there on the construction site so that its materials, when unloaded, would be conveniently placed for the skilled workers who would need them—failed to leave me, at the end of the day, with the feeling that I had fully realized my capabilities.

In the second paragraph of this essay, the writer begins with "I *learned*, first of all." In the third, he begins with "more important, I *found*." In this paragraph, he starts with "Most important perhaps, I *discovered*." Notice that "discovered," an alternative for "found" and "learned," refers, like "found," to the thesis in paragraph 1 and helps achieve coherence between paragraph 4 and the three preceding paragraphs. "Most important perhaps" has the same effect, since it reminds us of the points the writer made in the two preceding paragraphs. Saving the most important point for the end is also a commendable strategy.

In paragraph 4, as in paragraphs 2 and 3, the main idea is stated in the opening sentence. This idea is developed without digressions in the rest of the paragraph, and examples of the writer's jobs are given in the same order as in paragraph 2. The last part of the paragraph's last sentence, referring to the idea in its first part—a tactic that helps achieve coherence—is a rephrasing of that idea and a fitting summary of and conclusion to the paragraph.

Here is the essay's last paragraph:

₅   Just what these were I hardly knew at the time; nor am I convinced now that I know just what they are. Nonetheless, I do know that without a skill, or a craft, or a profession, my options of ways to earn a living are limited to jobs that are poorly paying, boring, and unfulfilling. This much I did learn from my three years of work after graduation from high school.

Coherence between this paragraph and the preceding one is achieved by *pronoun reference:* the use of a pronoun or pronouns in one sentence to refer to a noun in a previous sentence. Here, "They" in the first sentence refers to "capabilities" in the previous paragraph. Coherence within the paragraph is helped by the transition word "nonetheless." Fittingly, for a concluding paragraph, the second sentence restates and amplifies the essay's thesis and includes the details of the lesson the writer learned and wrote about in the body (paragraphs 2, 3, and 4) of the essay:

> . . . I do know that without a skill, or a craft, or a profession, my options of ways to earn a living are limited to jobs that are poorly paying, boring, and unfulfilling.

The paragraph is comparable to the essay in that each should have unity, completeness, order, and coherence. Sometimes, an author will write a short essay in a single paragraph, as you saw in Maeve Brennan's "Painful Choice" (page 12) and will see again in John Updike's "Beer Can" (page 60). A good paragraph, whether it is a one-paragraph essay or part of a larger essay, is an integrated unit. Paragraphs have been called, rightly—by Richard M. Weaver in "The Function of the Paragraph"—"compositions in miniature."

WHAT I HAVE LIVED FOR
Bertrand Russell

Bertrand Russell (1872–1970), recipient of the Nobel Prize for Literature in 1950, was a British mathematician, philosopher, and social reformer. In this passage from his autobiography, he summarizes his personal philosophy.

---

1   Three passions, simple but overwhelmingly strong, have governed my life: the longing for love, the search for knowledge, and unbearable pity for the suffering of mankind. These passions, like great winds, have blown me hither and thither, in a wayward course, over a deep ocean of anguish, reaching to the very verge of despair.

From *The Autobiography of Bertrand Russell: 1872–1914*. George Allen and Unwin (Publishers) Ltd. By permission.

2   I have sought love, first, because it brings ecstasy—ecstasy so great that I would often have sacrificed all the rest of life for a few hours of this joy. I have sought it, next, because it relieves loneliness —that terrible loneliness in which one shivering consciousness looks over the rim of the world into the cold unfathomable lifeless abyss. I have sought it, finally, because in the union of love I have seen, in a mystic miniature, the prefiguring vision of the heaven that saints and poets have imagined. This is what I sought, and though it might seem too good for human life, this is what—at last—I have found.

3   With equal passion I have sought knowledge. I have wished to understand the hearts of men. I have wished to know why the stars shine. . . . A little of this, but not much, I have achieved.

4   Love and knowledge, so far as they were possible, led upward toward the heavens. But always pity brought me back to earth. Echoes of cries of pain reverberate in my heart. Children in famine, victims tortured by oppressors, helpless old people a hated burden to their sons, and the whole world of loneliness, poverty, and pain make a mockery of what human life should be. I long to alleviate the evil, but I cannot, and I too suffer.

5   This has been my life. I have found it worth living, and would gladly live it again if the chance were offered me.

Questions About "Paragraphs"

1. How does Russell achieve coherence in paragraph 1? In paragraph 2?

2. Considering the writer's purpose in paragraph 2, explain whether the paragraph is complete.

3. What is the topic sentence of paragraph 3? Of paragraph 4?

4. What does the phrase "with equal passion" (par. 3) contribute to the coherence of the essay?

5. What is the writer's purpose in writing "but" (par. 4)?

6. Explain whether paragraph 5 fulfills the requirement(s) of a concluding paragraph.

Questions on Diction and Writing Techniques

1. How does your dictionary define "passion"? What does the phrase "like great winds" (par. 1) contribute to your understanding of the word's meaning?

2. Define the following words and write sentences using each of them appropriately: ecstasy (par. 2), unfathomable (par. 2), abyss (par. 2), mystic (par. 2), reverberate (par. 4), mockery (par. 4).

3. What is the thesis of this piece?

4. How are the central ideas of paragraphs 2, 3, and 4 related to the main idea of the essay?

5. Comment on the essay's unity. Where, if at all, does the writer digress?

For Discussion, Reading, and Writing

1. This essay is mainly about (circle one):

   A. Russell's longing for love.

   B. Russell's search for knowledge.

   C. Russell's unbearable pity for the suffering of mankind.

   D. The three passions that governed Russell's life.

   E. Russell's wish to live his life over again.

2. What passions have governed your life? Write about one of them in a single paragraph that is unified, orderly, coherent, and complete.

3. Write a short essay on any subject—sports, hobbies, music, or anything else—imitating the organization of Russell's essay. Include (a) a statement in an introductory paragraph of three related ideas to be developed; (b) development of the ideas in separate paragraphs; and (c) a summary in a concluding paragraph.

REMEMBERING JIMMY
Ralph Ellison

Ralph Ellison (born 1914) won the National Book Award and a
literary reputation with his novel **Invisible Man**. He is acclaimed
as one of the two most important living black American novelists,
the other being James Baldwin (born 1924).

---

1   In the old days the voice was high and clear and poignantly
lyrical. Steel-bright in its upper range and, at its best, silky smooth,
it was possessed of a purity somehow impervious to both the stress
of singing above a twelve-piece band and the urgency of Rushing's
own blazing fervor. On dance nights, when you stood on the rise of
the school grounds two blocks to the east, you could hear it jetting
from the dance hall like a blue flame in the dark; now soaring high
above the trumpets and trombones, now skimming the froth of
reeds and rhythm as it called some woman's anguished name—or
demanded in a high, thin, passionately lyrical line, "Baaaaay-bay,
Bay-aaaay-bay! Tell me what's the matter now!"—above the shouting of the swinging band.

2   Nor was there need for the by now famous signature line:
"If anybody asks you who sang this song / Tell 'em / it was little
Jimmy Rushing / he's been here and gone"—for everyone on Okla-
homa City's "East Side" knew that sweet, high-floating sound.
"Deep Second" was our fond nickname for the block in which
Rushing worked and lived, and where most Negro business and entertainment were found, and before he went to cheer a wider world
his voice evoked the festive spirit of the place. Indeed, he was the
natural herald of its blues-romance, his song the singing essence of
its joy. For Jimmy Rushing was not simply a local entertainer, he
expressed a value, an attitude about the world for which our lives

afforded no other definition. We had a Negro church and a segregated school, a few lodges and fraternal organizations, and beyond these there was all the great white world. We were pushed off to what seemed to be the least desirable side of the city (but which some years later was found to contain one of the state's richest pools of oil), and our system of justice was based upon Texas law, yet there was an optimism within the Negro community and a sense of possibility which, despite our awareness of limitation (dramatized so brutally in the Tulsa riot of 1921), transcended all of this; and it was this rock-bottom sense of reality, coupled with our sense of the possibility of rising above it, which sounded in Rushing's voice.

3   And how it carried! In those days I lived near the Rock Island roundhouse, where, with a steady clanging of bells and a great groaning of wheels along the rails, switch engines made up trains of freight unceasingly. Yet often in the late-spring night I could hear Rushing as I lay four blocks away in bed, carrying to me as clear as a full-bored riff on "Hot Lips" Paige's horn. Heard thus, across the dark blocks lined with locust trees, through the night throbbing with the natural aural imagery of the blues, with high-balling trains, departing bells, lonesome guitar chords simmering up from a shack in the alley—it was easy to imagine the voice as setting the pattern to which the instruments of the Blue Devils Orchestra and all the random sounds of night arose, affirming, as it were, some ideal native to the time and to the land. When we were still too young to attend night dances, but yet old enough to gather beneath the corner street lamp on summer evenings, anyone might halt the conversation to exclaim, "Listen, they're raising hell down at Slaughter's Hall," and we'd turn our heads westward to hear Jimmy's voice soar up the hill and down, as pure and as miraculously unhindered by distance and earthbound things as is the body in youthful dreams of flying.

4   "Now, that's the Right Reverend Jimmy Rushing preaching now, man," someone would say. And rising to the cue another would answer, "Yeah, and that's old Elder 'Hot Lips' signifying along with him; urging him on, man." And, keeping it building, "Huh, but though you can't hear him out this far, Ole Deacon Bigun [the late Walter Page] is up there patting his foot and slapping on his big belly [the bass viol] to keep those fools in line." And we

might go on to name all the members of the band as though they were the Biblical four-and-twenty elders, while laughing at the impious wit of applying church titles to a form of music which all the preachers assured us was the devil's potent tool.

⁵   Our wit was true, for Jimmy Rushing, along with the other jazz musicians whom we knew, had made a choice, had dedicated himself to a mode of expression and a way of life no less "righteously" than others dedicated themselves to the church. Jazz and the blues did not fit into the scheme of things as spelled out by our two main institutions, the church and the school, but they gave expression to attitudes which found no place in these and helped to give our lives some semblance of wholeness. Jazz and the public jazz dance was a third institution in our lives, and a vital one; and though Jimmy was far from being a preacher, he was, as official floor manager or master-of-the-dance at Slaughter's Hall, the leader of a public rite.

Questions About "Paragraphs"

1. Explain how Ellison achieves coherence in paragraph 1.

2. ". . . Jimmy Rushing was not simply a local entertainer, he expressed a value" (par. 2). Comment on whether the writer, in paragraph 2, sufficiently explains this idea for you to be convinced of its validity.

3. Is paragraph 3 unified? What is its central idea? Does the writer give in the paragraph enough information to make the idea clear to you? Explain.

4. What is the function of "and," with which Ellison begins sentences 2, 3, and 4 of paragraph 4?

5. Comment on the coherence between paragraphs in this selection.

Questions on Diction and Writing Techniques

1. Define the following words and write sentences using each of

them appropriately: lyrical (par. 1), impervious (par. 1), essence (par. 2), transcended (par. 2), rite (par. 5).

2. Ellison uses "steel-bright" and "silky smooth" (par. 1) to describe the quality of the sound of Rushing's voice. Comment on the effect on you of three or more other words or phrases he chooses to describe the voice.

For Discussion, Reading, and Writing

1. Fill the blanks in this passage from "Remembering Jimmy" to make it intelligible:

   "Deep Second" was our fond nickname for the _____ in which

   Rushing worked and lived, and where most _____ business and entertainment were found, and before he went to cheer a wider world

   his _____ evoked the festive _____ of the place. Indeed, he was

   the natural herald of its blues-romance, his _____ the singing

   essence of its _____.

   Compare your choice of words with those in paragraph 2.

2. What, according to Ellison, was the value that Jimmy Rushing expressed? Using at least two devices to achieve coherence, write a paragraph that gives enough information to make clear to a reader the value that any musician or other artist expresses to you.

3. Making sure to establish coherence, write a paragraph about an institution, other than church and school, that does not "fit into the scheme of things spelled out" by them but gives your life or the life of anyone you know "some semblance of wholeness."

DARKNESS AT NOON
Harold Krents

Harold Krents, a graduate of Harvard College and Harvard Law School, is a practicing attorney and an advocate of the employment of handicapped people.

---

1   Blind from birth, I have never had the opportunity to see myself and have been completely dependent on the image I create in the eye of the observer. To date it has not been narcissistic.

2   There are those who assume that since I can't see, I obviously also cannot hear. Very often people will converse with me at the top of their lungs, enunciating each word very carefully. Conversely, people will also often whisper, assuming that since my eyes don't work, my ears don't either.

3   For example, when I go to the airport and ask the ticket agent for assistance to the plane, he or she will invariably pick up the phone, call a ground hostess and whisper: "Hi, Jane, we've got a 76 here." I have concluded that the word "blind" is not used for one of two reasons: Either they fear that if the dread word is spoken, the ticket agent's retina will immediately detach, or they are reluctant to inform me of my condition of which I may not have been previously aware.

4   On the other hand, others know that of course I can hear, but believe that I can't talk. Often, therefore, when my wife and I go out to dinner, a waiter or waitress will ask Kit if "*he* would like a drink" to which I respond that "indeed *he* would."

5   This point was graphically driven home to me while we were in England. I had been given a year's leave of absence from my Washington law firm to study for a diploma in law degree at Oxford University. During the year I became ill and was hospitalized.

Immediately after admission, I was wheeled down to the X-ray room. Just at the door sat an elderly woman – elderly I would judge from the sound of her voice. "What is his name?" the woman asked the orderly who had been wheeling me.

6   "What's your name?" the orderly repeated to me.

7   "Harold Krents," I replied.

8   "Harold Krents," he repeated.

9   "When was he born?"

10   "When were you born?"

11   "Nov. 5, 1944," I responded.

12   "Nov. 5, 1944," the orderly intoned.

13   This procedure continued for approximately five minutes at which point even my saint-like disposition deserted me. "Look," I finally blurted out, "this is absolutely ridiculous. Okay, granted I can't see, but it's got to have become pretty clear to both of you that I don't need an interpreter."

14   "He says he doesn't need an interpreter," the orderly reported to the woman.

15   The toughest misconception of all is the view that because I can't see, I can't work. I was turned down by over forty law firms because of my blindness, even though my qualifications included a cum laude degree from Harvard College and a good ranking in my Harvard Law School class.

16   The attempt to find employment, the continuous frustration of being told that it was impossible for a blind person to practice law, the rejection letters, not based on my lack of ability but rather on my disability, will always remain one of the most disillusioning experiences of my life.

17   Fortunately, this view of limitation and exclusion is beginning to change. On April 16, the Department of Labor issued regulations that mandate equal-employment opportunities for the handicapped. By and large, the business community's response to offering employment to the disabled has been enthusiastic.

18   I therefore look forward to the day, with the expectation that it is certain to come, when employers will view their handicapped workers as a little child did me years ago when my family still lived in Scarsdale.

19   I was playing basketball with my father in our backyard according to procedures we had developed. My father would stand

beneath the hoop, shout, and I would shoot over his head at the basket attached to our garage. Our next-door neighbor, aged five, wandered over into our yard with a playmate. "He's blind," our neighbor whispered to her friend in a voice that could be heard distinctly by Dad and me. Dad shot and missed. I did the same. Dad hit the rim. I missed entirely. Dad shot and missed the garage entirely. "Which one is blind?" whispered back the little friend.

20   I would hope that in the near future when a plant manager is touring the factory with the foreman and comes upon a handicapped and nonhandicapped person working together, his comment after watching them work will be, "Which one is disabled?"

Questions About "Paragraphs"

1. Krents expresses two ideas in paragraph 2. What is the first of these? How does he support it? How does he signal to you that the paragraph contains a second idea? What is the idea?

2. What is Krents' purpose in writing paragraph 3? How does he signal that purpose to you?

3. If this were your essay, would you begin paragraph 3 with the last sentence of paragraph 2? Combine paragraphs 2 and 3? Leave the two paragraphs as they are? Why?

4. How does Krents achieve coherence between paragraphs 3 and 4? Between paragraphs 4 and 5?

5. Why, in paragraph 4, does Krents write "therefore"? Find, elsewhere in this essay, his use of that word for a similar purpose.

6. What is the topic sentence of paragraph 15? Of paragraph 17?

7. Is paragraph 20 an apt concluding paragraph? Why?

8. This essay was written for and edited by a daily newspaper. How does this fact help to explain its paragraphing?

Questions on Diction and Writing Techniques

1. Define, in your own way, any words in this essay that are new to you, but whose meaning you can surmise from their context. Then compare your definitions with those in your dictionary. Also, write in your text the dictionary definitions of all other words that are new to you. Use the words in both groups in sentences.

2. Is the thesis of this essay expressed or implied? If expressed, state where. If implied, state it in your own words.

3. What does the anecdote in paragraph 19 contribute to an explanation of the essay's main idea?

4. To better appreciate the organization of this essay and the progression of its ideas, summarize it in a coherent paragraph of not over one hundred words.

For Discussion, Reading, and Writing

1. What, according to Krents, was the toughest misconception of all?

2. Fill the blanks in this sentence to make it intelligible:

   I would hope that in the near future _____ a plant manager is touring the _____ with the foreman and comes upon a _____ and nonhandicapped person _____ together, his comment after _____ them work will be, "Which one of them is _____?"

   Compare your choice of words with those in paragraph 20.

3. Think about the difference between lack of ability and disability, making notes as you do. Then, (a) write a one-paragraph letter on the subject to a friend; (b) write a one-paragraph letter to the president of a company in support of a real or imaginary person's application for a job.

A FABLE FOR TOMORROW
Rachel Carson

Rachel Carson (1907–1964) was a marine biologist and author.
She was the first scientist to document the dangers of insecticides,
in **Silent Spring** (1962), in which this essay appeared.

1   There was once a town in the heart of America where all life
seemed to live in harmony with its surroundings. The town lay in
the midst of a checkerboard of prosperous farms, with fields of
grain and hillsides of orchards where, in spring, white clouds of
bloom drifted above the green fields. In autumn, oak and maple
and birch set up a blaze of color that flamed and flickered across a
backdrop of pines. Then foxes barked in the hills and deer silently
crossed the fields, half hidden in the mists of the fall mornings.

2   Along the roads, laurel, viburnum and alder, great ferns and
wildflowers delighted the traveler's eye through much of the year.
Even in winter the roadsides were places of beauty, where countless
birds came to feed on the berries and on the seed heads of the dried
weeds rising above the snow. The countryside was, in fact, famous
for the abundance and variety of its bird life, and when the flood of
migrants was pouring through in spring and fall people traveled
from great distances to observe them. Others came to fish the
streams, which flowed clear and cold out of the hills and contained
shady pools where trout lay. So it had been from the days many
years ago when the first settlers raised their houses, sank their wells,
and built their barns.

3   Then a strange blight crept over the area and everything began
to change. Some evil spell had settled on the community: mysterious
maladies swept the flocks of chickens; the cattle and sheep sickened
and died. Everywhere was a shadow of death. The farmers spoke

of much illness among their families. In the town the doctors had become more and more puzzled by new kinds of sickness appearing among their patients. There had been several sudden and unexplained deaths, not only among adults but even among children, who would be stricken suddenly while at play and die within a few hours.

4   There was a strange stillness. The birds, for example—where had they gone? Many people spoke of them, puzzled and disturbed. The feeding stations in the backyards were deserted. The few birds seen anywhere were moribund; they trembled violently and could not fly. It was a spring without voices. On the mornings that had once throbbed with the dawn chorus of robins, catbirds, doves, jays, wrens, and scores of other bird voices there was now no sound; only silence lay over the fields and woods and marsh.

5   On the farms the hens brooded, but no chicks hatched. The farmers complained that they were unable to raise any pigs—the litters were small and the young survived only a few days. The apple trees were coming into bloom but no bees droned among the blossoms, so there was no pollination and there would be no fruit.

6   The roadsides, once so attractive, were now lined with browned and withered vegetation as though swept by fire. These, too, were silent, deserted by all living things. Even the streams were now lifeless. Anglers no longer visited them, for all the fish had died.

7   In the gutters under the eaves and between the shingles of the roofs, a white granular powder still showed a few patches; some weeks before it had fallen like snow upon the roofs and the lawns, the fields and streams.

8   No witchcraft, no enemy action had silenced the rebirth of new life in this stricken world. The people had done it themselves.

9   This town does not actually exist, but it might easily have a thousand counterparts in America or elsewhere in the world. I know of no community that has experienced all the misfortunes I describe. Yet every one of these disasters has actually happened somewhere, and many real communities have already suffered a substantial number of them. A grim specter has crept upon us almost unnoticed, and this imagined tragedy may easily become a stark reality we all shall know.

Questions About "Paragraphs"

1. How does Carson try to convince the reader of the validity of the main idea of paragraph 3?

2. What is the main idea of paragraph 4? Where is it expressed?

3. The topic sentence of paragraph 5 is implied. Write a suitable topic sentence for the paragraph.

4. What is the main idea of paragraph 6? How does Carson make the idea clear to you?

5. Find examples of Carson's use of transition words in paragraphs 4, 5, and 9.

Questions on Diction and Writing Techniques

1. Mark in your text all words in this essay that, though new to you, you understood from their context. Define them in your own words. Compare your definitions with those in your dictionary. Look up in your dictionary all other words that are new to you. Use the words in both groups in sentences.

2. What is Carson's purpose in writing "in fact" (par. 2)?

3. Why does she write "once so attractive" (par. 6)?

4. This essay may be divided into three parts: paragraphs 1-2, 3-8, and 9. Explain the function of each part.

For Discussion, Reading, and Writing

1. The first and last sentences of this passage are complete. Fill in the blanks in the other sentences.

This town does not actually exist, but it might easily have a thousand counterparts in America or elsewhere in the world. I know of no _____ that has experienced all the _____ I describe. _____ every one of these _____ has actually happened somewhere, and many real _____ have already _____ a substantial number of _____. A grim specter has crept upon us almost unnoticed, and this imagined tragedy may easily become a stark reality we all shall know.

Compare your choice of words with those in paragraph 9.

2. A fable is a short, uncomplicated story told to point a moral. What is Carson's message in this essay?

3. Starting out with a clearly stated topic sentence, write a paragraph (one that you might want to see published) to the editor of your school's newspaper, explaining your views on environmental abuse of your college campus or of some place such as a park, wood, or lake.

Sentences

YOU have been using sentences all your life and probably know more about them than you realize. The purposes of this section are to make you conscious of what you already know, to describe techniques of sentence building that may be unfamiliar, and to increase your awareness of the variety of possibilities for constructing the units of composition called "sentences."

The most common sentence — the *standard sentence* — consists of two parts: a subject and a predicate. The *predicate* is the part of a sentence that tells us something about the *subject*. "Bill Smith [subject] hit the ball [predicate]" is a standard sentence, but the amount of information it contains is small. This amount — the *density* of the sentence — can be increased by *modification, subordination* (a form of modification), and *coordination*.

Modification

"To modify" means to limit or describe a grammatical element. In the sentence,

Powerful Bill Smith hit the ball.

we modify "Bill Smith" with an adjective. In

After two bunting attempts, powerful Bill Smith hit the ball *over the head of Jake Johnson.*

we expand the sentence more by modifying "hit" with "after two bunting attempts," a prepositional phrase (a preposition, its object, and any modifier of the object) and with another prepositional phrase, "over the head of Jake Johnson." We could continue to rewrite, using adjectives, adverbs, phrases, and clauses—building to an information-packed sentence:

After two bunting attempts and two foul tips, league-leading State U.'s slugging center fielder, powerful Bill Smith, hit the ball *over the head of A. & M.'s Jake (alias "Flatfoot") Johnson, past the right-field fence of Kennedy Stadium to the top row of the stands where a proud State supporter speared the speeding sphere.*

By means of *modification*, we have expanded the original sentence, increasing the amount of information it contains by adding specific details.

To learn how writers utilize modification, consider these four sentences:

1. America needs a new kind of college.
2. I do not really live in that world.
3. I observed two large ants.
4. A saxophone player stands on the sidewalk.

These sentences are the cores and main clauses (constructions containing a subject and a predicate that can stand alone as a sentence) of enlarged sentences:

1. America needs a new kind of college, *in which the teachers are not drawn primarily from the academic profession, and the pedagogy does not rely primarily on classrooms* [Christopher Jencks, "An Anti-Academic Proposal"].

2. And I do not really live in that world, *so narrow and so trivial, so cruel and so unconscious; I was a mere visitor* [Katherine Anne Porter, "The Bullfight"].

3. *One day when I went out to my woodpile, or rather my pile of stumps,* I observed two large ants, *the one red, the other much larger, nearly half an inch long, and black, fiercely contending with one another* [Henry David Thoreau, *Walden*].

4. *Each afternoon in New York a rather seedy* saxophone player, *his cheeks blown out like a spinnaker,* stands on the sidewalk *playing Danny Boy in such a sad, sensitive way that he soon has half the neighborhood peeking out of windows tossing nickels, dimes and quarters at his feet* [Gay Talese, "New York"].

In each instance, the writer—by adding details—made the main clause more specific. Jencks stated the characteristics of "a new kind of college." Porter listed attributes of "that world" she referred to. Thoreau described the "two large ants." Talese particularized his subject. Each writer, by means of modification, increased the amount of information in the sentence and thereby made it of greater interest to readers.

Subordination

Adjectives, adverbs, phrases, and clauses that limit or describe other elements in a sentence are subordinate—of less importance, secondary—to them. Their placement in modifying roles is called *subordination.*

Often, writers use this technique to de-emphasize one idea while emphasizing another. Compare the first two examples with the third:

1. Bill Smith attempted two bunts. He hit a home run.

2. Bill Smith attempted two bunts, and then he hit a home run.

3. *After two attempts to bunt,* Bill Smith hit a home run.

Two sentences in the first example and two main clauses in the second example describe actions whose importance is not differentiated. In the third example the writer de-emphasized one of the actions by making it subordinate, in a modifying prepositional phrase (in italics), to the action in the sentence's main clause, "Bill Smith hit a home run." The writer could change the relative importance of the two actions by reversing their roles in the sentence, placing the idea of bunting in the main clause and the idea of hitting a home run in a modifying phrase:

Before hitting a home run, Bill Smith attempted to bunt twice.

Here are some other examples of the use of subordination to show which idea the writer wishes to emphasize (subordinate, de-emphasized elements in italics):

Even though Secretary of War Stimson opposed the move, President Truman ordered the A-bombing of Japan.

When the Japanese surrendered, most American troops in the Pacific were returned to the United States.

Except for those who chose to make soldiering their career, returning American troops were discharged from the Army.

Many veterans were able to go to college *because of the G.I. Bill.*

Older and more mature than most of the other college students, many veterans distinguished themselves in college.

Although World War II is long since past, the war's combat veterans still remember its horrors.

Useful in signaling a subordinate element in a sentence are words like "even though," "when," "except for," "because of," and "although."

Generally, a writer, when using subordination to increase the density of a sentence, has a choice of ways to construct the expanded sentence. Consider how this information might be merged in a sentence:

a. The mile race was run in Madison Square Garden.
b. Twenty thousand spectators were there.
c. Tom Jones trailed during most of the contest.
d. He reached the tape five yards ahead of his nearest rival.
e. He won the race in four minutes flat.

Among the possible combinations are:

1. After trailing during most of the contest held in Madison Square Garden before twenty thousand spectators, Tom Jones won the mile race in four minutes flat, reaching the tape five yards ahead of his nearest rival.

2. Tom Jones won the mile race in four minutes flat, reaching the tape five yards ahead of his nearest rival after trailing during most of the contest held in Madison Square Garden before twenty thousand spectators.

3. After trailing during most of the contest held in Madison Square Garden before twenty thousand spectators, Tom Jones reached the tape five yards ahead of his nearest rival to win the mile race in four minutes flat.

In these sentences, the writer indicates the importance of the information in sentences (a) through (e) by putting secondary information in modifying elements — prepositional phrases introduced by "after" and "before" and a participial phrase introduced by "reaching" — that are subordinated to the main clauses in the sentences.

This is not all the writer does. He also increases or decreases the emphasis of the information in sentences (a) through (e) by the place assigned to it in the expanded sentences.

The beginning and the end are a sentence's most emphatic positions — especially the end, for what we read last we remember best. In sentence 1, even though the beginning and end are subordinate to the main clause, the writer de-emphasizes the main clause by placing it in the less emphatic middle position. In sentence 2, he emphasizes the information in the main clause by putting it in the beginning, but the emphasis is diminished by the stress achieved by the information placed at the end. In sentence 3, the writer better emphasizes the idea in the main clause — that Jones won the mile race in four minutes flat — by putting it at the end.

For another example of the function and effect of subordination, consider how the author of "Menial Jobs Taught Me a Lot" (presented in its entirety in "Paragraphs," pages 31–34) might have written its first paragraph:

Original	*Alternate*
1. When I graduated from high school I decided that, having spent fourteen years without interruption in grammar school and secondary schools, I would take a year or two, perhaps more, away from school before going on to college.	1. I spent fourteen years without interruption in grammar and secondary schools. 2. Then I graduated from high school. 3. I decided I would take a year or two, perhaps more, away from school before going on to college.

The alternate sentences, all grammatically correct, contain the information that is in the first sentence of the original paragraph. But, regardless of the importance of the information they contain, the emphasis is the same in the three individual sentences. In the first sentence of the original paragraph, however, one idea is stressed and the others are de-emphasized by means of subordination.

In sentence 1 of the original, the writer assigned less importance to the ideas in alternate sentences 1 and 2—"*when* I graduated from high school"; "*having* spent fourteen years without interruption in grammar and secondary schools"—than he did to the idea in alternate sentence 3, which he emphasized by putting its idea in the original sentence's main clause: "I decided that I would take a year or two, perhaps more, away from school before going on to college."

Original	*Alternate*
2. Now, after three years of nondescript jobs, I am convinced that my decision to take a long break between high school and college was wise.	4. I had nondescript jobs for three years. 5. I am convinced that my decision to take a long break between high school and college was wise.

The writer's construction of the original sentence 2 reveals the importance he assigns to the ideas expressed in the alternate paragraph's sentences 4 and 5: In sentence 2, a prepositional phrase—"after three years in nondescript jobs"—is subordinate to the sentence's main clause, "I am convinced . . ."

Original	Alternate
3. From the menial jobs I had I learned a valuable lesson.	6. The jobs I had were menial. 7. But I learned a valuable lesson.

The writer makes clear the relative importance of the ideas in sentence 3 of the original by subordinating sentence 6 of the alternate in a prepositional phrase, "*from* the menial jobs I had," that modifies the idea in sentence 7, originally expressed — and emphasized — in a main clause: "I learned a valuable lesson."

A comparison of the two groups of sentences just discussed will reveal another benefit of subordination: the alleviation of monotony, which may result from a series of short, standard sentences with little modification. It must not be concluded, however, that a sentence is necessarily less desirable because it is uncomplicated or short. The sentences in paragraph 2 of "Menial Jobs Taught Me a Lot" are relatively simple and short, averaging eighteen words per sentence, six less than the average length of the sentences in the first paragraph of the essay. They are, nonetheless, sound sentences.

The criteria for judging whether a sentence is good are the exactness with which it expresses its writer's ideas and the clarity with which it communicates them to the reader. Thus the second sentence of paragraph 3, containing six words, and the last sentence of paragraph 4, containing eighty-nine words (seventy-two of them subordinated to its seventeen-word split main clause: "My last job . . . failed to leave me . . . with the feeling that I had fully realized my capabilities"), are equally good.

The short second sentence in paragraph 3 not only adds variety — an antidote to monotony — but also makes an impact because of the staccato effect of its brevity. It draws attention to itself and the idea it contains. The long last sentence in paragraph 4 has the virtue of emphasizing its main idea and of serving as the climax of the sentence (and of the paragraph as well). The writer achieved these effects by postponing the completion of the main idea until the end of the sentence, a construction that produces a *periodic sentence.*

The effect that a writer can achieve with a periodic sentence can be highlighted by comparing one with a *standard sentence,* also called a *loose sentence.* A loose sentence does not end with the completion of its main clause but continues with additional information; the writer attaches information that modifies and is subordinate to the sentence's main clause. In this example, the main clause is in italics (added):

> *January 11, 1965, was a bright warm day in Southern California,* the kind of day when California floats on the Pacific horizon and the air smells of orange blossoms and it is a long way from the bleak and difficult East, a long way from the cold, a long way from the past [Joan Didion, *Slouching Towards Bethlehem*].

The reader of a periodic sentence, in contrast, is held in suspense because grammatical construction and meaning are not complete until the end Again, the main clauses are in italics (added):

> If neither men nor gadgets nor both combined can control the earth from the earth, *we fail to see how they will do so from the moon* [Eric Sevareid, "The Dark of the Moon"].

> In an era when huge television audiences watch surgical operations in the comfort of their living rooms, when, thanks to the animated cartoon, the geography of the digestive system has become familiar territory even to the nursery school set, in a land where the satisfaction of curiosity about almost all matters is a national pastime, *the secrecy surrounding embalming can, surely, hardly be attributed to the inherent gruesomeness of the subject* [Jessica Mitford, *The American Way of Death*].

Coordination

In addition to modification and subordination, the writer may use *coordination* to expand a sentence. Instead of writing

> Smith stepped into the batter's box. He faced the pitcher.

she might combine the two sentences by giving them a common subject and pairing the two predicates:

> Smith stepped into the batter's box and faced the pitcher.

Instead of writing

Johnson checked first base. He turned to the batter. He raised his arm. He threw a screwball.

she might combine these sentences by giving them a common subject and linking their predicates:

Johnson checked first base, turned to the batter, raised his arm, and threw a screwball.

Coordination is the joining of grammatical elements of identical construction in pairs or series. It is often signaled by the conjunctions "and," "but," "for," "nor," "or," and "yet":

. . . among these are Life, Liberty *and* the Pursuit of Happiness.
He studied hard, *but* flunked the course.
He ran all the way, *for* he was eager to get home in time for dinner.
Neither snow, *nor* rain, *nor* heat, *nor* gloom of night stays these couriers from the swift completion of their appointed rounds.
Give me liberty *or* give me death.
She was outgoing, *yet* had few friends.

There are examples of coordination in paragraph 3 of "Menial Jobs Taught Me a Lot."

I had *to unload* by hand from trailers and *to stack* in orderly piles [pair of coordinate infinitives] . . . material such as rough *lumber,* roofing *shingles,* and *kegs* of nails [coordinate nouns in a series].
. . . I was obliged *to clean up rubbish . . . load it on my truck,* and then *unload it* [coordinate series of infinitive phrases] . . .

Notice that the coordinate elements are of the same grammatical kind; "to unload" and "to stack," for example, are both infinitives. Unlike subordination, which makes one element less important than another, coordination combines in pairs or series elements — single words, phrases, or clauses — that are similar in kind and function and equal in importance.

These sentences are diagrammed to point out examples of coordinate (1) verbs, (2) nouns, (3) prepositional phrases and nouns, (4) gerund phrases, and (5) predicates (all in italics):

1. Having once got hold they never let go, but
   struggled and
   wrestled and
   rolled
                                 on the chips incessantly.[1]

2. One hundred years later,
   the life of the Negro is
   still badly crippled by
                 the manacles of segregation and
                 the chains of discrimination.[2]

3. It is his privilege
   to help man endure
             by lifting his heart,
             by reminding him of the
                           courage and
                           honor and
                           hope and
                           pride and
                           compassion and
                           pity and
                           sacrifice

   which have been the glory of his past.[3]

4. We observe today not a
   victory of a party but
   a celebration of freedom—
                 symbolizing an end as well as a beginning—
                 signifying renewal as well as change.[4]

5. He has
             plundered our seas,
             ravaged our coasts,
             burnt our towns, and
             destroyed the lives of our people.[5]

[1] Henry David Thoreau, *Walden.*
[2] Martin Luther King, "I Have a Dream."
[3] William Faulkner, "Man Will Prevail."
[4] John F. Kennedy, "Inaugural Address."
[5] Thomas Jefferson, "Declaration of Independence."

Observe that each writer, by using similar elements, shows which ideas belong together and thereby conveys them succinctly and with clarity to the reader. Notice too that each sentence draws attention to itself and to its ideas by the repetition of similar elements.

Another effect that a writer can achieve with coordination is shown in example 5. The writer arranged the coordinate elements so that the sentence's most important idea comes at the end, where it makes the longest-lasting impression on the reader.

I have discussed modification, subordination, and coordination —three major methods of expanding a sentence—separately merely for convenience. Coordinate elements, as you have observed in the examples just presented, may modify and be made subordinate to other elements in a sentence just as other elements may modify and be made subordinate to them.

BEER CAN
John Updike

John Updike (born 1932), American novelist and short-story writer, contributes to **The New Yorker** magazine, where you will find some of the most consistently meticulous contemporary prose. Here is one of his single-paragraph pieces that appeared there; it is as concise as Maeve Brennan's "Painful Choice" (page 12).

₁ This seems to be an era of gratuitous inventions and negative improvements. ₂Consider the beer can. ₃It was beautiful—as beautiful as the clothespin, as inevitable as the wine bottle, as dignified and reassuring as the fire hydrant. ₄A tranquil cylinder of delightfully resonant metal, it could be opened in an instant, requiring only the application of a handy gadget freely dispensed by every grocer. ₅Who can forget the small, symmetrical thrill of those two triangular punctures, the dainty *pffff,* the little crest of suds that foamed eagerly in the exultation of release? ₆Now we are given, instead, a top beetling with an ugly, shmoo-shaped "tab," which, after fiercely resisting the tugging, bleeding fingers of the thirsty man, threatens his lips with a dangerous and hideous hole. ₇However, we have discovered a way to thwart Progress, usually so unthwartable. ₈*Turn the beer can upside down and open the bottom.* ₉The bottom is still the way the top used to be. ₁₀True, this operation gives the beer an unsettling jolt, and the sight of a consistently inverted beer can might make people edgy, not to say queasy. ₁₁But the latter difficulty could be eliminated if manufacturers would design cans that looked the same whichever end was up, like playing cards. ₁₂What we need is Progress with an escape hatch.

Questions About "Sentences"

1. Updike's first sentence is an example of coordination: "of *gratuitous inventions* and *negative improvements.*" Find in the paragraph two other sentences that combine similar grammatical elements into pairs or series.

2. What is the main idea of sentence 4? What ideas does Updike subordinate to it? He might have written the sentence: "It was a tranquil cylinder of delightfully resonant metal. It could be opened in an instant. It required only the application of a handy gadget freely dispensed by every grocer." What purpose is served by combining these sentences as he did? Which version do you prefer? Why?

3. Updike might have written sentence 11 like this: "But if manufacturers would design beer cans that looked the same whichever end was up, like playing cards, the latter difficulty would be eliminated." Which version do you prefer? Why?

Questions on Diction and Writing Techniques

1. Define the following words and write sentences using each of

them appropriately: gratuitous, symmetrical, exaltation, thwart, queasy.

2. What do the italicized words contribute to your understanding of the idea in sentence 3: "It was beautiful — as beautiful *as the clothespin*, as inevitable *as the wine bottle*, as dignified and reassuring *as the fire hydrant*"?

3. What are the transitional words in Updike's paragraph? What is the function of each?

4. What does "like playing cards" contribute to your understanding of the idea in the sentence in which it appears?

5. "Most paragraphs have an internal unity, and they can be analyzed as compositions in miniature. . . . They will have a relative self-containment, or basic unity and coherence, and they will emphasize some point or idea" (Richard M. Weaver, *Composition*). Comment on Updike's one-paragraph essay as a composition "in miniature."

For Discussion, Reading, and Writing

1. Write a sentence that, except for "beer can," is like Updike's sentence 2 (for example, "Consider the Model T Ford"). Then write a sentence containing a series of coordinate elements and beginning with "It was beautiful —."

2. Imitating the structure of Updike's fourth sentence, write a standard sentence with a simple subject-predicate arrangement and then expand it by placing a modifying element before it and another after it.

3. Take any standard sentence and expand it in any way you can. For example, starting with "John likes Mary," you might end up with

John, the handsome star offensive quarterback, who is this year's leading contender for the Alumni Trophy given annually to the outstanding player on Gopher College's football team, likes Mary, its vigorous, effusive cheerleader, because she owns a brand-new two-seater bicycle on which they can ride to school together.

4 . Can you think of other "gratuitous inventions and negative improvements" to which you might apply Updike's conclusion, "What we need is Progress with an escape hatch"? If so, imitating the organization of "Beer Can," write a one-paragraph essay about one of them.

5. The beer can would seem to be too lowly an object to be a fitting topic for an essay and yet Updike managed to write a successful piece about it. Select as another possible topic for a one-paragraph essay — among whose sentences are examples of modification, subordination, and coordination — a ball-point pen, a paper clip, an alarm clock, a calendar, a wall poster, a wastebasket, or any object often taken for granted.

ON THE BLUE WATER
Ernest Hemingway

Ernest Hemingway (1899–1961), American novelist and short-story writer, is the author of many books, including the novels **A Farewell to Arms** (1929) and **For Whom the Bell Tolls** (1940) and the short novel **The Old Man and the Sea** (1952). He won the Nobel Prize for Literature in 1954.

---

1 Because the Gulf Stream is an unexploited country, only the very fringe of it ever being fished, and then only at a dozen places in thousands of miles of current, no one knows what fish live in it, or how great size they reach or what age, or even what kinds of fish and animals live in it at different depths. When you are drifting, out of sight of land, fishing four lines, sixty, eighty, one hundred and one hundred fifty fathoms down, in water that is seven hundred fathoms deep you never know what may take the small tuna

Ernest Hemingway. From, "On the Blue Water: A Gulf Stream Letter," in *By-Line: Ernest Hemingway,* edited by William White. Copyright © 1967 By-Line Ernest Hemingway, Inc. (New York: Charles Scribner's Sons, 1967) Reprinted with the permission of Charles Scribner's Sons.

that you use for bait, and every time the line starts to run off the reel, slowly first, then with a scream of the click as the rod bends and you feel it double and the huge weight of the friction of the line rushing through that depth of water while you pump and reel, pump and reel, pump and reel, trying to get the belly out of the line before the fish jumps, there is always a thrill that needs no danger to make it real. It may be a marlin that will jump high and clear off to your right and then go off in a series of leaps, throwing a splash like a speedboat in a sea as you shout for the boat to turn with him watching the line melting off the reel before the boat can get around. Or it may be a broadbill that will show wagging his great broadsword. Or it may be some fish that you will never see at all that will head straight out to the northwest like a submerged submarine and never show and at the end of five hours the angler has a straightened-out hook. There is always a feeling of excitement when a fish takes hold when you are drifting deep.

₂   In hunting you know what you are after and the top you can get is an elephant. But who can say what you will hook sometime when drifting in a hundred and fifty fathoms in the Gulf Stream? There are probably marlin and swordfish to which the fish we have seen caught are pygmies; and every time a fish takes the bait drifting you have a feeling perhaps you are hooked to one of these.

Questions About "Sentences"

1. As you read it, were you aware of the length of the first sentence of paragraph 1? How many words long is it? Did you have any difficulty in reading or comprehending it? Can you say why? Underline the part of the sentence that expresses its main idea.

2. Underline the portion of sentence 2 that expresses its main ideas.

3. Find in paragraph 1 standard sentences to which information has been added. Underline the main clause in each.

Questions on Diction and Writing Techniques

1. What do "like a speedboat" and "like a submerged submarine" (par. 1) contribute to your understanding of the meaning of the sentences in which they appear?

2. What is the purpose and effect of the repetition of "it may be" in paragraph 1?

3. What is the function of "or" in paragraph 1?

For Discussion, Reading, and Writing

1. "On the Blue Water" is mainly about (circle one):

   A. the great variety of fish in the Gulf Stream.

   B. never knowing what you will hook while drifting in the Gulf Stream.

   C. the feeling of excitement when a fish takes hold of the bait.

   D. the Gulf Stream's being an unexploited country.

   E. Hemingway's passion for deep sea fishing.

2. By subordination, combine the following into one sentence:

   John is my best friend. He is twenty-one-years old. He has been tinkering with engines since he was a kid. He has been building his own stock racing cars for five years. During this time he rose to the top rank of racing-car drivers in the state. He earns a meager living. But he is content.

   Using the same material, write another sentence with a different idea in its main clause. Write a third sentence, using the same material, with still another idea expressed in its main clause. Underline the main clauses in each.

3. Revise any paragraph you have written so far this term in any of your classes by combining its short sentences into one or more longer, denser sentences.

THE FACE OF THE
WATER

Mark Twain

Mark Twain is the pen name of Samuel L. Clemens
(1835–1910). Among his numerous works is **Life on the
Mississippi** (1883), based on his experience as a steamboat pilot
on the Mississippi River.

1   The face of the water, in time, became a wonderful book—a
book that was a dead language to the uneducated passenger, but
which told its mind to me without reserve, delivering its most cher-
ished secrets as clearly as if it uttered them with a voice. And it was
not a book to be read once and thrown aside, for it had a new story
to tell every day. Throughout the long twelve hundred miles there
was never a page that was void of interest, never one that you
could leave unread without loss, never one that you would want to
skip, thinking you could find higher enjoyment in some other
thing. There never was so wonderful a book written by man; never
one whose interest was so absorbing, so unflagging, so sparklingly
renewed with every reperusal. The passenger who could not read it
was charmed with a peculiar sort of faint dimple on its surface (on
the rare occasions when he did not overlook it altogether); but to
the pilot that was an *italicized* passage; indeed, it was more than
that, it was a legend of the largest capitals, with a string of shouting
exclamation-points at the end of it, for it meant that a wreck or a
rock was buried there that could tear the life out of the strongest
vessel that ever floated. It is the faintest and simplest expression the
water ever makes, and the most hideous to a pilot's eye. In truth,
the passenger who could not read this book saw nothing but all
manner of pretty pictures in it, painted by the sun and shaded by
the clouds, whereas to the trained eye these were not pictures at all,
but the grimmest and most dead-earnest of reading-matter.

2   Now when I had mastered the language of this water, and had come to know every trifling feature that bordered the great river as familiarly as I knew the letters of the alphabet, I had made a valuable acquisition. But I had lost something, too. I had lost something which could never be restored to me while I lived. All the grace, the beauty, the poetry, had gone out of the majestic river! I still kept in mind a certain wonderful sunset which I witnessed when steamboating was new to me. A broad expanse of the river was turned to blood; in the middle distance the red hue brightened into gold, through which a solitary log came floating, black and conspicuous; in one place a long, slanting mark lay sparkling upon the water; in another the surface was broken by boiling, tumbling rings, that were as many-tinted as an opal; where the ruddy flush was faintest, was a smooth spot that was covered with graceful circles and radiating lines, ever so delicately traced; the shore on our left was densely wooded, and the somber shadow that fell from this forest was broken in one place by a long, ruffled trail that shone like silver; and high above the forest wall a clean-stemmed dead tree waved a single leafy bough that glowed like a flame in the unobstructed splendor that was flowing from the sun. There were graceful curves, reflected images, woody heights, soft distances; and over the whole scene, far and near, the dissolving lights drifted steadily, enriching it every passing moment with new marvels of coloring.

3   I stood like one bewitched. I drank it in, in a speechless rapture. The world was new to me, and I had never seen anything like this at home. But as I have said, a day came when I began to cease from noting the glories and the charms which the moon and the sun and the twilight wrought upon the river's face; another day came when I ceased altogether to note them. Then, if that sunset scene had been repeated, I should have looked upon it without rapture, and should have commented upon it, inwardly, after this fashion: "This sun means that we are going to have wind to-morrow; that floating log means that the river is rising, small thanks to it; that slanting mark on the water refers to a bluff reef which is going to kill somebody's steamboat one of these nights, if it keeps on stretching out like that; those tumbling 'boils' show a dissolving bar and a changing channel there; the lines and circles in the slick water over yonder are a warning that that troublesome place is shoaling up dangerously; that silver streak in the shadow of the forest is the

'break' from a new snag, and he has located himself in the very best place he could have found to fish for steamboats; that tall dead tree, with a single living branch, is not going to last long, and then how is a body ever going to get through this blind place at night without the friendly old landmark?"

₄   No, the romance and beauty were all gone from the river. All the value any feature of it had for me now was the amount of usefulness it could furnish toward compassing the safe piloting of a steamboat. Since those days, I have pitied doctors from my heart. What does the lovely flush in a beauty's cheek mean to a doctor but a "break" that ripples above some deadly disease? Are not all her visible charms sown thick with what are to him the signs and symbols of hidden decay? Does he ever see her beauty at all, or doesn't he simply view her professionally, and comment upon her unwholesome condition all to himself? And doesn't he sometimes wonder whether he has gained most or lost most by learning his trade?

Questions About "Sentences"

1. Instead of writing sentence 1 of paragraph 1 as he did, Mark Twain might have written "The face of the water, in time, became a wonderful book." Which version do you prefer? Why?

2. What is Mark Twain's purpose in the repetition of similar grammatical elements in the second half of sentence 3 of paragraph 1?

3. Rewrite the first sentence of paragraph 2, placing its main clause at the beginning. Which version gives greater emphasis to the sentence's main idea?

4. What are the purpose and the effect of the short second sentence in paragraph 2? Find, in paragraph 3, a short sentence used for a similar reason.

Questions on Diction and Writing Techniques

1. Mark in your text all words in this essay that, though new to you, you understood from their context. Define them in your

own words. Compare your definitions with those in your dictionary. Look up in your dictionary any other words that are new to you. Use the words in both groups in sentences.

2. What does Twain achieve with his comparison of "the face of the water" with "a wonderful book"? Throughout paragraph 1 and in paragraph 2 he amplifies the comparison, using such phrases as "a book that was *a dead language* to the uneducated passenger" and "it had *a new story* to tell every day." Underline in your text three or more examples of Twain's use of this technique to make his meaning clear in those paragraphs.

For Discussion, Reading, and Writing

1. Why was the book of the river not to be read once and thrown aside?

2. What did Mark Twain say he lost from "mastering the language of this water"?

3. Why has he pitied doctors?

4. Which of these sentences better emphasizes its main idea?

   A. The doctor advised Jones to stop smoking immediately, after examining the x-rays of his lungs and checking his medical record.

   B. The doctor, after examining the x-rays of Jones' lungs and checking his medical record, advised him to stop smoking immediately.

5. Revise these sentences to emphasize the most important ideas in each:

   A. Patrick Henry, the patriot who became governor of Virginia during the Revolutionary War, said, "Give me liberty or give me death," a phrase familiar to all Americans.

   B. The clerk of the court said that the jury would not leave the room until it reached a verdict, except to return to the courtroom to ask the judge for further instructions or to go out for lunch.

C. Frank Jones won an astounding election victory, beating the incumbent congressman, Walter Brown, by three thousand votes after trailing during most of the evening's counting of the ballots that was slowed down by a power failure in the lower part of the state.

THE SAN FRANCISCO EARTHQUAKE
Jack London

Jack London (1876–1916) was a popular writer of stories such as **The Call of the Wild** (1903), based on romantic adventures. His ability to report vividly his observations is evident in this account of the great San Francisco earthquake of 1906.

1   The earthquake shook down in San Francisco hundreds of thousands of dollars worth of walls and chimneys. But the conflagration that followed burned up hundreds of millions of dollars worth of property. There is no estimating within hundreds of millions the actual damage wrought.

2   Not in history has a modern imperial city been so completely destroyed. San Francisco is gone. Nothing remains of it but memories and fringe of dwelling houses on its outskirts. Its industrial section is wiped out. Its social and residential section is wiped out. The factories and warehouses, the great stores and newspaper buildings, the hotels and palaces of the nabobs, all are gone. Remains only the fringe of dwelling houses on the outskirts of what was once San Francisco.

3   Within an hour after the earthquake shock, the smoke of San Francisco's burning was a lurid tower visible a hundred miles away. And for three days and nights this lurid tower swayed in the sky, reddening the sun, darkening the day, and filling the land with smoke.

From *Collier's*, May 5, 1906, pp. 22–23.

₄ On Wednesday morning at quarter past five came the earthquake. A minute later the flames were leaping upward. In a dozen different quarters south of Market Street, in the working class ghetto and in the factories, fires started. There was no opposing the flames. There was no organization, no communication. All the cunning adjustments of a twentieth century city had been smashed by the earthquake. The streets were humped into ridges and depressions, and piled with the debris of fallen walls. The steel rails were twisted into perpendicular and horizontal angles. The telephone and telegraph systems were disrupted. And the great water mains had burst. All the shrewd contrivances and safeguards of man had been thrown out of gear by thirty seconds' twitching of the earthcrust.

₅ By Wednesday afternoon, inside of twelve hours, half the heart of the city was gone. At that time I watched the vast conflagration from out on the bay. It was dead calm. Not a flicker of wind stirred. Yet from every side wind was pouring in upon the city. East, west, north, and south, strong winds were blowing upon the doomed city. The heated air rising made an enormous suck. Thus did the fire of itself build its own colossal chimney through the atmosphere. Day and night this dead calm continued, and yet, near to the flames, the wind was often half a gale, so mighty was the suck.

₆ Wednesday night saw the destruction of the very heart of the city. Dynamite was lavishly used, and many of San Francisco's proudest structures were crumbled by man himself into ruins, but there was no withstanding the onrush of the flames. Time and again successful stands were made by the firefighters, and every time the flames flanked around on either side, or came up from the rear, and turned to defeat the hard won victory.

₇ An enumeration of the buildings destroyed would be a directory of San Francisco. An enumeration of the buildings undestroyed would be a line and several addresses. An enumeration of the deeds of heroism would stock a library and bankrupt the Carnegie medal fund. An enumeration of the dead — will never be made. All vestiges of them were destroyed by the flames. The number of the victims of the earthquake will never be known.

Questions About "Sentences"

1. What is London's purpose in writing the short sentence "San Francisco is gone" (par. 2)? Find in paragraph 5 two examples of his use of sentences to achieve the same effect.

2. London might have written the next-to-last sentence of paragraph 2 like this: "Gone are all the factories and warehouses, the great stores and newspaper buildings, the hotels and the nabobs." Which version better emphasizes the writer's main idea?

3. What effect does London achieve with coordination in sentence 3 of paragraph 4? Find in that paragraph two other sentences structured similarly to achieve the same effect.

4. Rewrite sentence 3 of paragraph 4 as a standard, or loose, sentence. Which version is more suspenseful? Why?

5. By what means does London achieve the effect of paragraph 7?

Questions on Diction and Writing Techniques

1. Define "nabobs" (par. 2) and write a sentence using it appropriately.

2. What is the effect of similarly constructed sentences 4 and 5 of paragraph 2?

3. What do "lurid tower" (par. 3) and "colossal chimney" (par. 5) contribute to your understanding of the ideas the writer is trying to communicate in the sentences in which they appear?

4. Does London give you enough information in paragraph 4 to convince you to accept as true the main idea of the paragraph? Explain.

5. By what means does London establish order among paragraphs 4, 5, and 6? Are the paragraphs coherent?

For Discussion, Reading, and Writing

1. Which of these statements, according to London, are true (T), which false (F)?

   A. _____ Insurance company adjustors came close to estimating the damage wrought by the earthquake.

   B. _____ If dynamite had been used, many of San Francisco's proudest structures might have been saved.

   C. _____ An enumeration of the buildings destroyed would be a directory of San Francisco.

   D. _____ The number of the victims of the earthquake will never be known.

   E. _____ Jack London suffered minor injuries.

2 Imitating London's construction and length of sentences and his use of sentence variety to achieve his purpose, write an essay — in about six hundred words (the length of this piece) — about a dramatic event to which you were an eyewitness.

Words

ONE of the benefits of reading is an increase in the supply of words that you can draw upon to express your ideas. You no doubt have met in this text words that were new to you. The meaning of some of them was reasonably clear from their contexts. The meaning of others you found in your dictionary. When you come across them another time, you likely will recognize them and know what they mean. To make new words a part of your active vocabulary it is a good idea to practice using them. List them and, when appropriate in your writing, try them out.

Words have primary or explicit meanings, *denotations*, which we find (along with information about pronunciation and derivation) in dictionaries. They have *connotations* as well—secondary, implied meanings based on associations. "Hearth," for example, is defined as the floor of a fireplace, but the word may *suggest* warmth and friendship. "Beach" means a stretch of sand or pebbles along a seashore, but the word may suggest expansiveness or freedom from restraint. When choosing a word, you must take into account both its explicit and its implicit meanings.

The choice of words is called *diction*. Good diction requires the writer to select words with care and take pains to arrange them in a way that will best convey meaning. You should not assume that your reader is a mind reader and must not lay on him or her the burden of trying to unravel the meaning of what you have written. Your job is to sort out ideas and then, utilizing suitable words, to express them clearly to the reader.

No word is in itself bad. But any word you choose must be apt, meaningful, consistent with the rest of the words you use, and appropriate for your audience and the occasion of your writing.

Words may usefully be grouped as *ambiguous* or *vague, specific* or *general, abstract* or *concrete*.

Ambiguous and Vague Words

Ambiguous words are words that can be understood in more than one sense. An example is "un-American." The word is ambiguous because it may mean different things to different people. Using a word without making clear which of its meanings you intend can confuse your reader. (I will discuss the need for definition to avoid misunderstanding in "Definition," pages 276–300.)

Vague words are words that do not communicate an exact meaning. "Fantastic," as in "He's a *fantastic* person," is vague because it doesn't specifically modify "person." Among the more precise words that might be substituted for it are "charming," "outgoing," and "enthusiastic."

Among the many words that beginning writers often use inaccurately are "cool," "marvelous," "remarkable," "terrific," and "wonderful." These words, as your dictionary will reveal, have precise meanings, but in certain contexts they are inexact. Compare their use in these sentences with the possible alternative words in parentheses:

Jane's party was cool (lively, unusual, uproarious).

Mr. Smith is a marvelous (knowledgeable, understanding, helpful) teacher.

I had a remarkable (fulfilling, relaxing, instructive) weekend.

The movie was terrific (entertaining, enlightening, terrifying).

Sarah has a wonderful (loving, supportive, compassionate) father.

In each instance, the more definite alternative conveys more exact meaning.

Specific and General Words

In addition to differentiating between vague and precise words, we can classify words according to whether they are specific or general. Specific words—for example, "hamburger," "jeans," "house," "dog," "quarterback"—convey more particular meaning than do general words: "food," "clothing," "building," "animal," "athlete." "The cook served John a *hamburger*" creates a better defined image than does "The cook served John *food*."

"Specific" and "general" are relative terms, as you can see from this series:

substance, food, meat, beef, hamburger

"Food" is more specific than "substance" but more general than "meat," and "beef" is more specific than "meat" but more general than "hamburger." Here are more examples of the gradation of words from general to specific:

clothing, outerwear, trousers, jeans, Levis

structure, building, dwelling, house, dormitory

animal, mammal, dog, poodle, Fido

animal, man, athlete, football player, quarterback

You can make a specific word more specific by adding one or more modifiers. "*Broiled* hamburger" is more specific than "hamburger"; "*charcoal-broiled* hamburger" is still more specific; "*medium-rare charcoal-broiled* hamburger" is more specific yet.

Compare the image called forth by

The cook served John a hamburger

with the one evoked by

The cook served John a *medium-rare charcoal-broiled* hamburger.

To appreciate the function and effect of specific diction, compare the words in these different reports of the same event:

The men walked into the bank with guns drawn. One stayed near the door while the other went behind the counter and put currency into a bag.

The masked gunmen rushed into the Main Street branch of the United Bank and Trust Company, brandishing Colt .45s. One bandit stationed himself just inside the front door while the other desperado leaped over the teller's counter and stuffed bundles of brand-new 10-, 20-, and 50-dollar bills into a brown paper bag.

To emphasize more the importance of the writer's carefully choosing specific words to convey meaning vividly, here are the two sentences arranged schematically:

The men	The masked gunmen
walked	rushed
into the bank	into the Main Street branch of the United Bank and Trust Company
with guns drawn.	brandishing Colt .45s.
One	One bandit
stayed	stationed himself
near the door	just inside the front door
while the other	while the other desperado
went behind	leaped over
the counter	the teller's counter
and put	and stuffed
currency	bundles of brand-new 10-, 20-, and 50-dollar bills
into a bag.	into a brown paper bag.

The specific words in the right-hand column depict in detail what happened and give the reader a more precise picture than do the words in the left-hand column.

Abstract and Concrete Words

Words may be classified as abstract or concrete. The words in the first column denote abstractions—intangibles, ideas. The words in the second column are concrete—relating to the experience of our senses, to things that are actual or real.

friendship	handshake
love	embrace
femininity	woman
beauty	rainbow
calamity	earthquake
color	blue

Like "specific" and "general," "abstract" and "concrete" are relative terms. Consider, for example, this series:

justice, the law, rules of the road, speeding limit, 55 M.P.H.

When writers deal with concepts they will of course have occasion to use abstract words: "We hold these *truths* to be sacred and undeniable. . . ." But to convey particulars they will use concrete words because, like specific words, concrete words are more vivid.

Imagery

Another way to enliven your writing is with imagery. "Imagery" refers to mental pictures representing an actual scene and to the nonliteral use of language in figures of speech such as *simile* and *metaphor*.
    Here are examples of simile:

. . . he was *as nervous as a race horse* fretting to be on the track [Willa Cather, "When I Knew Stephen Crane"].

The visitor was lively and eager; her mind lay open and orderly, *like a notebook ready for impressions* [Mary McCarthy, "America the Beautiful"].

> O, my luve is *like a red, red rose,*
> That's newly sprung in June
> [Robert Burns, "A Red, Red Rose"]

Notice that in each instance a comparison is expressed between dissimilar things (a man with a nervous race horse; a mind with a notebook; a beloved with a rose) and that, as in most similes, the comparisons are introduced by "as" or "like."

A metaphor is an implied comparison that identifies one thing with an unlike other thing. If Burns had written, "my luve *is* a rose," instead of "my luve is *like* a rose," he would have created a metaphor. Here are two examples of metaphor:

> . . . we drove my father through a *wilderness* of smashed plate glass [James Baldwin, *Notes of a Native Son*].

> In the middle of the *journey* of our life I came to myself within a dark wood where the straight way was lost [Dante Alighieri, *Inferno*].

Here the streets of Harlem covered with smashed plate glass after a riot are identified with a wilderness, and life with a journey. Like similes, metaphors animate writing by evoking visual images.

Formal and Informal Language

Another distinction between types of diction is formal and informal language. Formal language is likely to contain scholarly, multisyllabic, and abstract words; informal language, everyday, short, concrete words, as well as some slang.

Just as the attire you would choose for a church wedding or a funeral would differ from what you would wear to a tennis match or a picnic, the selection of formal or informal words will depend on the occasion. Would you use the same language in a letter to the admissions officer of a graduate school as you would in a letter to a fellow student? When writing to a friend, you probably would use everyday language and slang, language that is very informal. However informal your letter to the admissions officer, you most likely would not use slang.

Degrees of formality and informality, in descending order, may be observed in these passages:

This was the American Dream: a sanctuary on the earth for individual man: a condition in which he could be free not only of the old established closed-corporation hierarchies of arbitrary power which had oppressed him as a mass, but free of that mass into which the hierarchies of church and state had compressed and held him individually thralled and individually impotent [William Faulkner, "On Privacy"].

There are two ways in which one can own a book. The first is the property right you establish by paying for it, just as you pay for clothes and furniture. But this act of purchase is only the prelude to possession. Full ownership comes only when you have made it a part of yourself, and the best way to make yourself a part of it is by writing in it. An illustration may make the point clear. You buy a beefsteak and transfer it from the butcher's icebox to your own. But you do not own the beefsteak in the most important sense until you consume it and get it into your bloodstream. I am arguing that books, too, must be absorbed in your bloodstream to do you any good [Mortimer J. Adler, "How to Mark a Book"].

Richard Nixon's Vice President, Spiro Agnew, writing about Attica under his byline in *The New York Times* newspaper the other day, said: "To compare the loss of life by those who violate society's law with the loss of life of those whose job it is to uphold it—represents not simply an assault on human sensibility but an insult to reason."

Beautiful. I think it was the greatest article I read in my whole life. . . . Because of it I finally was able to brush off the last shreds of the stupid ideas Sister Anna Gertrude outfitted us with in St. Benedict Joseph Labre School, Queens, New York City.

That silly Jesus Christ. The way that old nun made us learn it, Jesus spent the whole last morning of his Life standing in Part XXXII with a real bum named Barabbas. Instead of making a deal to sink Barabbas, Christ stood around rooting for Barabbas to get his case severed and dropped. One description of Barabbas was that he was a boss of thieves in Jerusalem. The first Jewish button man. I used to sit in class and picture Barabbas as Lepke [a notorious American gangster] with a beard [Jimmy Breslin, "The Greatest Article I Read in My Whole Life"].

Observe in the last passage the writer's use of ordinary, everyday words, among them the informal "bum" and "making a deal" and the slangy "button man." These words are not improper in themselves; no words ever are. The propriety of a word depends on the writer's purpose and the occasion of its use.

Inflated Language

Some people try to use language to impress their audience. In an article that appeared not too long ago in the newspaper of a university in southern New England, a young man wrote, "As a graduate student . . . I have come to realize the blatant dysfunctionality of this process we call education." Not satisfied with a simple word such as "fault," the writer—trying to score a verbal home run—stretched beyond the possible three-syllable "dysfunction" to the six-syllable "dysfunctionality," which is not a word at all, in an attempt to wow his audience.

In the same essay there is this sentence: "I arrived at school with open arms and an open mind." "With open arms" and "an open mind" are *clichés*—overused, colorless expressions like "fit as a fiddle," "water over the dam," "call a spade a spade," and "no flies on him"—which writers use to avoid the mental exertion needed to clarify their own thinking and to make their meaning clear to their readers. "What," a reader has the right to ask, "do you mean by 'with open arms and an open mind'? That you were eager to learn? That you were not prejudging school?"

The young man also wrote in his article, "As an impressionable 17-year-old high school student, ideas of materiality pervaded my world. The pursuance of a college degree and the 'rewards' associated with it seemed to me an entirely pragmatic outlook." This is gobbledegook—pretentious, long-winded, unintelligible, and dull. What the writer probably meant to say is: "When I was 17 years old, possessions were important where I lived, and getting a college degree in order to make money seemed proper."

The same student finally managed to work into his article the currently popular and overused "viable." He wrote, "At this time I can't offer any viable alternatives," instead of saying simply that he has no alternatives.

Wordiness is of course not limited to students. "At this point in time" is widely used as a substitute for "now." Edwin Newman, the television commentator, in *Strictly Speaking*, reminds us that a former White House press secretary requested an extension of time so that the President's attorney could "evaluate and make a judgment in terms of a response." What he meant was that the attorney "wanted more time to think about it."

Careful writers use language economically. Knowing what they want to communicate, they put ideas into as few precise, apt words as possible. Not:

> I intend to express my own opinions, hoping with them to make clear to the reader of this paper the background and origins, the whys and wherefores of the deterioration and decline in the viability in the marketplace of our currency at this time.

But:

> My purpose is to explain the present decline in the purchasing power of the dollar.

The first of these sentences, containing forty-four words, is meandering, pretentious, and unintelligible. The second, of fifteen words, is compact and meaningful.

In lieu of a twenty-seven-word sentence with needless introductory phrases and useless repetition of words with similar meaning, such as

> In my opinion it seems necessary to point out that the plaintiff in this case is making statements that are lies, untrue, and not at all believable.

the effective writer creates a concise, forceful sentence of four words:

> The plaintiff is lying.

Wordiness

Wordiness is the use of more words than are necessary to make one's meaning clear. In your writing, make a special effort to eliminate needless words when you rewrite your first draft. Here is how you might revise wordy sentences:

Original:

Concerning the question of whether or not the power of the legislative branch of the government should be allowed to proliferate, it seems to me that it depends basically on the crucial factor of how great you want the strength of the executive branch of the government to be. (49 words)

Revised:

Whether congressional power should be increased depends on how strong you want the presidency to be. (16 words)

At least five common faults appear in the original sentence.

1. *Useless phrases* — that is, phrases that contribute nothing to the meaning of a sentence: "concerning the question of" and "it seems to me that."

2. *Redundancy* — unneeded repetition of words: "or not" ("whether" implies "or not").

3. *A useless word* — one that contributes nothing to the meaning of the sentence containing it: "basically."

4. *A vague word:* "factor."

5. *Pretentious diction* — words used to impress the reader: "crucial factor."

Containing only a third as many words as the original, the revised sentence conveys concisely and more clearly as much information as the original does.

Original:

For the period of a year, there has been no observable improvement in the area of crime for the simple reason that there has not been a fundamental change for the better in crime prevention capability. (36 words)

Revised:

For a year the rate of crime has been stable because the police force is still inadequate. (17 words)

The original sentence contains at least three common faults:

1. *Circumlocutions* – roundabout expressions: "for the period of a year" and "for the simple reason that."

2. *Needless words:* "in the area of," "observable," and "fundamental."

3. *Pretentious diction:* "crime prevention capability."

In the revised sentence, the writer has replaced the vague and uneconomical "there has not been a fundamental change for the better in crime prevention capability" with the precise, concise, and vigorous "the police force is still inadequate."

Original:

With reference to your question, I came to discover at that point in time that I was definitely a religious person due to the fact that I was completely impressed concerning the matter of a belief in a life after death among the people in my family. (47 words)

Revised:

I discovered that I was religious then because I was impressed with my family's belief in a life after death. (20 words)

This original sentence has at least four common faults:

1. *Useless beginning:* "with reference to your question."

2. *Useless words:* "came to" and "among the people."

3. *Circumlocutions:* "at that point in time" and "due to the fact that."

4. *Unnecessary qualifiers,* which fail to achieve the intended emphasis: "definitely" and "completely."

The revised sentence is simple and direct.

The best comment on wordiness that I know, and a model of brevity itself (sixty-three words), is E. B. White's quotation of his composition teacher at Cornell, William Strunk, Jr., in *The Elements of Style:*

> Vigorous writing is concise. A sentence should contain no unnecessary words, a paragraph no unnecessary sentences, for the same reason that a drawing should have no unnecessary lines and a machine no unnecessary parts. This requires not that the writer make all his sentences short, or that he avoid all detail and treat his subjects only in outline, but that every word tell.

Make "every word tell." See how much meaning Abraham Lincoln packed into the 173 words of the Gettysburg Address.

About every word you put on paper ask yourself, "What does it contribute to the meaning, clarity, and conciseness of my writing?"

THE DEATH OF BENNY PARET
Norman Mailer

Norman Mailer wrote the important World War II novel **The Naked and the Dead** (1948). His nonfiction works include the Pulitzer Prize–winning **Armies of the Night** (1968), written in the style of the so-called new journalism (see page 316).

---

1   On the afternoon of the night Emile Griffith and Benny Paret were to fight a third time for the welterweight championship, there

From *The Presidential Papers* by Norman Mailer. Reprinted by permission of the author and the author's agents, Scott Meredith Literary Agency, Inc., 845 Third Avenue, New York, N.Y. 10022.

was murder in both camps. "I hate that kind of guy," Paret had said earlier to Pete Hamill about Griffith. "A fighter's got to look and talk and act like a man." One of the Broadway gossip columnists had run an item about Griffith a few days before. His girl friend saw it and said to Griffith, "Emile, I didn't know about you being that way." So Griffith hit her. So he said. Now at the weigh-in that morning, Paret had insulted Griffith irrevocably, touching him on the buttocks, while making a few more remarks about his manhood. They almost had their fight on the scales.

₂ The rage in Emile Griffith was extreme. I was at the fight that night, I had never seen a fight like it. It was scheduled for fifteen rounds, but they fought without stopping from the bell which began the round to the bell which ended it, and then they fought after the bell, sometimes for as much as fifteen seconds before the referee could force them apart.

₃ Paret was a Cuban, a proud club fighter who had become welterweight champion because of his unusual ability to take a punch. His style of fighting was to take three punches to the head in order to give back two. At the end of ten rounds, he would still be bouncing, his opponent would have a headache. But in the last two years, over the fifteen-round fights, he had started to take some bad maulings.

₄ This fight had its turns. Griffith won most of the early rounds, but Paret knocked Griffith down in the sixth. Griffith had trouble getting up, but made it, came alive and was dominating Paret again before the round was over. Then Paret began to wilt. In the middle of the eighth round, after a clubbing punch had turned his back to Griffith, Paret walked three disgusted steps away, showing his hindquarters. For a champion, he took much too long to turn back around. It was the first hint of weakness Paret had ever shown, and it must have inspired a particular shame, because he fought the rest of the fight as if he were seeking to demonstrate that he could take more punishment than any man alive. In the twelfth, Griffith caught him. Paret got trapped in a corner. Trying to duck away, his left arm and his head became tangled on the wrong side of the top rope. Griffith was in like a cat ready to rip the life out of a huge boxed rat. He hit him eighteen right hands in a row, an act which took perhaps three or four seconds, Griffith making a pent-up whimpering sound all the while he attacked, the right hand whipping like a piston rod which has broken through the crankcase, or like a baseball bat demolishing a pumpkin. I was sitting in the second row of that corner—they were not ten feet away from me, and like everybody else, I was hypnotized. I had never seen one man hit another so hard and so many times. Over the referee's face came a look of woe as if some spasm had passed its way through him, and then he leaped on Griffith to pull him away. It was the act of a brave man. Griffith was uncontrollable. His trainer leaped into the ring, his manager, his cut man, there were four people holding Griffith, but he was off on an orgy, he had left the Garden, he was back on a hoodlum's street. If he had been able to break loose from his handlers and the referee, he would have jumped Paret to the floor and whaled on him there.

And Paret? Paret died on his feet. As he took those eighteen punches something happened to everyone who was in psychic range of the event. Some part of his death reached out to us. One felt it hover in the air. He was still standing in the ropes, trapped as he had been before, he gave some little half-smile of regret, as if he were saying, "I didn't know I was going to die just yet," and then, his head leaning back but still erect, his death came to breathe about him. He began to pass away. As he passed, so his limbs descended beneath him, and he sank slowly to the floor. He went down more slowly than any fighter had ever gone down, he went down like a large ship which turns on end and slides second by second into its grave. As he went down, the sound of Griffith's punches echoed in the mind like a heavy ax in the distance chopping into a wet log.

Questions About "Words"

1. Instead of "murder" (par. 1), Mailer might have written "bad feelings." Which do you prefer? Why?

    Mailer might have written "reaction" instead of "rage" (par. 2). Why did he choose the word he did?

3. Why is the word "maulings" (par. 3), in the context of this essay, an apt choice?

4. In paragraph 4, Mailer wrote "wilt" and "clubbing punch." He might have written, instead, "to slow up" and "heavy blow." Which words express more meaning? Explain.

5. What is the effect on you of "like a cat ready to rip the life out of a huge boxed rat" (par. 4)? Find three more examples in this essay of Mailer's use of a similar figure of speech for the same purpose.

6. What is your feeling about the Griffith-Paret fight? Does Mailer, by his choice of words, try to affect your attitude toward it? Explain.

Questions on Diction and Writing Techniques

1. Mailer might have written sentence 1 of paragraph 3: "Paret, a proud club fighter who had become a welterweight champion because of his unusual ability to take a punch, was a Cuban." Which version better emphasizes the main idea of the sentence? Why?

2. "Griffith caught him in the twelfth." Does this version of a sentence in paragraph 4 better emphasize the main idea of the sentence? Why or why not?

3. Is there any point in this essay where your interest wanes? If so, explain why.

For Discussion, Reading, and Writing

1. What was the first hint of weakness Paret showed?

2. Why do you think boxing attracts such a large audience?

3. Does Mailer, in this essay, express or imply a comment about boxing? Explain.

4. Write a draft of a paragraph about any violent encounter you

have observed. In a second draft, add one or more similes or metaphors.

5. Attend a sports event, or any other kind of event. Using as many apt, vivid words as possible, write a short essay about it.

SUMMER

Mimi Sheraton

Mimi Sheraton, food and restaurant critic of **The New York Times**, has written books about cooking. **From My Mother's Kitchen**, from which this essay is taken, includes recipes and reminiscences of a family that indulged in good eating.

1   Summer was always my favorite season, not only because I loved heat, but because school was closed and I was free.

2   Flatbush was beautiful in summer, and a visit there only a short while ago proved that it still is. The small streets with their amply spreading maple trees are dappled with sun and shade, and the somewhat unprepossessing builders' houses are set in velvety lawns and flowery borders. And occasionally, one still hears the giggles of children in bathing suits running under hissing lawn sprinklers in backyards.

3   Our house was cool and dark in summer, and the faint, exotic aromas of camphor and tar paper hung in the air, adding to the out-of-season relaxed feeling, though I suppose some people might find those odors stifling. All the furniture was covered with the same slipcover fabric, a teal-blue and natural striped Belgian linen, fine, heavy, and glossy, piped in orange. Even the upright piano and its bench wore their shrouds from early June to late September.

From "Summer" (pp. 108–110) from *From My Mother's Kitchen* by Mimi Sheraton. Copyright © 1979 by Mimi Sheraton. Reprinted by permission of Harper and Row, Publishers, Inc.

Oriental rugs were rolled on poles and wrapped in tar paper and slid up to the attic, to be replaced by white and flowered Indian druggets that stank to high heaven on damp days.

4   Most of our time was spent at the Brooklyn beaches, Manhattan and Oriental, which were then private, and where the name bands of the late thirties—Benny Goodman, the Dorsey Brothers, Glenn Miller, and more—played every afternoon on week-long engagements.

5   We took wonderful sandwiches to those beaches—big, squashy and crisp poppy-seed rolls or sliced rye bread piled with egg salad made with minced green pepper; salmon or tuna salad with celery and parsley; thick slices of home cooked pickled tongue with fiery mustard; rare roast beef with both mustard and butter; tomato herring with slices of Bermuda onion and butter; and others. I say wonderful now, but I remember the embarrassment I felt at the rye bread sandwiches and how I wished for neat, squared-off sandwiches on packaged white bread, which I considered more American and, therefore, classier.

6   The problem with the rye bread was its shape—the standard loaf that tapered toward both ends. My mother cut it on the diagonal to make larger slices, and because the loaf tapered, no two slices were the same size, so the edges of my sandwiches did not "match." They were, I thought, sloppy Jewish sandwiches, and what wouldn't I do to be eating one even as I write?

7   In addition to our own, we ate other food sold at the beach. Not only hot dogs and ice cream, but the local specialty—hot, freshly made waffles, which we sprinkled with lots of vanilla-scented confectioner's sugar as we held them between sheets of glassine paper.

8   There were marvelous summer dinners, too—fried chicken at room temperature, assortments of salads, perhaps an all-dairy dinner with blintzes and sour cream as a combination main course and dessert, or sour cream and pot cheese mixed with chopped radishes, scallions, and cucumbers, slices of cold roast beef with homemade pepper slaw and potato salad. But one summer dinner stands for all others in my memory.

9   It took place when I was very young—about nine or so—and had spent the day with a friend seeing the movie *It Happened One Night*, with Clark Gable and Claudette Colbert. One look at Gable

sans undershirt (the famous scene that sent undershirt sales plummeting), and even at nine I was hooked.

10 We ate in the dining room that very hot night because it was cooler than the kitchen. There were only three of us (my brother was too young to eat with us and was already asleep), and the table was huge, so my mother set only half of it, drawing the ivory-colored crocheted lace cloth back and placing a pad and white damask cloth over the half at which we sat.

11 The menu was cold beet borscht with sour cream and hot boiled potatoes, cold fried flounder with just hints of cinnamon and hot paprika in its crisp breading, hot buttered corn, pepper slaw, a fresh peach kuchen in a deep dish bathed with thick, heavy un whipped sweet cream, and a pitcher of iced tea with lemon slices and sprigs of mint from the back yard.

12 As my father, mother, and I sat down, I announced that I knew who I would marry.

13 "Really? Who?" asked my mother.

14 "Clark Gable," I answered emphatically.

15 "Over my dead body," my mother said with shock and a disturbing firmness in her voice.

16 "Why not?" I asked, amazed that such a simple announcement should touch off such an obvious wellspring of disapproval.

17 "Because he's not Jewish, and Jewish girls marry Jewish boys," she answered.

18 "Then I won't be Jewish. I think that's stupid," I answered, and the argument was on.

19 Midway through dinner my father, whose temper was shorter than usual in hot weather, shouted "Quiet! Quiet!" and to me, "Look, if you want to marry Clark Gable, marry Clark Gable. I'll pay for the wedding."

20 This was more than my mother could stand, and she flared up at him, yelling, "Sure, you give her ideas—go ahead, go ahead, encourage her. Very nice for a rabbi's granddaughter!"

21 This time my father blew up, banging for quiet on the table with such force that his borscht flew up out of his bowl on to the white cotton cloth. As the argument continued I watched the slow, inevitable spread of the pink stain as it bled out on the cloth.

22 "You're crazier than she is," he said to my mother. "Imagine arguing with a nine-year-old child because she wants to marry one

of the country's top movie stars. She'll never even meet him," he said.

23   He was wrong, for about twenty-five years later I did meet Clark Gable. It was on a movie set in Rome, where I worked for a few minutes as an extra. We talked for a while, he complaining about having had all of his guns stolen during a recent hunting trip in Austria, and I noting that even though he was obviously aging and that his thick figure was stiffly corseted, the King was still the King. I like to think that the possibility of our marriage was not quite as remote as my father had thought it to be.

Questions About "Words"

1. Find, in paragraphs 2 and 3, examples of Sheraton's use of sensory words — words that relate to the senses.

2. Are "wonderful" (par. 5) and "marvelous" (par. 8) apt diction? Explain.

3. Sheraton might have written the sentence in paragraph 11: "The menu was borscht, flounder, corn, slaw, a kuchen, and tea." Which version do you prefer? Why? Imitating Sheraton's style, start with a sentence such as "Breakfast consisted of juice, eggs, bacon, and coffee" and make its diction more specific; for example: "Breakfast consisted of a tall glass of just-squeezed cold orange juice, two large fresh eggs, sunny-side up, three pieces of crisp tangy bacon, heavily-buttered warm hard rolls, and piping-hot coffee with sugar and cream."

Questions on Diction and Writing Techniques

1. Explain what dialogue contributes to the effectiveness of the storytelling.

2. What portrait of the parents emerges from the dialogue? Describe them in a paragraph of not over 100 words.

For Discussion, Reading, and Writing

1. Which of these statements are true (T), which false (F)?

   A. _____ Summer was Sheraton's favorite season because it was a time of wonderful food.

   B. _____ The problem with the rye bread was that it had to be cut diagonally to make larger slices.

   C. _____ In addition to their own food, Sheraton and her family ate hamburgers sold at the beach.

   D. _____ One summer dinner was especially memorable for its outstanding assortment of wonderful food.

   E. _____ Sheraton's mother called her father "crazy" because he lost his temper, banged on the table, spilled the borscht, and stained the white cotton tablecloth.

2. Write a draft of a short essay about any memorable meal you have had. Revise your writing, including words that make it as vivid as possible.

AMERICANS AND THE LAND
John Steinbeck

John Steinbeck (1902–1968) wrote, among other works, **The Grapes of Wrath** (1939), a sociological novel that put him in the front rank of twentieth-century American writers. He won the Nobel Prize for Literature in 1962.

₁   I have often wondered at the savagery and thoughtlessness with which our early settlers approached this rich continent. They came at it as though it were an enemy, which of course it was. They burned the forests and changed the rainfall; they swept the buffalo from the plains, blasted the streams, set fire to the grass, and ran a reckless scythe through the virgin and noble timber. Perhaps they felt that it was limitless and could never be exhausted and that a man could move on to new wonders endlessly. Certainly there are many examples to the contrary, but to a large extent the early people pillaged the country as though they hated it, as though they held it temporarily and might be driven off at any time.

₂   This tendency toward irresponsibility persists in very many of us today; our rivers are poisoned by reckless dumping of sewage and toxic industrial wastes, the air of our cities is filthy and dangerous to breathe from the belching of uncontrolled products from combustion of coal, coke, oil, and gasoline. Our towns are girdled with wreckage and the debris of our toys—our automobiles and our packaged pleasures. Through uninhibited spraying against one enemy we have destroyed the natural balances our survival requires. All these evils can and must be overcome if America and Americans are to survive; but many of us still conduct ourselves as our ancestors did, stealing from the future for our clear and present profit. . . .

₃   On the East Coast, and particularly in New England, the colonists farmed meager lands close to their communities and to safety. Every man was permanently on duty for the defense of his family and his village; even the hunting parties went into the forest in force, rather like raiders than hunters, and their subsequent quarrels with the Indians, resulting in forays and even massacres, remind us that the danger was very real. A man took his gun along when he worked the land, and the women stayed close to their thick-walled houses and listened day and night for the signal of alarm. The towns they settled were permanent, and most of them exist today with their records of Indian raids, of slaughter, of scalpings, and of punitive counter-raids. The military leader of the community became the chief authority in time of trouble, and it was a long time before danger receded and the mystery could be explored.

₄   After a time, however, brave and forest-wise men drifted westward to hunt, to trap, and eventually to bargain for the furs which were the first precious negotiable wealth America produced for trade and export. Then trading posts were set up as centers of collection and the exploring men moved up and down the rivers and crossed the mountains, made friends for mutual profit with the Indians, learned the wilderness techniques, so that these explorer-traders soon dressed, ate, and generally acted like the indigenous people around them. Suspicion lasted a long time, and was fed by clashes sometimes amounting to full-fledged warfare; but by now these Americans attacked and defended as the Indians did.

5   For a goodly time the Americans were travelers, moving about the country collecting its valuables, but with little idea of permanence; their roots and their hearts were in the towns and the growing cities along the eastern edge. The few who stayed, who lived among the Indians, adopted their customs and some took Indian wives and were regarded as strange and somehow treasonable creatures. As for their half-breed children, while the tribe sometimes adopted them they were unacceptable as equals in the eastern settlements.

6   Then the trickle of immigrants became a stream, and the population began to move westward—not to grab and leave but to settle and live, they thought. The newcomers were of peasant stock, and they had their roots in a Europe where they had been landless, for the possession of land was the requirement and the proof of a higher social class than they had known. In America they found beautiful and boundless land for the taking—and they took it.

7   It is little wonder that they went land-mad, because there was so much of it. They cut and burned the forests to make room for crops; they abandoned their knowledge of kindness to the land in order to maintain its usefulness. When they had cropped out a piece they moved on, raping the country like invaders. The topsoil, held by roots and freshened by leaf-fall, was left helpless to the spring freshets, stripped and eroded with the naked bones of clay and rock exposed. The destruction of the forests changed the rainfall, for the searching clouds could find no green and beckoning woods to draw them on and milk them. The merciless nineteenth century was like a hostile expedition for loot that seemed limitless. Uncountable buffalo were killed, stripped of their hides, and left to rot, a reservoir of permanent food supply eliminated. More than that, the land of the Great Plains was robbed of the manure of the herds. Then the plows went in and ripped off the protection of the buffalo grass and

opened the helpless soil to quick water and slow drought and the mischievous winds that roamed through the Great Central Plains. There has always been more than enough desert in America; the new settlers, like overindulged children, created even more.

Questions About "Words"

1. What is the effect on you of the language: *"reckless* scythe" (par. 1), *"helpless* soil" (par. 7), *"mischievous* winds" (par. 7)?

2. What purpose does Steinbeck reveal by his choice of words: *"noble* timber" (par. 1), *"pillaged* the country" (par. 1), *"stealing* from the future" (par. 2), *"raping* the country *like invaders"* (par. 7)?

3. Find examples of metaphor and simile in paragraphs 6 and 7. What is the purpose of these figures of speech?

Questions on Diction and Writing Techniques

1. How, in paragraph 1, does Steinbeck support the idea of "the savagery and thoughtlessness with which our early settlers approached this rich continent"? Would the paragraph be as, more, or less effective if its third sentence were omitted? Explain. How, in paragraph 2, does the writer explain the generalization, "This tendency toward irresponsibility persists in very many of us today"?

2. How does Steinbeck achieve coherence in paragraph 1?

3. How does "this" help achieve coherence between paragraphs 1 and 2?

4. Find examples of coordination in the first sentence of paragraph 2.

5. How does Steinbeck achieve coherence between paragraphs 3 and 4?

6. Steinbeck uses "then," a word that signals a change in time, in

paragraph 4. Find examples of its use in paragraphs 6 and 7. What does the word contribute to order?

For Discussion, Reading, and Writing

1. "This tendency toward irresponsibility persists in very many of us today . . ." Using one or more of the examples of "irresponsibility" Steinbeck gives in paragraph 2, or any other you are familiar with, write a short essay in which you use specific details to explain your thesis and precise, specific, concrete diction to convey your meaning clearly to your readers.

2. What does Steinbeck mean by "packaged pleasures" (par. 2)? Can you cite examples of some? Why does he say that "our automobiles and our packaged pleasures" are "toys"? Do you agree? Why?

3. Trying to affect and to control the response of your readers by your choice of words, write a short essay about your hometown, using a topic related to this subject: "Our towns are girdled with wreckage and the debris of our toys—our automobiles and our packaged pleasures."

THE GREAT YANKEE STADIUM HOLDUP
Shirley Povich

Shirley Povich, sports editor of **The Washington Post** at the age of twenty, has to his credit columns that have won awards for fine sports writing. Typical of that writing is this report of a prize fight for the heavyweight championship.

From *Best Sports Stories 1977*, eds. Irving T. Marsh and Edward Fine (New York: Dutton, 1977), pp. 19–21.

1   They staged the great Yankee Stadium holdup Tuesday night
when they held up the arm of Muhammad Ali and called him the
winner at the end of 15 rounds.

2   The victim of this violence to simple justice was Ken Norton,
the challenger to Ali's heavyweight boxing crown. Norton had just
exposed Ali as a tired old relic of the prize ring wars who now talks
a better fight than he fights.

3   But Ali was reendowed with the title he lost in the ring by
two judges and a referee intimidated by the old shibboleth that the
decision can't go against the champ if the fight is close. Norton was
jobbed. The fight wasn't close, and their logic is baseless, anyway. If
you've overdrawn at the bank, even by a dollar, you're overdrawn.

4   Once more it was Ali getting the benefit of some sacred quality
attributed to him. Norton licked him in their second fight three
years ago, but it was close enough to bring Ali the decision. The
vote could have gone against him in that bummer fight with Jimmy
Young in Washington a few months back, but it didn't.

5   Before the bell rang for Round 15 Tuesday night, there was
scribbling on this scoreboard. It read: "Ali needs this one big. A KO
or we got new champ."

6   But he blew the fifteenth round, too, to a tireless Norton who
managed to catch up with Ali's defensive dance and fetch him a left
hook and two rights that were the only telling punches of the
round. Ali's title had surely slipped away. On this scorecard, it was
8–6–1 for Norton.

7   Then came Norton's biggest jolt of the fight. Justice had been
kicked in the butt. Norton, who had won the title in the ring, lost
it to those little pencils that were marking the official scoring.

8   Ali was all talk, little fight. Between rounds, he repeatedly
went to the ropes, sometimes on all four sides of the ring, to exhort
his fans in his own cry, "Norton must fall." But Norton was the
most unpsyched opponent Ali has ever faced. With an assurance that
stemmed largely from the fact that he had punished Ali in their previous two bouts, Norton was unafraid and more than faintly con-
temptuous of this cheerleader who was trying to lick him. This guy
wasn't George Foreman, who could level a man with one punch.

9   As a prizefighter, the only thing classic about Norton is his su-
perbly sculptured body that tapers in lines that make Ali look thick-
waisted. Norton's fighting style is mostly pursuit, and a bit on the

awkward side, with too many roundhouse rights, but unlike Ali, he came to fight.

10   At thirty-four, Ali had lost the speed that meant everything to him. The fleshiness at 222 pounds is more than baby fat. His performance against Foreman was his own recognition he can't move like he used to. From the opening bell, he was a defensive fighter. Alternately, he went into his dance and his rope-a-dope for long periods, no way to score points except in the glee of his admirers who take almost everything Ali does in the ring.

11   "Norton will fall in five," Ali had said repeatedly before the fight.

12   When Round Five commenced, he was warned for holding again. He blew that round, too, with his defensive rope-a-dope, and when, near the bell, he ventured out into the middle of the ring, he got popped with a Norton right.

13   Ali was winning the delighted shouts of his fans with his new gimmick, a shimmy of the buttocks that he introduced in the third round to taunt Norton, but meanwhile he was losing that round, too. Norton won all five rounds from the fourth to the ninth, and two of the last three, only to be fouled by the ring official at the finish.

14   Ali miscalculated when he went into his rope-a-dope coverup against Norton for long stretches in the belief that Norton's flailing would bring on the weariness that finally caught up with Foreman in Zaire.

15   But the thirty-one-year-old Norton was perfectly conditioned for this night, and he didn't weary, and he was slipping in some decent punches in his assaults on Ali's peekaboo defense. When Ali in desperation, tried to break it off, he was clubbed in the head.

16   Norton was guilty of only one, unfortunate mistake of no special importance. That was in the thirteenth round when, believing he was completely in command, he mimicked Ali's rope-a-dope retreat into his own corner, and dared Ali to come to him. He didn't bring it off very well, and in fact he lost the round, but that was the last round he lost on this scorecard, despite the official scoring that showed eight of nine markings in the last three rounds in favor of Ali.

17   Ali's performance was a $6 million fraud on the viewing public. That was his guarantee, and he rarely tried to earn it. The clos-

est he came to having Norton in any serious trouble was in a late round when Norton had to recover from a thumb in his eye. Norton was charging forward in every round with the faith that he was fighting a man who couldn't hurt him, and that was the size of it. Faced with a moving target, Ali had little punch, and his overriding desire was not to get hurt.

18   The new Ali buttocks wriggle even drew a rebuke from his manager and spiritual leader, Herbert Muhammad, who was at ringside. "Tell him to cut that stuff out."

19   Ali's corner was a study of depression after they brought Ali in at the final bell. None of the customary joy there, but a terrible fear that Ali had lost this one. Good-bye to that $10 million gate with Foreman. Good-bye title. Ali was awfully tired, and looked merely resigned. Then, Norton got hit, simultaneously by three robbers pulling loaded scorecards on him.

Questions About "Words"

1. What does the pun in paragraph 1 reveal about Povich's attitude toward the fight? What is revealed by "tired old relic" (par. 2)? Find other choices of words that reveal the writer's attitude toward his subject.

2. Define the following words and write sentences using each of them appropriately: shibboleth (par. 3), jobbed (par. 3).

3. What kind of language is "bummer" (par. 4)? Find three more examples of similar diction in this essay.

4. Substitute other words for "those little pencils" (par. 7). Which version do you prefer? Why? In the context of this essay, is Povich's choice of words appropriate? Explain.

5. Find a figure of speech in paragraph 7.

6. Do you know the meaning of "rope-a-dope" (par. 14)? Can you find the word in any dictionary? Is Povich justified in using it?

7. What experience of yours, if any, does Povich evoke with "peek-aboo defense" (par. 15)? Comment on the aptness of this phrase.

8. Is the writer consistent in this essay in the kind of language he uses? Cite examples to support your answer.

9. Is the very informal diction in this essay appropriate to the writer's subject and audience? Explain.

Questions on Diction and Writing Techniques

1. Does paragraph 1 fulfill the purposes of an opening paragraph? Explain.

2. What is the topic sentence of paragraph 8? Is the paragraph unified? Explain.

3. Does Povich explain to you clearly the meaning of the topic sentence of paragraph 17? If so, how?

4. Does paragraph 19 fulfill the purposes of a concluding paragraph? Explain.

5. What was the effect on you of the relatively short paragraphs of this essay?

6. Are the short paragraphs appropriate to Povich's audience?

7. What is the main idea of this essay? Does the writer express it explicitly? If so, where? If not, state it in your own words.

For Discussion, Reading, and Writing

1. Observe and be prepared to discuss in class, making reference to apt instances, Povich's use of language that communicates his attitude toward his subject, that is chosen to affect the reader's attitude toward the subject, and that is vivid and concise.

2. Using diction appropriate to your topic and your audience, write in the style of Povich a short article that you might want to submit for publication in your college's newspaper or elsewhere on a subject such as

    Sports event

    Movie

    Chess match

Local character
Club meeting
Theatrical performance
New book
Show on TV

3. Povich's conclusion is (circle one):

A. Crime does not pay.

B. Norton was jobbed.

C. Ali showed off.

D. Ali was all talk, little fight.

E. The three robbers should go to jail.

3

Sources of Material

Personal Experience

AT one time or another you very likely have asked yourself, "What do I have to write about?" If so, you've shared the feeling of many beginning writers. Most of them, however, have more to write about than they realize, for on the subject of themselves they are the most knowledgeable. Henry David Thoreau, at the beginning of *Walden*, based on personal experience, put it this way (italics at end added):

> In most books, the *I*, or first person, is omitted; in this it will be retained; that, in respect to egotism, is the main difference. We commonly do not remember that it is, after all, always the first person that is speaking. *I should not talk so much about myself if there were anybody else I knew as well.*

"Personal experience," it might be claimed, is a redundancy because experience means a personal encounter. But, since observation is a variety of experience, it is useful to use the term "personal experience" to differentiate between the two kinds of experience.

Observation, in my distinction, refers to awareness of what goes on outside of the writer. By personal experience I mean what goes on within the mind of the writer: his or her consciousness of thoughts and ideas and involvement with incidents, persons, places, and things. (The distinction is sometimes elusive. We will consider it again in "Observation," pages 116–133.)

Much of what we know is an accumulation in memory of sensory experiences since infancy. This repository of information is a major source of writing material. Here is a paragraph, written many years after the occasion, filled with recollected details:

> By sundown the streets were empty, the curtains had been drawn, the world put to rights. Even the kitchen walls had been scrubbed and now gleamed in the Sabbath candles. On the long white tablecloth were the "company" dishes, filled for some with *gefilte* fish on lettuce leaves, ringed by red horseradish, sour and half-sour pickles, tomato salad with a light vinegar dressing; for others, with chopped liver in a bed of lettuce leaves and white radishes; the long white *khalleh*, the Sabbath loaf; chicken soup with noodles *and* dumplings; chicken, meat loaf, prunes, and sweet potatoes that had been baked all day into an open pie; compote of prunes and quince, apricots and orange rind; applesauce; a great brown nutcake filled with almonds, the traditional *lekakh*; all surrounded by glasses of port wine, seltzer bottles with their nozzles staring down at us waiting to be pressed; a samovar of Russian tea, *svetouchnee* from the little red box, always served in tall glasses, with lemon slices floating on top. My father and mother sipped it in Russian fashion, through lumps of sugar held between the teeth [Alfred Kazin, *A Walker in the City*].

Your earliest experiences are of course those of childhood. Embedded in memory, they await evocation by you now and could be reported as Simone de Beauvoir does hers in *Memoirs of a Dutiful Daughter:*

> I retain only one confused impression from my earliest years: it is all red, and black, and warm. Our apartment was red: the carpet was red, the Renaissance dining room was red, the figured silk hangings over the stained-glass doors were red, and the velvet cur-

tains in Papa's study were red too. The furniture in this awesome
sanctum was made of black pearwood; I used to creep into the
kneehole under the desk and wrap myself in its dusty gloom; it
was dark and warm there, and the red of the carpet pleased my
eyes. That is how I passed the early days of infancy. Safely shel-
tered, I watched, I touched, and I took stock of the world.

Here the writer's reminiscence of early childhood, recalled by her
in maturity, consists almost entirely of sensory impressions.

   Another example of writing based on personal experience illustrates the writer's consciousness of the meaning of a childhood
experience:

   Whenever we children came to stay at my grandmother's house,
   we were put to sleep in the sewing room, a bleak, shabby, utilitar-
   ian rectangle, more office than bedroom, more attic than office,
   that played to the hierarchy of chambers the role of a poor relation. It was a room seldom entered by the other members of the
   family, seldom swept by a maid, a room without pride; the old
   sewing machine, some castoff chairs, a shadeless lamp, rolls of
   wrapping paper, piles of cardboard boxes that might someday
   come in handy, papers of pins, and remnants of material united
   with the iron folding cots put out for our use and the bare floor
   boards to give an impression of intense and ruthless temporality.
   Thin white spreads, of the kind used in hospitals and charity institutions, and naked blinds at the windows reminded us of our orphaned condition and of the ephemeral character of our visit;
   there was nothing here to encourage us to consider this our home
   [Mary McCarthy, *Memories of a Catholic Girlhood*].

Like Simone de Beauvoir, Mary McCarthy is describing a place
that made an impression on her as a child. But McCarthy conveys
more meaning and makes a poignant comment on her childhood
by making the sewing room in her grandmother's house—"that
played to the hierarchy of chambers the role of a poor relation"—symbolic of her and her brother's orphaned condition.

   Many people are so busy *doing,* they have little or no time for
reflection. And yet men and women, uniquely, are contemplative
animals embarked on a continuing search for meaning. When writ-

ing about a personal experience, you have the opportunity to review the thing experienced and your response to it with the intention of finding, perhaps for the first time, its importance to you and, going beyond that, its possible significance to others.

Such a viewing of one's past is exemplified by a passage from *A Man Called White* by Walter White, who describes himself in the book's beginning: "I am a Negro. My skin is white, my eyes are blue, my hair is blond. The traits of my race are nowhere upon me." On a day in September 1906, when he was thirteen, he and his family were about to be attacked in their home in Atlanta during a race riot:

> In the flickering light the mob swayed, paused, and began to flow toward us. In that instant there opened up within me a great awareness; I knew then who I was. I was a Negro, a human being with an invisible pigmentation which marked me a person to be hunted, hanged, abused, discriminated against, kept in poverty and ignorance, in order that those whose skin was white would have readily at hand a proof of their superiority, a proof patent and inclusive, accessible to the moron and the idiot as well as to the wise man and the genius. No matter how low a white man fell, he was superior to two-thirds of the world's population, for those two-thirds were not white.

After commenting on his mental response to the threat of the mob —a sudden insight about his own status in Atlanta—the writer, at the end of this passage, makes a more generally significant observation about the cause of race riots.

Since most of us live uneventfully, what occurs to us and our responses to it may seem humdrum and not worthy of reporting. Yet, if we can find meaning in our lives for ourselves, we can make out of seemingly ordinary experiences effective essays.

In an essay based on your personal experiences, you have an opportunity to review your past, to evaluate it in order to discover its significance to you, and in doing so to make your past interesting to your readers. However you evaluate it, whether explicitly or implicitly, you should be aware that personal experience is a major source of the essay writer's material. This source is like a well that never runs dry. It is a reservoir that is replenished daily. It requires no trips to the library, no research. What you have experienced thus far today, or even in the last hour, may provide you all the ideas you need for an essay. And, in the well of your past, there is a large supply of material waiting to be drawn upon.

CHEWING TOBACCO
Mark Twain

Mark Twain (see page 66) is unsurpassed in American literature as a storyteller. Among his continually popular novels are **The Adventures of Tom Sawyer** (1876) and **The Adventures of Huckleberry Finn** (1884).

1   The country schoolhouse was three miles from my uncle's farm. It stood in a clearing in the woods and would hold about twenty-five boys and girls. We attended the school with more or less regularity once or twice a week, in summer, walking to it in the cool of the morning by the forest paths and back in the gloaming at the end of the day. All the pupils brought their dinners in baskets— corn dodger, buttermilk and other good things—and sat in the shade of the trees at noon and ate them. It is the part of my education which I look back upon with the most satisfaction. My first visit to the school was when I was seven. A strapping girl of fifteen, in the customary sunbonnet and calico dress, asked me if I "used tobacco"—meaning did I chew it. I said no. It roused her scorn. She reported me to all the crowd and said:

2   "Here is a boy seven years old who can't chaw tobacco."

3   By the looks and comments which this produced I realized that I was a degraded object; I was cruelly ashamed of myself. I determined to reform. But I only made myself sick; I was not able to

learn to chew tobacco. I learned to smoke fairly well but that did not conciliate anybody and I remained a poor thing and character-less. I longed to be respected but I never was able to rise. Children have but little charity for one another's defects.

Questions About "Personal Experience"

1. Where in this piece does Mark Twain evaluate his experience? What significance, if any, does he attach to it?

2. If the writer had omitted the last sentence, would this piece have a different effect on you than it does? Explain.

Questions on Diction and Writing Techniques

1. Is "gloaming" (par. 1) an apt word? Why? What synonyms might be more appropriate in an essay you might write?

2. What purpose is served by the short sentence, "I said no" (par. 1)?

3. Mark Twain might have concluded paragraph 1 like this: "She reported to all the crowd that, although I was seven years old, I couldn't chew tobacco." What does he add to his writing by the use of direct quotation?

For Discussion, Reading, and Writing

1. If you have ever experienced a lack of charity in children to-ward your "defects," tell about it in about 250 words (the length of this piece), incorporating in your writing, if appro-priate, one or more direct quotations.

2. Write a short essay about any single incident in your child-hood, making sure to state why the experience was meaningful to you and therefore might be of interest to your reader.

3. Agree with a student in your composition class to share an ex-perience such as going together to a ball game, a supermarket, a museum, a movie, or a restaurant. After making separate first drafts, write jointly an essay based on the common experience.

THE VALUE OF UNORIGINAL REMARKS
S. I. Hayakawa

S. I. Hayakawa, formerly professor of English and
president of San Francisco State College, was in 1976
elected U.S. Senator from California.

1   An incident in my own experience illustrates how necessary it
sometimes is to give people the opportunity to agree. Early in
1942, a few weeks after the beginning of the war and at a time
when rumors of Japanese spies were still widely current, I had to
wait two or three hours in a railroad station in Oshkosh, Wisconsin,
a city in which I was a stranger. I became aware as time went on
that the other people waiting in the station were staring at me sus-
piciously and feeling uneasy about my presence. One couple with a
small child were staring with special uneasiness and whispering to
each other. I therefore took occasion to remark to the husband that
it was too bad that the train should be late on so cold a night. The
man agreed. I went on to remark that it must be especially difficult
to travel with a small child in winter when train schedules were so
uncertain. Again the husband agreed. I then asked the child's age
and remarked that the child looked very big and strong for his age.
Again agreement—this time with a slight smile. The tension was
relaxing.

2   After two or three more exchanges, the man asked, "I hope
you don't mind my bringing it up, but you're Japanese, aren't you?
Do you think the Japs have any chance of winning this war?"

3   "Well," I replied, "your guess is as good as mine. I don't know
any more than I read in the papers. (This was true.) But the way I
figure it, I don't see how the Japanese, with their lack of coal and

steel and oil and their limited industrial capacity, can ever beat a powerfully industrialized nation like the United States."

4   My remark was admittedly neither original nor well informed. Hundreds of radio commentators and editorial writers were saying exactly the same thing during those weeks. But just because they were, the remark *sounded familiar* and was *on the right side*, so that it was easy to agree with. The man agreed at once, with what seemed like genuine relief. How much the wall of suspicion had broken down was indicated in his next question. "Say, I hope your folks aren't over there while the war is going on."

5   "Yes, they are. My father and mother and two young sisters are over there."

6   "Do you ever hear from them?"

7   "How can I?"

8   "Do you mean you won't be able to see them or hear from them till after the war is over?" Both he and his wife looked troubled and sympathetic.

9   There was more to the conversation, but the result was that within ten minutes after it had begun they had invited me to visit them in their city and have dinner with them in their home. And the other people in the station, seeing me in conversation with people who *didn't* look suspicious, ceased to pay any attention to me and went back to reading their papers and staring at the ceiling.

Questions About "Personal Experience"

1. What conclusion does Hayakawa draw from his experience?

2. Can you justify placing elsewhere in this essay Hayakawa's comment about the significance he attaches to his experience as, for example, where Mark Twain places his evaluation of his experience in "Chewing Tobacco" (page 108)?

3. What is Hayakawa's purpose in this essay? Does he achieve this purpose? Explain.

Questions on Diction and Writing Techniques

1. What is the function of "therefore" in paragraph 1?

2. Point out the words relating to time that Hayakawa uses to order chronologically the events related in paragraph 1.

3. How do "Japanese" and "Japs" (par. 2) differ?

4. What does Hayakawa achieve by using dialogue?

For Discussion, Reading, and Writing

1. Using dialogue as much as possible, write a short essay beginning with "An incident in my own experience illustrates . . ."

2. After visiting any public place—a bus station, museum, sports stadium, chess club, department store—and speaking with one or more persons there, report the incident in a short essay that states explicitly or shows by implication the significance of the experience.

MY FIRST LESSON IN HOW TO LIVE AS A NEGRO
Richard Wright

Richard Wright (1908–1960), author of **Native Son** (1940), is among the most important black American novelists.

---

1 My first lesson in how to live as a Negro came when I was quite small. We were living in Arkansas. Our house stood behind the railroad tracks. Its skimpy yard was paved with black cinders. Nothing green ever grew in that yard. The only touch of green we could see was far away, beyond the tracks, over where the white folks lived. But cinders were good enough for me and I never missed the green growing things. And anyhow cinders were fine weapons. You could always have a nice hot war with huge black cinders. All

you had to do was crouch behind the brick pillars of a house with your hands full of gritty ammunition. And the first woolly black head you saw pop out from behind another row of pillars was your target. You tried your very best to knock it off. It was great fun.

₂   I never fully realized the appalling disadvantages of a cinder environment till one day the gang to which I belonged found itself engaged in a war with the white boys who lived beyond the tracks. As usual we laid down our cinder barrage, thinking that this would wipe the white boys out. But they replied with a steady bombardment of broken bottles. We doubled our cinder barrage, but they hid behind trees, hedges, and the sloping embankments of their lawns. Having no such fortifications, we retreated to the brick pillars of our homes. During the retreat a broken milk bottle caught me behind the ear, opening a deep gash which bled profusely. The sight of blood pouring over my face completely demoralized our ranks. My fellow-combatants left me standing paralyzed in the center of the yard, and scurried for their homes. A kind neighbor saw me and rushed me to a doctor, who took three stitches in my neck.

₃   I sat brooding on my front steps, nursing my wound and waiting for my mother to come from work. I felt that a grave injustice had been done me. It was all right to throw cinders. The greatest harm a cinder could do was leave a bruise. But broken bottles were dangerous; they left you cut, bleeding, and helpless.

₄   When night fell, my mother came from the white folks' kitchen. I raced down the street to meet her. I could just feel in my bones that she would understand. I knew she would tell me exactly what to do next time. I grabbed her hand and babbled out the whole story. She examined my wound, then slapped me.

₅   "How come yuh didn't hide?" she asked me. "How come yuh awways fightin'?"

₆   I was outraged, and bawled. Between sobs I told her that I didn't have any trees or hedges to hide behind. There wasn't a thing I could have used as a trench. And you couldn't throw very far when you were hiding behind the brick pillars of a house. She grabbed a barrel stave, dragged me home, stripped me naked, and beat me till I had a fever of one hundred and two. She would smack my rump with the stave, and, while the skin was still smarting, impart to me gems of Jim Crow wisdom. I was never to throw cinders any more. I was never to fight any more wars. I was never, never, under any conditions, to fight *white* folks again. And they were absolutely right in clouting me with the broken milk bottle. Didn't I know she was working hard every day in the hot kitchens of the white folks to make money to take care of me? When was I ever going to learn to be a good boy? She couldn't be bothered with my fights. She finished by telling me that I ought to be thankful to God as long as I lived that they didn't kill me.

7　　All that night I was delirious and could not sleep. Each time I closed my eyes I saw monstrous white faces suspended from the ceiling, leering at me.

8　　From that time on, the charm of my cinder yard was gone. The green trees, the trimmed hedges, the cropped lawns grew very meaningful, became a symbol. Even today when I think of white folks, the hard, sharp outlines of white houses surrounded by trees, lawns, and hedges are present somewhere in the background of my mind. Through the years they grew into an overreaching symbol of fear.

Questions About "Personal Experience"

1. What is Wright's purpose in writing paragraph 8? Would this piece be more, less, or equally effective if the paragraph were left out? Explain.

Questions on Diction and Writing Techniques

1. What alternative language might Wright have chosen in lieu of "pop out" and "knock it off" (par. 1)? Which verbs are more vivid?

2. What is the main idea of paragraph 2? Does Wright give you enough information to convince you of its validity? Explain.

3. In paragraph 1, writing about the fight between his gang and other black children, Wright uses "weapons," "ammunition," "target." Find similar diction in paragraph 2. Do these words help convey to you his personal experience? Explain.

4. What does "Jim Crow" (par. 6) denote (see page 74)? What is its derivation? Why does Wright call his mother's advice "Jim Crow wisdom"?

For Discussion, Reading, and Writing

1. Rewrite paragraph 6, incorporating in your version as much dialogue as possible.

2. Filling the blank spaces with language reflecting your own experience, write a short essay beginning with "My first lesson in . . . came when I was . . ." End the essay with a fitting conclusion drawn from the experience.

3. Using personal experience as your source of material, write an essay about an incident that shaped or helped shape your present attitude toward a person, a class of people, an institution, God, or anything else.

4. Write a short essay that relates an incident or series of events that occurred in your childhood and that might be of interest to others. Try to tell about the experience as you perceived it then. If it seems humorous now, try to make your readers see it that way.

Observation

WRITERS for whom personal experience is a major source of material can increase the effectiveness of their writing by reporting in detail what they perceive, but the emphasis in such writing is on what goes on *within* the writer. In contrast, the emphasis in writing for which observation is a major source of material is on what goes on *outside* the writer.

Through the senses—hearing, sight, smell, taste, and touch— we become aware of the world around us: the ring of a telephone, the flicker of a flame, the aroma of fresh bread, the taste of chewing gum, the coldness of an ice cube. Our awareness of the elements of our environment varies. We are likely to be most perceptive when highly motivated: to identify a strange sound when bedded down outdoors at night in unfamiliar surroundings; to find an item of jewelry lost on a beach; to detect a friend on an arriving train; to discover the ingredients of a dish prepared by a fine cook; to savor the bouquet of an unusual wine.

Training also increases one's ability to notice more. A hunter, a botanist, or a bird watcher is likely to be more aware of the environment on a walk through the woods than is someone who is not initiated in the lore of nature. A doctor, a sailor, a farmer, an orchestra conductor, an editor, an automobile mechanic — each, in his or her specialty, is likely to see details that others might not observe. You surely see things keenly in your fields of interest. To be an effective writer, you must train yourself by practice to be more observant, with all your senses, more of the time.

A good exercise in observation is to place a notebook and pencil beside you on the table while having a meal in any eating place and to jot down in a word, phrase, or sentence what you perceive with your five senses, including snatches of conversation. Or take notes of what you observe at a party, during a class, in a locker room. Better yet, do one of these exercises with a friend, together or separately, and then compare notes.

There is a correlation between careful observation and good writing. Consider the effect on you of the specific details in this passage; count the number of them the writer observed and reports to his readers:

> It was in Burma, a sodden morning of the rains. A sickly light, like yellow tinfoil, was slanting over the high walls into the jail yard. We were waiting outside the condemned cells, a row of sheds fronted with double bars, like small animal cages. Each cell measured about ten feet by ten and was quite bare within except for a plank bed and a pot for drinking water. In some of them brown, silent men were squatting at the inner bars, with their blankets draped around them. These were the condemned men, due to be hanged within the next week or two [George Orwell, "A Hanging"].

I find these specific details:

1. A sodden morning of the rains

2. A sickly light

3. Slanting over the high walls into the jail yard

4. A row of sheds

5. Fronted with double bars

6. Each cell measured about ten feet by ten

7. Quite bare within except for a plank bed

8. And a pot for drinking water

9. Brown, silent men

10. Squatting at the inner bars

11. With their blankets draped around them

By making his writing concrete, the writer makes it more vigorous.

A beginning writer will often settle for a quick impression instead of observing with care and then reporting the specific details on which that impression is based. She might report of her subject, merely: "He looked disreputable." Here, by contrast, is how an attentive writer reported her observations of Stephen Crane, American novelist, poet, and short-story writer:

> He was thin to emaciation, his face was gaunt and unshaven, a thin dark moustache straggled on his upper lip, his black hair grew low on his forehead and was shaggy and unkempt. His gray clothes were much the worse for wear and fitted him so badly it seemed unlikely he had ever been measured for them. He wore a flannel shirt and a slovenly apology for a necktie, and his shoes were dusty and worn gray about the toes and were badly run over at the heel. I had seen many a tramp printer come up the *Journal* stairs to hunt a job, but never one who presented such a disreputable appearance as this storymaker man [Willa Cather, "When I Knew Stephen Crane"].

Cather supports in detail her conclusion that Crane's appearance was "disreputable" and thereby gives her readers the information needed to make it credible.

I have been using the word "observation" so far in the sense of recognizing and noting facts or occurrences. Here are examples of facts:

John is six feet tall.

Mary weighs one hundred and ten pounds.

This morning the sun rose in London at 6:30 A.M.

An inch of rain fell in Chicago yesterday.

The Yankees scored four runs in the ninth inning of their last game with the Red Sox.

The driver of the green Buick was caught driving in the southbound lane of U.S. Route 1 at seventy miles per hour.

These are statements about what is known. They can be verified. We say that they are *facts*.

"Observation" has another meaning. According to an old chestnut, "Where there's smoke there's fire." We may see smoke, but even without seeing fire we conclude that it must be there. You fail to find your car in a parking lot and say it has been stolen. You hear the sound of a siren and say it comes from an ambulance. You detect the smell of charcoal burning and say your neighbor is having a cookout. You taste a hamburger and say the cook has been too lavish with the salt. In each instance, you are observing, or you are coming to a conclusion, by a process of reasoning called *inferring*. An *inference*, in the words of S. I. Hayakawa, is "a statement about the unknown made on the basis of the known. . . . The common characteristic of inferences is that they are statements about matters which are not directly known, made on the basis of what has been observed."

Much of our knowledge of our environment is the result of inference, conclusion, judgment. Through observation, in both senses of the term, we attain awareness of the real world.

How objective—unaffected by personal feelings or prejudice—can or should we be? (I will return to this question in "Description," pages 193–212.) According to Thoreau:

There is no such thing as pure *objective* observation. Your observation, to be interesting, *i.e.*, to be significant, must be *subjective*. The sum of what the writer of whatever class has to report is simply some human experience . . . Senses that take cognizance of outward things merely are of no avail [Henry David Thoreau, *Journal*, May 6, 1854].

In the light of Thoreau's comment, consider this report:

One afternoon in late August, as the summer's sun streamed into
the car and made little jumping shadows on the windows, I sat gazing out at the tenement-dwellers, who were themselves looking
out of their windows from the gray crumbling buildings along the
tracks of upper Manhattan. As we crossed into the Bronx, the
train unexpectedly slowed down for a few miles. Suddenly from
out of my window I saw a large crowd near the tracks, held back
by two policemen. Then, on the other side from my window, I
saw a sight I would never be able to forget: a little boy almost severed in halves, lying at an incredible angle near the track. The
ground was covered with blood, and the boy's eyes were opened
wide, strained and disbelieving in his sudden oblivion. A policeman stood next to him, his arms folded, staring straight ahead at
the windows of our train. In the orange glow of late afternoon
the policeman, the crowd, the corpse of the boy were for a brief
moment immobile, motionless, a small tableau to violence and
death in the city. Behind me, in the next row of seats, there was a
game of bridge. I heard one of the four men say as he looked out
at the sight, "God, that's horrible." Another said, in a whisper,
"Terrible, terrible." There was a momentary silence, punctuated
only by the clicking of the wheels on the track. Then, after the
pause, I heard the first man say: "Two hearts" [Willie Morris,
North Toward Home].

Notice the number of concrete details the objective reporter chooses
to make us see and feel the scene he portrays. These, being part of
"some human experience" (in Thoreau's words), elicit a subjective
response, implied in the last few sentences, that makes the writer's
observations interesting and significant: that to the four men in the
car the death of a fellow human being is of less concern than a game
of cards.

This passage exemplifies the point that the distinction between
observation (the awareness of what goes on outside a writer) and
personal experience (what goes on within the mind of the writer) is
sometimes elusive. There is such a close connection between the
world outside of the writer and his or her response to it that often
it is difficult to keep the two apart.

Forceful writing depends in large measure on reporting details.
Thus the more observant you are, the more effective are your essays

likely to be; among the important tools of the successful writer are the five senses. But, as Thoreau suggests, writers—you among them —are not machines. You have a right to report your unique perception of the world around you and to include in writing that uses observation as your main source of material your feelings and your interpretation of your experience.

AN UGLY NEW FOOTPRINT IN THE SAND
A. B. C. Whipple

A. B. C. Whipple—contributor to **Life** and other magazines— has written, besides a book about the poets Byron and Shelley, two books about the sea. In this essay, he tells about oil's pollution of a wild and lonely beach.

1   There were strangers on our beach yesterday, for the first time in a month. A new footprint on our sand is nearly as rare as in *Robinson Crusoe*. We are at the very edge of the Atlantic; half a mile out in front of us is a coral reef, and then nothing but 3,000 miles of ocean to West Africa. It is a wild and lonely beach, with the same surf beating on it as when Columbus came by. And yet the beach is polluted.

2   Oil tankers over the horizon have fouled it more than legions of picknickers could. The oil comes ashore in floating patches that stain the coral black and gray. It has blighted the rock crabs and the crayfish and has coated the delicate whorls of the conch shells with black goo. And it has congealed upon itself, littering the beach with globes of tar that resemble the cannonballs of a deserted battlefield. The islanders, as they go beachcombing for the treasures the sea has washed up for centuries, now wear old shoes to protect their feet from the oil that washes up too.

₃   You have to try to get away from pollution to realize how bad
it really is. We have known for the last few years how bad our cities
are. Now there is no longer an escape. If there is oil on this island
far out in the Atlantic, there is oil on nearly every other island.

₄   It is still early here. The air is still clear over the island, but it
won't be when they build the airstrip they are talking about. The
water out over the reef is still blue and green, but it is dirtier than it
was a few years ago. And if the land is not despoiled, it is only because there are not yet enough people here to despoil it. There will
be. And so for the moment on this island we are witnesses to the
beginning, as it were, of the pollution of our environment. . . .

₅   Until the pollution of our deserted beach, it seemed simple to
blame everything on the "population explosion." If the population
of this island, for example, could be stabilized at a couple of hundred, there would be very little problem with the environment in
this secluded area. There would be no pollution of the environment
if there were not too many people using it. And so if we concentrate on winning the war against overpopulation, we can save the
earth for mankind.

₆   But the oil on the beach belies this too-easy assumption.
Those tankers are not out there because too many Chinese and Indians are being born every minute. They are not even out there because there are too many Americans and Europeans. They are delivering their oil, and cleaning their tanks at sea and sending the residue
up onto the beaches of the Atlantic and Pacific, in order to fuel the
technology of mankind—and the factories and the power plants,
the vehicles and the engines that have enabled mankind to survive
on his planet are now spoiling the planet for life.

₇   The fishermen on this island are perfectly right in preferring
the outboard motor to the sail. Their livelihood is involved, and the
motor, for all its fouling smell, has helped increase the fisherman's
catch so that he can now afford to dispense with the far more ob-
noxious outdoor privy. But the danger of technology is in its escalation, and there has already been a small amount of escalation here.
You can see the motor oil slicks around the town dock. Electric
generators can be heard over the sound of the surf. And while there
are only about two dozen automobiles for the ten miles of road, already there is a wrecked jeep rusting in the harbor waters where it
was dumped and abandoned. The escalation of technological pollu-

tion is coming here just as surely as it came to the mainland cities that are now shrouded by fly ash.

8   If the oil is killing the life along the coral heads, what must it not be doing to the phytoplankton at sea which provide 70% of the oxygen we breathe? The lesson of our fouled beach is that we may not even have realized how late it is already. Mankind, because of his technology, may require far more space per person on this globe than we had ever thought, but it is more than a matter of a certain number of square yards per person. There is instead a delicate balance of nature in which many square miles of ocean and vegetation and clean air are needed to sustain only a relatively few human beings. We may find, as soon as the end of this century, that the final despoliation of our environment has been signaled not by starvation but by people choking to death. The technology—the machine —will then indeed have had its ultimate, mindless, all-unintended triumph over man, by destroying the atmosphere he lives in just as surely as you can pinch off a diver's breathing tube.

9   Sitting on a lonely but spoiled beach, it is hard to imagine but possible to believe.

Questions About "Observation"

1. By means of which sense(s) does Whipple observe the escalation of technology on his island? Cite examples from the text to illustrate your response.

2. Explain whether the harm to the phytoplankton at sea implied in paragraph 8 is a fact or an inference.

3. Are facts and inferences equally reliable? Support your judgment with examples from this selection and from your own experience.

Questions on Diction and Writing Techniques

1. What purpose is served by the writer's use in paragraph 1 of metaphor? What by the allusions to *Robinson Crusoe* and Columbus?

2. What is the effect of the short last sentence of paragraph 1?

3. Does paragraph 1 function well as an introductory paragraph? (See page 30.) Explain.

4. Whipple uses pronoun reference—"it"—to help achieve coherence in paragraph 2. Find another example in this essay of this technique to achieve coherence within a paragraph (see pages 27–28).

5. Are "goo" and "cannonballs of a deserted battlefield" (par. 2) apt diction? Why or why not?

For Discussion, Reading, and Writing

1. Which of the following best states Whipple's conclusion (circle one)?

   A. We may find that the final despoliation of our environment will be signaled by people choking to death.

   B. You can't escape pollution by living on a remote island.

   C. If we concentrate on winning the war against over-population, we can save the earth for humankind.

   D. Because of lack of food we may require far more space per person on this globe than we had ever thought.

   E. Technology—the machine—will triumph over man.

2. On the basis of your own observations, prepare to comment in class on the good and bad effects of technology.

3. Choose a place on or near your campus where you have noticed evidence of pollution. Go there and make notes of what you see and of what you infer from the facts. Write a short essay about what you observed.

4. If you have had occasion to observe the blighting over a period of years of a place you know well, report your observations in a short essay, using as many specific details as possible.

WHAT DO CATS AND WRITERS HAVE IN COMMON?

John Lacy

A newspaperman ever since graduating from college, John Lacy now writes a column regularly for **The Hartford Courant**.

1   The Mark Twain home on Farmington Avenue had more than a dozen cats around when the author and his family lived there in the previous century.

2   And when Ernest Hemingway resided in Key West in the '30s, his house was inhabited by 50 cats (even today, a visitor to this tourist site must wade through as many as 40 feline descendants).

3   It is no mere coincidence for such great writers to have had access to so many cats. Even an ordinary, everyday typewriter pounder can see the worth of a cat as companion. The cat has many of the qualities a writer may wish for himself.

4   A cat is always listening. If only the writer could stretch out on a sunny windowsill, appearing to be in a nap, but with his ears twitching this way and that, ever alert for the first chirp or rustle of feathers that will interrupt monotony.

5   A cat is a researcher beyond compare. Open a door for a cat and it does not rush through willy-nilly. The cat inspects new territory, looking left and right; it places one paw forward, carefully, and until that paw is down, firmly, it doesn't bring the second one forward, and then, only with care.

6   A cat is a patient observer of life. Offered a choice of vantage points, a cat takes a high post—atop a wood pile, on the hood of a car, on the roof of a shed. From there, the cat studies the unfolding of the world's patterns—the track of the mouse in the field, the course of the bird through the trees.

₇ And if a cat leaps on a fence, it is to sharpen its claws and to take a position. Public opinion will show the way for the cat's next move. What essayist or writer of editorials doesn't admire the skill with which a cat keeps things in balance?

₈ A cat appears aloof. In this stance of objectivity, it is clear the cat does not curry favor. It may accept some tuna, yes. But it will, just as quickly, disappear without composing one kind phrase about the event.

₉ A cat is not a scene-stealer. The cat does not disturb the natural flow of a happening by thrusting notepaper, camera or microphone into the middle of things. There's no end to what a reporter might learn if he had the ability to slink around a crowded room's perimeter, pausing here and there beneath a chair, and sitting, immobile, for an hour behind a curtain.

₁₀ A cat insists on being a solitary worker. Cats do not run in packs. A cat prefers to do its job without distraction, and only when it feels the need will it climb into a soft lap for a stroking. Who among us doesn't require that kind of cuddling now and then?

₁₁ Cats are not blabbermouths. A cat doesn't boast about the story just completed; it quietly goes to the doormat and leaves the headline—a well-dressed mole, perhaps—as the only evidence of pride. This doesn't mean the cat isn't having fun in the pursuit of its task. Many times I have been in a mood for juggling rodents.

₁₂ One may wonder if Twain and Hemingway grew their whiskers in admiration of the cat. We have no record to tell us whether they used their facial hair for testing unfamiliar openings.

₁₃ With all their cats, Twain and Hemingway found success. At present, I am only a two-cat writer. And sometimes I get the uneasy feeling that these two spayed females—who might have preferred to continue bearing litters—are staring at me as if to say: "We told you so."

Questions About "Observation"

1. Mark all the statements Lacy makes that prove he is a keen observer of the behavior of cats.

Questions on Diction and Writing Techniques

1. Lacy might have written "moving" instead of "twitching" (par. 4). Which verb conveys more meaning? Find in paragraph 9 an example or examples of his use of vivid verbs.

2. Does Lacy express his thesis clearly and precisely? Explain.

3. To better understand the organization of this essay, divide it into sections consisting of one or more paragraphs. What is the function of each section?

4. Mark those paragraphs that have clearly stated topic sentences. Underline the topic sentences.

For Discussion, Reading, and Writing

1. Fill the blanks in this passage from memory to make it intelligible:

    Cats are not _____. A cat doesn't _____ about the story just completed; _____ quietly goes to the doormat and _____ the headline—a well-dressed mole, perhaps—as the only evidence of _____. This doesn't mean the cat isn't having _____ in the pursuit of its task. Many times _____ been in a mood for juggling _____.

    Compare your words with those in paragraph 11.

2. Observe carefully any animal or person. Imitating Lacy's approach, write an essay in which you characterize it by its behavior.

WHEN THE YOUNG HAVE IT GOOD
Robert Ardrey

Robert Ardrey has had a varied career as playwright, screenwriter, and anthropologist.

1   The African hunting dog, known in the early days as the Cape hunting dog, is perhaps the world's most successful predator, excluding only man. It is not a dog at all, not even a member of the family *Canidae,* but has four toes on his foot, ears like ping-pong paddles, and bears the scientific name *Lycaon pictus.* It looks like a dog, however, and not a very large one, since it weighs about forty pounds. Its success as a hunter has been based entirely on a capacity to outrun any animal in Africa, together with the superb coordination of its hunting pack. But despite its success, or because of it, the hunting dog is a rare animal today. Since the early times of settlement in the Cape, three hundred years ago, its reputation has been so terrifying that men have hunted it, even poisoned it, as vermin.

2   The hunting dog has terrified not only men but other animals. I have watched Thomson's gazelle graze within two hundred yards of a hungry cheetah, the fastest of land animals. But in 1966, when Eliot Elisofon and I had the chance to photograph a large hunting-dog pack for three days, dawn to dusk, no antelope approached close enough to be identified without binoculars. Within our view was perhaps thirty square miles of flat, open, treeless plain; along the margins animals grazed. Just once four zebras strolled by at a distance of several hundred yards. Since they had the confidence, one must assume that the margin was sufficient for escape. But also the pack was sleeping.

3   At that time a study of one pack, over a period of a few months, was all that science had yet collected in the way of reliable observa-

tion. When I returned to the Serengeti two years later, however, Kruuk and Schaller, as by-products of their hyena and lion specialties, had collected more information on the entire predator community than science had ever possessed before. It is information which, although largely unpublished, I am permitted to use before this investigation closes. Now, in terms of adult-young relations of almost shocking amiability, I wish simply to describe one hunt.

4   Schaller, by the summer of 1968, had followed twenty-two packs. He came by my cottage about four o'clock one afternoon, having spotted a pack which he judged would hunt about five thirty By four thirty we had found it, sleeping in the midst of a rolling area of plain parched by the dry season, burned black by fire. We animal-watched, waited, talked. There were ten adults and fourteen pups well over half grown. Schaller had known the pack when the pups were born six months earlier and there had been sixteen. They had lost only two. It was an infant mortality rate so low as to be difficult to believe. Finally three adults were stirring, nosing the others to their feet. All went to the pups, and now there was a rolling pell-mell of play, adults and pups together, and the strange twittering sound, like a flock of sparrows, that the dogs make when excited.

5   "War dance," said Schaller. And like a ritual it was, for the dogs when sufficiently excited were all on their feet. The three leaders headed off, other adults behind them, then the pups, and last a disabled adult on three legs. It was precisely five thirty; whether they had heard a factory whistle blow or Schaller earlier had given them instructions, I do not know. One of the most memorable sights in nature, however, is that of a pack strung out in single file almost a quarter of a mile long, headed into the late, gray light with white-tipped tails upraised like beacons to make following easier.

6   They trotted. The hunting dog—like the albatross, the elephant seal, and few other species—has no least fear of men, and one may drive beside the pack as if one were not there. We checked the Land Rover's speedometer, and they were doing fifteen miles an hour. The pups kept the pace with ease, as did the adult on three legs. Now the leaders speeded up to a run. The speedometer read twenty-five miles an hour. Still the pups and the three-legged rear guard kept even. But now the leaders were putting on pressure and a gap was widening between adults and pups.

7   Since game flee an area in which a pack is running, a common

tactic is to approach a rise at high speed on the chance of surprising prey on the far side. Such speed for the three leaders, with whom none could keep up, was over forty miles an hour. They outdistanced us, and by the time we reached the rise the three had stopped, the others were catching up, and across the empty valley beyond, Thomson's gazelles were stotting half a mile away. The word was being spread. Hunting dogs kill by surprise in ten or fifteen minutes or have a long search ahead through a forewarned world. Yet 85 percent of all hunts observed by Schaller have been successful, a record to stun a lion pride.

8 The leaders were moving again in a new direction at a modest run, the whole torchlight parade of bouncing white tails reassembled behind them. Then the leaders were digging in at full run and we could see three large wart hogs ahead running at an angle to our left toward their hole. That monstrous machine, the Land Rover, will survive cross-country driving at such speed, but only with difficulty will its human occupants. I lost the wart hogs. Within my view, however, the dogs were beginning one of their notable maneuvers. When prey curves in its flight, each dog in the file sets a separate course so that the pack is like narrowly set spokes in a wheel. They are not following; that is left to the leaders. They are setting courses of interception along the probable curve. But now there was no necessity. The wart hogs had vanished and we thought they had made it underground. But the leaders were struggling, for they had caught the last one by the hind legs and all one could hear was the squealing of the wart hog.

9 "Poor pig," said Schaller. Like a first-class nightmare, one is unlikely to forget a hunting-dog kill, since it does not kill but eats its prey alive. Nothing has so contributed to hunting-dog horror as the long-drawn manner of its prey's death. But in truth the dog cannot kill. He is small, and his teeth are small, even for his size. He has forty-two, and they are designed for slicing, not killing. Only the cats have killing teeth; even the wolf, taking caribou or moose, will proceed as does the hunting dog. And yet, while nature may provide its explanations, the spectacle remains other than nice.

10 I find it a subject for meditation that within my limited career of animal-watching, the two images most horrid and sublime were separated by little over sixty seconds. By now the hundred-pound

wart hog's viscera were torn open and he was finished, though still squealing. Then the fourteen pups arrived, crowding into the living feast. And with their arrival every adult stepped back, none with more than a mouthful of meat. They were undoubtedly hungry, for their bellies were lean. Now and again they would string themselves out in hunting formation at some hint of further prey. But in the hour and fifteen minutes that Schaller and I sat beside the kill, no adult took another mouthful of meat. The food was exclusively for the pups.

11   We sat in the gathering darkness in the middle of a plain emptied of all living creatures by fear of these formidable little beasts. And we discussed what course of natural selection could have produced such inhibition favoring the young. Only a very high adult death rate could place such selective value on the successful raising of young to maturity. I speculated on disability. In the lion pride all cubs eat last, and if kills are few or small, they starve. But the adult lion is very nearly invulnerable. The hunting dog, small and relatively fragile, may suffer a high casualty rate when attacking prey more formidable than wart hogs. Schaller shook his head. "I think disease," he said.

12   When it grew too dark to stay longer, we drove away. And six months later Schaller wrote me that distemper had hit the pack, leaving only nine survivors. When the young have it good, there is a reason somewhere.

Questions About "Observation"

1. Cite three or more specific details that indicate how carefully Ardrey observed his surroundings.

2. What does Ardrey infer from the strolling by of four zebras at a distance of several hundred yards?

Questions on Diction and Writing Techniques

1. In paragraph 1 there is an example of simile: "like ping-pong

paddles." Find other examples of simile in paragraphs 4, 5, and 9.

2. In paragraphs 4 and 5, Ardrey chooses temporal diction to guide his readers through a time sequence: "finally" (par. 4); "then" and "last" (par. 5). List at least five more examples of his use of such words in the rest of the selection.

3. Ardrey might have written the last sentence in paragraph 5: "One of the most memorable sights in nature, however, is that of a pack strung out, headed into the late light with tails upraised." Which of the versions of the sentence do you prefer? Why?

4. The paragraphs in this essay might be grouped 1–3, 4–10, and 11–12. What is the function of each group in Ardrey's plan of organization?

5. Does Ardrey give you enough information to make clear to you why the African hunting dog is successful as a hunter? Explain.

6. Does Ardrey make clear to you "what course of natural selection could have produced such inhibition favoring the young" (par. 11)?

7. Does Ardrey give you sufficient specific information for you to accept as valid his general statement "When the young have it good, there is a reason somewhere" (par. 12)? Explain.

For Discussion, Reading, and Writing

1. To what does Ardrey attribute the African hunting dog's success as a hunter?

2. How does Ardrey explain the terror that the African hunting dog holds for other animals?

3. Write a paragraph or two about the adult-young relations of any creatures you have had occasion to observe.

4. Prepare to write a short essay by observing with care any part of your school or other environment. Make notes of what you observe. From your observations, note-taking, and thinking about your subject, find a suitable thesis (such as Ardrey's, "When the young have it good, there is a reason somewhere."). Write the essay.

Diaries and Journals

A renowned concert pianist is said to have remarked, "When I don't practice one day, I know it. When I miss practice two days, my wife knows it. When I fail to practice three days, my audience knows it." Skill in writing also requires continual practice. One way of achieving it is by keeping a diary or journal.

"Diary" and "journal" are virtually synonymous terms. If there is a useful distinction between them, it is that a diary may be more private, more intimate than a journal and that in a journal the writer is more likely not only to record, but also to reflect on what took place.

If you are among the beginning writers who are self-conscious or hypercritical of their writing, the privacy of a diary may help you to write more freely. In your diary you need not be concerned about grammar, spelling, punctuation, or anything else—such as the possibility of adverse criticism by your composition teacher—that might inhibit putting your ideas on paper.

One reason for keeping a diary is it can be a repository of information that you might incorporate in more formal writing—to fulfill, for example, writing assignments in your courses in college. Thus a diary can be—in addition to a kind of writing—a source of material. In it you might incorporate information and ideas derived from personal experience and observation.

Other reasons for keeping a diary or journal are

1. To keep a record of one's activities

2. To record a personal experience and one's feelings and thoughts about it

3. To evaluate an experience and to discover its significance

4. To train oneself to become more observant

5. To become more reflective

By allowing one to give vent to feelings that might otherwise be bottled up, keeping a diary can also be useful as a sort of therapy.

An entry in Thoreau's *Journal* illustrates the opportunity a journal or diary offers for reflection:

> It occurred to me when I awoke this morning, feeling regret for intemperance of the day before in eating fruit, which had dulled my sensibilities, that man was to be treated as a musical instrument, and if any viol was to be made of sound timber and kept well tuned always, it was he, so that when the bow of events is drawn across him he may vibrate and resound in perfect harmony. A sensitive soul will be continually trying its strings to see if they are in tune. A man's body must be rasped down exactly to a shaving. It is of far more importance than the wood of a Cremona violin [Henry David Thoreau, *Journal*, September 12, 1853].

Thoreau might have written merely

> Woke up today feeling ill. Overindulged the day before.

Instead he mulls over his experience and, illuminating his conclusion with an apt analogy, writes a cogent statement about how one should care for one's body.

When should you write in your diary? As often as appeals to

you, during any free time you have. If you're like most people, you probably won't find time unless you make up your mind to write daily or on alternate days at the same time each day.

How much should you write? Consider a few consecutive entries Nathaniel Hawthorne made in his journal in August 1850:

August 8th

E. P. Whipple & wife took tea.

August 12th

Seven chickens hatched. Afternoon, J. T. Headley and brother called.—Eight chickens.

August 19th

Monument Mountain, in the early sunshine; its base enveloped in mist, parts of which are floating in the sky; so that the great hill looks really as if it were founded on a cloud. Just emerging from the mist is seen a yellow field of rye, and above that, forest.

August 21st (Wednesday)

Eight more chickens hatched.—Ascended a mountain with wife; a beautiful, mellow, autumnal sunshine.

August 24th

In the afternoons, now-a-days, this valley in which I dwell seems like a vast basin, filled with golden sunshine as with wine.

Don't frown upon trivial entries. Anything that comes to mind, however seemingly insignificant, could be included. One reason for this is that your ability to write will improve with any writing you do regularly. (See Peter Elbow's "Freewriting," pp. 331–332.)

Consider these short entries Virginia Woolf made in her diary in 1940:

Friday, June 7th

Just [back] from London this roasting hot evening. The great battle which decides our life or death goes on. Last night an air raid here. Today battle sparks. Up till 2:30 this morning.

Friday, August 23

Book flopped. Sales down to 15 a day since air raid on London. Is that the reason? Will it pick up?

Monday, September 2nd

There might be no war, the past two days. Only one air raid warning. Perfectly quiet nights. A lull after the attacks on London.

Entries may be brief notes or essays in miniature.

How factual should one be in a diary? Joan Didion, in "On Keeping a Notebook," wrote: "So the point of my keeping a notebook has never been, nor is it now, to have an accurate factual record of what I have been doing or thinking . . . *How it felt to me:* that is getting closer to the truth about a notebook . . . *Remember what it was to me:* that is always the point." But this is her view of what a notebook (journal or diary) should be like. It need not be yours.

Writing is a useful way for you to clarify your thinking; writing in a diary gives you a chance to do this before an audience that is always handy. Eric Hoffer was a longshoreman when he wrote, "I had to sort things out; to talk to somebody. So . . . I began a diary." He is now a well-known essayist, with several books to his credit. His diary, kept during 1958 and 1959, appeared as *Working and Thinking on the Waterfront*. These are its first entries:

June 1, 1958

5 A.M. I am getting self-righteous. This usually happens after a long stretch of work. I remember Tolstoi saying somewhere that work makes not only ants but men, too, cruel.

4 P.M. Went to the dentist to have my teeth cleaned. Lili and the boy met me afterwards and we went to the beach. We had a good, plentiful meal at the Hitchrack. It is long since I tasted such good liver. The boy has learned several dirty words. Lili does not seem alarmed.

Hoffer's entries demonstrate the range of material to be found in diaries—from the trivial ("Went to the dentist to have my teeth cleaned") to the philosophical ("I remember Tolstoi saying somewhere that work makes not only ants but men, too, cruel.").

PAPER IS PATIENT
Anne Frank

Anne Frank (1929–1945) and her family, Jews in hiding from the
German secret police in Nazi-occupied Amsterdam, were discovered and arrested on August 4, 1944. Eight months later Anne
died in the concentration camp at Bergen-Belsen. Her diary was
found by friends and published in the United States in 1952.

Saturday, 20 June, 1942

1   I haven't written for a few days, because I wanted first of all to
think about my diary. It's an odd idea for someone like me to keep
a diary; not only because I have never done so before, but because
it seems to me that neither I — nor for that matter anyone else — will
be interested in the unbosomings of a thirteen-year-old schoolgirl.
Still, what does that matter? I want to write, but more than that, I
want to bring out all kinds of things that lie buried deep in my heart.

2   There is a saying that "paper is more patient than man"; it
came back to me on one of my slightly melancholy days, while I sat
chin in hand, feeling too bored and limp even to make up my mind
whether to go out or stay at home. Yes, there is no doubt that
paper is patient and as I don't intend to show this cardboard-covered
notebook, bearing the proud name of "diary," to anyone, unless I
find a real friend, boy or girl, probably nobody cares. And now I
come to the root of the matter, the reason for my starting a diary:
it is that I have no such real friend.

3   Let me put it more clearly, since no one will believe that a girl
of thirteen feels herself quite alone in the world, nor is it so. I have
darling parents and a sister of sixteen. I know about thirty people
whom one might call friends — I have strings of boy friends, anxious
to catch a glimpse of me and who, failing that, peep at me through

mirrors in class. I have relations, aunts and uncles, who are darlings too, a good home, no—I don't seem to lack anything. But it's the same with all my friends, just fun and joking, nothing more. I can never bring myself to talk of anything outside the common round. We don't seem to be able to get any closer, that is the root of the trouble. Perhaps I lack confidence, but anyway, there it is, a stubborn fact and I don't seem to be able to do anything about it.

4   Hence, this diary. In order to enhance in my mind's eye the picture of the friend for whom I have waited so long, I don't want to set down a series of bald facts in a diary like most people do, but I want this diary itself to be my friend, and I shall call my friend Kitty.

Questions About "Diaries and Journals"

1. What reasons for keeping a diary does Frank give?

2. Explain whether she achieves her purpose of avoiding setting down "a series of bald facts" (par. 4).

Questions on Diction and Writing Techniques

1. What is the derivation of "diary"?

2. How does Frank attain coherence between paragraphs 3 and 4?

3. What is the degree of formality of Frank's writing? Who is her audience? How are the two related?

For Discussion, Reading, and Writing

1. Fill the blanks in this passage from memory to make it intelligible:

   Hence, this _____. In order to enhance in my mind's eye the

   picture of the _____ for whom I have waited so long, I don't

   want to set down a series of bald _____ in a diary like most

   people do, but I want this _____ itself to be my _____, and
   I shall call my friend Kitty.

   Compare your words with those in paragraph 4.

2. Why does Frank say that it's an odd idea for her to keep a diary?

3. What do you take Frank to mean by "paper is patient" (par. 2)? Do you agree?

4. Do Frank's reasons for keeping a diary apply to you? Whether they do or not, explain in a paragraph or two why you will or will not keep one.

5. Whether or not you keep it up, start a diary and for a week or two make daily entries in it, however brief.

6. Write an entry in a diary in the form of a letter to a real or imaginary person on the subject of friendship.

FROM MAN TO BOY
John R. Coleman

John R. Coleman, during a sabbatical leave from the presidency of Haverford College, worked at a variety of menial jobs. The diary he kept was published in **Blue-Collar Journal** (1974).

Tuesday, March 27

1   One of the waitresses I find hard to take asked me at one point today, "Are you the boy who cuts the lemons?"

2   "I'm the man who does," I replied.

3   "Well, there are none cut." There wasn't a hint that she heard my point.

4   Dana, who has cooked here for twelve years or so, heard that exchange.

5   "It's no use, Jack," he said when she was gone. "If she doesn't

know now, she never will." There was a trace of a smile on his face, but it was a sad look all the same.

6 In that moment, I learned the full thrust of those billboard ads of a few years ago that said, "BOY. Drop out of school and that's what they'll call you the rest of your life." I had read those ads before with a certain feeling of pride; education matters, they said, and that gave a lift to my field. Today I saw them saying something else. They were untrue in part; it turns out that you'll get called "boy" if you do work that others don't respect even if you have a Ph.D. It isn't education that counts, but the job in which you land. And the ads spoke too of a sad resignation about the world. They assumed that some people just won't learn respect for others, so you should adapt yourself to them. Don't try to change them. Get the right job and they won't call *you* boy any more. They'll save it for the next man.

7 It isn't just people like this one waitress who learn slowly, if at all. Haverford College has prided itself on being a caring, considerate community in the Quaker tradition for many long years. Yet when I came there I soon learned that the cleaning women in the dormitories were called "wombats" by all the students. No one seemed to know where the name came from or what connection, if any, it had with the dictionary definition. *The American College Dictionary* says a wombat is "any of three species of burrowing marsupials of Australia . . . somewhat resembling ground hogs." The name was just one of Haverford's unexamined ways of doing things.

8 It didn't take much persuasion to get the name dropped. Today there are few students who remember it at all. But I imagine the cleaning women remember it well.

9 Certainly I won't forget being called a boy today.

Questions About "Diaries and Journals"

1. How does Coleman bring personal experience and observation to bear on this journal entry?
2. What conclusion does he arrive at?
3. Would his writing be as effective if he had not tried to find significance in the waitress's question? Explain.

Questions on Diction and Writing Techniques

1. Instead of reporting in the third person what the waitress and cook said, Coleman uses dialogue. Why?

2. What does he signal to you by using "but" (par. 6)? Find another instance of his use of this word in this essay for a similar reason.

3. What is the function of "yet" (par. 7)?

4. To better understand how Coleman organized his essay, divide it into parts consisting of one or more paragraphs and explain the function of each part.

For Discussion, Reading, and Writing

1. Why, according to Coleman, were the billboards in part untrue?

2. How, according to Coleman, were the students at Haverford College like the waitress?

3. Jot down notes, as in a journal entry, based on your recollection of an incident that you experienced or observed today. Think about the incident, considering its significance. Expand your notes into a draft of an essay. Develop them into a finished essay that you might want others to read.

LONELINESS
May Sarton

May Sarton, an American writer whose poetry, fiction, and essays have won her numerous awards, is an ardent diarist.

Reprinted from *The House By The Sea, A Journal*, by May Sarton, with the permission of W. W. Norton and Company, Inc. Copyright © 1977 by May Sarton.

Tuesday, January 28th

1 It is a queer winter, with a few warm days followed by cold, a few rainy days, then snow, and one can never settle down to good old winter! The crocuses are up . . . fatal!

2 Yesterday I had three letters from three friends, so different in every way that it was startling to find the same problem making for depression. One is a young married woman with two small children and a husband who is a company man. She feels shut out by his work, resents his cavalier way of bringing "friends," meaning clients, home without warning, but especially their lack of communication because there is never time. He is also away a lot on business. The second is a friend whose husband retired recently; on his retirement they moved away from the town where they had always lived to be near the ocean. He is at a loose end and she feels caught, angry and depressed without being able to define why. The third is a woman professor, quite young, who lives happily with a woman colleague but speaks of her "bone loneliness."

3 "Loneliness" for me is associated with love relationships. We are lonely when there is not perfect communion. In solitude one can achieve a good relationship with oneself. It struck me forcibly that I could never speak of "bone loneliness" now, though I have certainly experienced it when I was in love. And I feel sure that that poignant phrase would have described my mother often.

Questions About "Diaries and Journals"

1. What problem does Sarton find her three correspondents have in common?

2. What do her own experiences contribute to an understanding of the problem?

3. What are her conclusions?

Questions on Diction and Writing Techniques

1. Distinguish (with the help of your dictionary, if necessary)

between "communication" and "communion" and between "loneliness" and "solitude."

2. Sarton might have written her first sentence: "It is a queer winter." Which version do you prefer? Why?

3. Sarton expressed ideas similar to those in paragraph 3 in a paragraph in an essay ("The Rewards of Living a Solitary Life") she wrote for *The New York Times*:

> Loneliness is most acutely felt with other people, for with others, even with a lover sometimes, we suffer from our differences of taste, temperament, mood. Human intercourse often demands that we soften the edge of perception, or withdraw at the very instant of personal truth for fear of hurting, or of being inappropriately present, which is to say naked, in a social situation. Alone we can afford to be wholly whatever we are, and to feel whatever we feel absolutely. That is a great luxury!

Which writing do you think is more formal? How did you arrive at your conclusion?

For Discussion, Reading, and Writing

1. Compare the merits of telephoning and letter writing as means of communication.

2. Jot down anything that comes to mind on any subject. Find in the jotting the nucleus of a paragraph you might write. Write the paragraph.

3. Drawing on your own experience to explain your ideas, write a short essay that distinguishes between being alone and being lonely.

Reading and Interviews

FROM the time when someone first reads to us as children we receive information secondhand. From the printed page, whether reading randomly or purposefully, we get much information not otherwise available. Everything we read—in books, magazines, newspapers—adds to our knowledge of the world. The accumulation of information so attained is greater by far than that achieved by our own experiences and observations, however great these may be. Consider how much you have learned from books and other writings since you first began to read, on subjects as diverse as literature, history, geography, biology, mathematics, and religion. Reading is an important source of a writer's material.

In college, you probably read more thoughtfully than before—to acquire information and to achieve understanding. When you read for information, you are seeking facts. When you read for understanding, you are looking beyond the facts to their significance. Your reading is particularly purposeful when you read for immediate uses and toward a specific goal: to increase your knowledge of a subject in preparation for writing an essay, a report, or a research paper, or for taking an exam. The experience of a writer from Hartford, Connecticut, will illustrate this purposefulness.

Mary Smith (or so we'll call her), while interviewing a bridge engineer in the Connecticut Highway Department to get material for a proposed essay on covered bridges, learned by chance that the engineer had an interest in whales and a concern for them as an endangered species. The engineer, Mary learned, was a member of the Connecticut Cetacean Society, whose purpose is to preserve the order *Cetacea* (aquatic, chiefly marine animals, including whales, dolphins, and porpoises). Its members were to go on their annual whale-watching trip in Cape Cod Bay in the middle of May, then three months away. That whales stopped off the coast of Massachusetts during their migrations was a surprise to Mary. Seeing in the whale-watching trip an occasion for a weekend outing and the subject of an essay, she started to prepare herself by gathering information about whales.

First she turned to the *Encyclopaedia Britannica* (1967 edition) where she found a ten-and-a-half-page illustrated article on whales with sections such as "Whales in Legend and Literature," "Feeding Adaptations and Food," "Breeding and Reproduction," and "Migrations," and a bibliography of general and special references; a three-page article on whaling with sections such as "Early Whaling," "Modern Whaling," "Whale and Sperm Oils," and "Regulation"; and, in a long article on wildlife conservation, a short section on whales, giving a brief history of the measures taken to conserve them, including the creation of the International Whaling Commission (IWC). Then, for regional information about whales and whaling, Mary browsed through and read sections of books and pamphlets in the library of the Connecticut Historical Society in Hartford.

For up-to-date information about whales, she consulted *The New York Times Index*, where she discovered references to recent *Times* articles about whales and their conservation, and *The Readers' Guide to Periodical Literature*, where she found references to recent magazine articles on her subject.

On the weekend of May 13–14, Mary sailed from Provincetown on two four-hour trips in Cape Cod Bay on board *Dolphin III*. Sunday afternoon she spent at the whale and whaling exhibit at the Provincetown Museum and at the National Park Service building a few miles away, where she found and bought a useful slender volume, *Whale Fishery of New England.* Mary's reading and interviews (about which, more later), plus of course her personal experience and observations, resulted in an essay of about 1250 words. I reproduce it here, complete:

Watching the Great Whales

May is the time of year when the biggest animals on planet Earth visit southern New England. Offshore, sometimes within a mile of land, one may encounter creatures from 30 to 60 feet long, weighing from 30 to 60 tons—the great whales.

Great whales is a term used to designate the ten largest cetaceans (from *cetus,* Latin for whale). They range in length from the 30-foot-long minke to the 100-foot blue whale and are among the 80 or so species of the order *Cetacea,* which includes porpoises and dolphins, the smaller members of the whale family.

Whales are migratory animals. Some travel eight thousand miles each year, from feeding grounds to calving grounds and back. Genuses of the Northern Hemisphere make an annual pilgrimage north in the late winter and spring, some from tropical to polar latitudes where planktonic food proliferates in the summer. On their way north in the spring and again en route to the Caribbean and the equator in the fall, a number of them stop over in southern New England waters, using them as a picnic area where for a few weeks they enjoy a regional fare of plankton, herring, and the 3- to 4-inch-long sand lance or sand eel.

On a recent weekend a group of ninety Connecticut residents from many parts of the state, including New Britain, Glastonbury, Rocky Hill, Avon, and Hartford, went hunting for these whales in Cape Cod Bay on a trip sponsored by the Children's Museum of Hartford and led by its administrative director, Frank Gardner. These modern Queequegs—cameras in hand instead of harpoons—shipped out on two successive days on four-hour whale-watching trips aboard a latter-day *Pequod*: the trim, broad-beamed, 90-foot steel-hulled fisherman, *Dolphin III* out of Provincetown, Albert Avellar, Captain.

Most of them are members of the Connecticut Cetacean Society (CCS), a conservation organization founded in 1973 that now has over seven hundred members, two hundred of them from out of state, and that is the only state organization of its kind in the country. Perhaps best known for its promotion of the successful campaign to have the sperm whale designated by the state legislature in 1975 as the official animal of Connecticut, the Society has the aim of preserving members of the order *Cetacea* by seeking the abolition of the killing of all whales.

This attitude toward whales is a far cry from that of Connecticut Yankees of other years.

Interest in whaling, in Connecticut, goes back to the colonial period. For more than half a century, until the early 1700s, whaling by Nutmeggers, on a relatively modest scale, was concentrated offshore and in Long Island Sound, where whales often appeared. In 1712, a ship whaling in Nantucket Sound Shoals was blown during a storm far out to sea, where its captain sighted a school of sperm whales. This species' oil of exceptional quality, used to make fine candles, lured New England whalers farther and farther away from the mainland and ultimately all over the Seven Seas.

At the height of whaling in America, the middle third of the last century, New London—which in its whaling heyday is said to have had more millionaires than any other town or city in the country—was the third most active whaling port, after only New Bedford, by far the biggest, and Nantucket. In one year its shipping included seventy whalers. At least 820 whaling voyages originated there from 1784 to 1876.

In Connecticut, second to New London, with 130 sailings from 1830 to 1860, was Stonington; third, with 105 whaling sailings, was Mystic, whose seaport now permanently berths—for us and later generations to inspect—the *Charles W. Morgan,* the last of the great American whaling vessels. Other Connecticut ports such as East Haddam, New Haven, and Bridgeport also from time to time cleared whaling ships.

After the Civil War, in part due to the discovery of petroleum, whose by-product kerosene first supplanted candles for illumination, the New England whaling industry, and with it Connecticut's, declined. The last whaling voyage to originate in Connecticut started in New London in 1909.

Nonetheless, whaling on a large scale, with modern whale catchers and factory ships, has continued. It has been estimated that more whales were killed in the last fifty years than in all of whaling history going back to the ninth century. The right whale, one of the great whales, may have been hunted to the verge of extinction; it is rarely sighted today.

Concern for the future of whaling and for whales led to the creation in 1946 of the International Whaling Commission, whose purpose is to pool statistics and to set limits on whale catches. But policing of the whaling nations' observance of quotas is difficult. Conservationists are, understandably, disturbed.

Thus the organizing of CCS, some of whose members, led by Dr. Robbins Barstow, its executive director, were among the whale watchers on board the *Dolphin III* when its crew cast off her lines at Macmillan pier in Provincetown harbor to search for whales in Cape Cod Bay.

The Connecticut whale watchers sighted from twenty to thirty fin (finback) whales at different times and in different parts of the bay, some as long as 60 feet. The more distant ones were first identified by their spouts only. When these were spotted, one would hear from some of the landlubbers the proverbial "Thar she blows!" Captain Avellar eased his ship as close to the whales as he could, generally within 50 to 250 feet. Two whales, one of them a 60-ton finback, crossed within 30 feet of the bow of *Dolphin III*.

With the help of marine biologist Dr. Charles "Stormy" Mayo of U. Mass., one minke whale was identified. But, neither a humpback nor any of the other great whales — except finbacks — that have been seen in Cape Cod Bay in recent years made an appearance.

However, at the end of the first day's search Captain Avellar sighted a school of hundreds of white-sided dolphins about a mile off the hook of Provincetown, between Wood's End and Long Point Lighthouse. An endangered species themselves, the dolphins were feeding, as is nature's way, on schools of tiny sand lance.

Captain Avellar guided his ship among them, and the Connecticut whale watchers had the opportunity of seeing these cetaceans put on a spectacular marine acrobatic performance, as from time to time, while pursuing their evening meal, the 6- to 8-foot-long dolphins leaped out of the water, for a moment hung suspended in air, and then slowly slid back into the sea.

The reaction of those on board ship to the display was summed up by Eunice Wallace, of Hartford: "It was dramatically thrilling, like a ballet. Baryshnikov couldn't have done better."

While on board the *Dolphin III,* Mary made notes of what she saw and of what she heard in conversations with the ship's first mate and members of CCS. She listened carefully and recorded in a notebook the gist of a brief introductory talk by Dr. Mayo. She jotted down information that the marine biologist gave intermittently over a loudspeaker in his reports of and comments on his sightings of whales. Mary also introduced herself to Mr. Gardner and Dr. Barstow (who in turn introduced her to Dr. Mayo), asked them questions that came to mind about whales, and asked each if she might visit him in Hartford for an interview. Both readily and cordially agreed.

Back in Hartford, Mary decided to write a first draft of her essay before phoning to make appointments with Mr. Gardner and Dr. Barstow because (1) she had enough information to get started, (2) she could already see how to organize what material she had, and (3) the questions to be put to them would, she thought, be more specific and more thorough after she discovered in the course of writing a first draft what information she still needed to make her essay complete.

Mary made appointments over the phone to see Dr. Barstow at his place of work and Mr. Gardner at the Children's Museum. She then borrowed a tape recorder from the audiovisual department of her college. Having completed a first draft of her essay and through it having found what gaps in her knowledge of her subject seemed to remain, she made a list of questions she would ask the executive director of CCS, among them:

When was the CCS organized?

Who were its founders?

What prompted them to start it?

How many members did it start out with?

How many does CCS have now?

When did you join it? Why?

What is CCS's purpose?

How well is it fulfilling that aim?

Why are you concerned about the fate of the cetaceans?

Mary's list of questions for the administrative director of the Children's Museum, for the purpose of rounding out the information garnered previously, included:

Why do whales stop off in Cape Cod Bay during their migrations?

We saw during the weekend one minke and a number of finbacks. Has the humpback or any other of the great whales been sighted there in recent years?

What do whales feed on in Cape Cod Bay?

How many dolphins do you estimate we saw on Saturday?

How big do you think they were?

What were they feeding on?

Is there a rule for estimating the weight of a whale? If so, what is it?

Dr. Barstow and Mr. Gardner were not only willing, but eager to talk about their favorite subject in detail and at length. In addition to using the tape recorder, Mary jotted down notes on her sheet of questions, in part to remind herself to pursue lines of inquiry suggested by some of the responses and new ideas presented by the two men. Dr. Barstow gave her copies of recent issues of the CCS monthly bulletin and a copy of a little book that he and the president of CCS, Don Stineti, who did the artwork, had put together—*Meet the Great Ones: An Introduction to Whales and Other Cetaceans*. In response to Mary's final question, both men interviewed said, "Yes, if you need any more information, please don't hesitate to phone."

The interview is not often utilized in college writing. Yet it is a handy and fruitful source of material for a writer. From it you can get firsthand information and opinions on almost any subject, often from experts whose knowledge is invaluable. People like to talk about themselves and their concerns, and they enjoy being called upon to give information, whether specialized or not, and to state their opinions. They are generally flattered by being interviewed, willing to answer questions, and almost always cooperative.

The more you learn about your subject before the interview, the more definitive will your questions be. It is a good idea to bring to an interview a list of carefully prepared questions phrased to plug the gaps in your knowledge and a scheme—however tentative—for the organization of your material in a proposed essay. Nevertheless, you may find that the interview may take a turn that you did not anticipate. This may be all to the good, for the person interviewed may introduce material about which you did not have, and perhaps could not have had, prior knowledge. But if you want to control the direction the interview takes, it is best to follow as closely as possible the sequence of your prepared questions.

Note taking is always useful, but too much of it—especially if it delays proceedings—may distract the person interviewed and cause her or his interest to wane. In any case, a tape recorder—if the interviewee does not object to your using one—will be beneficial because of the ease and completeness with which it records conversation.

Even with carefully prepared questions and reasonably good responses, you may find, when you start to incorporate into your writing the information gathered in an interview, unexpected gaps in your knowledge. More likely than not, a phone call to the person you interviewed will get you the needed information.

The results make the interview worthwhile. It is indispensable when the information you seek is nowhere else available. Also, direct quotation—which must be done carefully and accurately—of an interviewee, even when the information is neither essential nor unique, is likely to sound more convincing than your own words. Knowledge given firsthand by the interviewee is likely to seem to your reader more immediate, vivid, and authoritative than your transcription of it.

JAILBREAK MARRIAGE
Gail Sheehy

Gail Sheehy is an award-winning reporter, essayist, and frequent contributor to magazines. Her books include **Passages** (1976), the source of this selection, which is about the "predictable crises of adult life."

1   Although the most commonplace reason women marry young is to "complete" themselves, a good many spirited young women gave another reason: "I did it to get away from my parents." Particularly for girls whose educations and privileges are limited, a *jailbreak marriage* is the usual thing. What might appear to be an act of rebellion usually turns out to be a transfer of dependence.

2   A lifer: that is how it felt to be Simone at 17, how it often feels for girls in authoritarian homes. The last of six children, she was caught in the nest vacated by the others and expected to "keep the family together." Simone was the last domain where her mother could play out the maternal role and where her father could exercise full control. That meant good-bye to the university scholarship.

3   Although the family was not altogether poor, Simone had tried to make a point of her independence by earning her own money since the age of 14. Now she thrust out her bankbook. Would two thousand dollars in savings buy her freedom?

4   "We want you home until you're 21."

5   Work, her father insisted. But the job she got was another closed gate. It was in the knitting machine firm where her father worked, an extension of his control. Simone knuckled under for a year until she met Franz. A zero. An egocentric Hungarian of pointless aristocracy, a man for whom she had total disregard. Except for one attraction. He asked her to marry him. Franz would be the getaway vehicle in her jailbreak marriage scheme: "I decided

From *Passages: Predictable Crises of Adult Life* by Gail Sheehy. Copyright © 1974, 1976 by Gail Sheehy. Reprinted by permission of the publisher, E. P. Dutton, Inc.

the best way to get out was to get married and divorce him a year later. That was my whole program."

6   Anatomy, uncontrolled, sabotaged her program. Nine months after the honeymoon, Simone was a mother. Resigning herself, she was pregnant with her second child at 20.

7   One day, her husband called with the news, the marker event to blast her out of the drift. His firm had offered him a job in New York City.

8   "Then and there, I decided that before the month was out I would have the baby, find a lawyer, and start divorce proceedings." The next five years were like twenty. It took every particle of her will and patience to defeat Franz, who wouldn't hear of a separation, and to ignore the ostracism of her family.

9   At the age of 25, on the seventh anniversary of her jailbreak marriage (revealed too late as just another form of entrapment), Simone finally escaped her parents. Describing the day of her decree, the divorcée sounds like so many women whose identity was foreclosed by marriage: "It was like having ten tons of chains removed from my mind, my body—the most exhilarating day of my life."

Questions About "Reading and Interviews"

1. What evidence is there in this piece that Sheehy used interviews as a source of her material?

2. What is Sheehy's purpose in this essay? How does the use of interviews help her achieve that purpose?

3. What impact does Sheehy's use of interview material have on you?

4. Rewrite one or two of Simone's remarks in the third person. Compare the effect on you of this method of reporting an interview with that of direct quotation, which Sheehy uses.

Questions on Diction and Writing Techniques

1. Define and use in sentences "domain" (par. 2) and "egocentric" (par. 5).

2. Comment on whether "jailbreak marriage" (par. 1) is an apt phrase. Find two other metaphors (see pages 78–79) that are consistent with "jailbreak."

3. Sheehy might have written the first sentence of paragraph 2 like this: "To Simone at 17 it felt like being a lifer, the way it often feels for girls in authoritarian homes." What was the writer's purpose in writing the sentence the way she did?

4. What is the derivation of "good-bye" (par. 2)?

5. Sheehy might have written the first sentence of paragraph 5 like this: "Her father insisted that she work." Why did she choose the inverted word order?

6. Combine sentences 3 ("Simone knuckled under . . .") through 7 (ending with "to marry him") of paragraph 5 into one sentence. Which version do you prefer? Why?

7. What words might Sheehy have chosen as alternatives to "sabotage" (par. 6)? Which verb do you prefer? Why?

For Discussion, Reading, and Writing

1. This essay is mainly about (circle one):

   A. Simone's marriage to Franz.

   B. Simone's distaste for Franz.

   C. Simone's attempt to find her own identity.

   D. why some women marry young.

   E. why some women run away from home.

2. Using the interview as your major source of material, write a paragraph or two about "an act of rebellion" (par. 1) by any person you know.

3. Interview young couples to gather your material and then write an essay on a restricted subject having to do with marriage.

4. Write an essay, based on interviews with your parents, grand-
    parents, teachers, or any other older persons, on some aspect of

    Birth control
    Motherhood without marriage
    Premarital sex
    Trial marriage
    Abortion

THROW-AWAY SOCIETY
Alvin Toffler

Alvin Toffler, editor, correspondent, and lecturer, is best known as
a social thinker. In **Future Shock** (1970), the source of this
excerpt, he writes about our system of values, about changes in
our industrial society and how we adapt to them.

1　　"Barbie," a twelve-inch plastic teen-ager, is the best-known and
best-selling doll in history. Since its introduction in 1959, the Barbie
doll population of the world has grown to 12,000,000 — more than
the human population of Los Angeles or London or Paris. Little
girls adore Barbie because she is highly realistic and eminently
dress-upable. Mattel, Inc., makers of Barbie, also sells a complete
wardrobe for her, including clothes for ordinary daytime wear,
clothes for formal party wear, clothes for swimming and skiing.

2　　Recently Mattel announced a new improved Barbie doll. The
new version has a slimmer figure, "real" eyelashes, and a twist-and-
turn waist that makes her more humanoid than ever. Moreover,
Mattel announced that, for the first time, any young lady wishing
to purchase a new Barbie would receive a trade-in allowance for her
old one.

₃   What Mattel did not announce was that by trading in her old doll for a technologically improved model, the little girl of today, citizen of tomorrow's super-industrial world, would learn a fundamental lesson about the new society: that man's relationships with *things* are increasingly temporary.

₄   The ocean of man-made physical objects that surrounds us is set within a larger ocean of natural objects. But increasingly, it is the technologically produced environment that matters for the individual. The texture of plastic or concrete, the iridescent glisten of an automobile under a streetlight, the staggering vision of a cityscape seen from the window of a jet — these are the intimate realities of his existence. Man-made things enter into and color his consciousness. Their number is expanding with explosive force, both absolutely and relative to the natural environment. This will be even more true in super-industrial society than it is today.

₅   That man-thing relationships are growing more and more temporary may be illustrated by examining the culture surrounding the little girl who trades in her doll. This child soon learns that Barbie dolls are by no means the only physical objects that pass into and out of her young life at a rapid clip. Diapers, bibs, paper napkins, Kleenex, towels, non-returnable soda bottles — all are used up quickly in her home and ruthlessly eliminated. Corn muffins come in baking tins that are thrown away after one use. Spinach is encased in plastic sacks that can be dropped into a pan of boiling water for heating, and then thrown away. TV dinners are cooked and often served on throw-away trays. Her home is a large processing machine through which objects flow, entering and leaving, at a faster and faster rate of speed. From birth on, she is inextricably embedded in a throw-away culture.

₆   The idea of using a product once or for a brief period and then replacing it, runs counter to the grain of societies or individuals steeped in a heritage of poverty. Not long ago Uriel Rone, a market researcher for the French advertising agency Publicis, told me: "The French housewife is not used to disposable products. She likes to keep things, even old things, rather than throw them away. We represented one company that wanted to introduce a kind of plastic throw-away curtain. We did a marketing study for them and

found the resistance too strong." This resistance, however, is dying
all over the developed world.

₇   Thus a writer, Edward Maze, has pointed out that many
Americans visiting Sweden in the early 1950's were astounded by
its cleanliness. "We were almost awed by the fact that there were
no beer and soft drink bottles by the roadsides, as, much to our
shame, there were in America. But by the 1960's, lo and behold,
bottles were suddenly blooming along Swedish highways . . . What
happened? Sweden had become a buy, use and throw-away society,
following the American pattern." In Japan today throw-away tissues are so universal that cloth handkerchiefs are regarded as old
fashioned, not to say unsanitary. In England for sixpence one may
buy a "Dentamatic throw-away toothbrush" which comes already
coated with toothpaste for its one-time use. And even in France,
disposable cigarette lighters are commonplace. From cardboard
milk containers to the rockets that power space vehicles, products
created for short-term or one-time use are becoming more numerous and crucial to our way of life.

₈   The recent introduction of paper and quasi-paper clothing carried the trend toward disposability a step further. Fashionable boutiques and working-class clothing stores have sprouted whole departments devoted to gaily colored and imaginatively designed paper
apparel. Fashion magazines display breathtakingly sumptuous
gowns, coats, pajamas, even wedding dresses made of paper. The
bride pictured in one of these wears a long white train of lace-like
paper that, the caption writer notes, will make "great kitchen curtains" after the ceremony.

₉   We develop a throw-away mentality to match our throw-
away products. This mentality produces, among other things, a set
of radically altered values with respect to property. But the spread
of disposability through the society also implies decreased durations
in man-thing relationships. Instead of being linked with a single object over a relatively long span of time, we are linked for brief
periods with the succession of objects that supplant it.

Questions About "Reading and Interviews"

1. Point out what material in this essay Toffler derived from interviews and what from reading.

2. How might Toffler have secured the information contained in paragraph 1?

3. How do the writer's sources of material in this essay relate to his purpose in writing it?

Questions on Diction and Writing Techniques

1. What does the amount of detailed information in paragraph 1 contribute to its effectiveness as an opening paragraph?

2. Define and use in sentences "humanoid" (par. 2), "boutiques" (par. 8), "sumptuous" (par. 8).

3. What purpose is served by "moreover" (par. 2), "however" (par. 6), "thus" (par. 7), "but" (par. 9)?

4. Find an example of metaphor in paragraph 4 and another in paragraph 5.

5. Toffler might have written sentence 3 of paragraph 4 like this: "The intimate realities of his existence are the texture of plastic or concrete, the iridescent glisten of an automobile under a streetlight, the staggering vision of a cityscape seen from the window of a jet." Which version better emphasizes the main idea he wants to convey to you?

6. What is the main idea of paragraph 5? Is any information that you need in order to understand and accept the idea not given?

7. What is the topic sentence of paragraph 7? Can you justify placing it elsewhere in the paragraph? Comment on whether it is well explained.

8. What words might Toffler have chosen instead of "sprouted" (par. 8)? Which do you prefer? Why?

9. What is the essay's thesis (see pages 2–9)? Where does the writer digress? Is the essay unified? Explain.

For Discussion, Reading, and Writing

1. Which of these statements, according to Toffler, are true (T), which false (F)?

   A. ____ Little girls like Barbie because she is unbreakable.

   B. ____ The new improved Barbie doll is more humanoid than ever.

   C. ____ Man's relationships with things are increasingly temporary.

   D. ____ Products created for short-term or one-time use are good for business.

   E. ____ We develop a throw-away mentality to match our throw-away products.

2. Might there be a correlation between "decreased durations in man-thing relationships" (par. 9) and decreased duration in man-woman relations? If this subject interests you, write an essay about it based on interviews with married, divorced, or single persons you know.

3. What benefit, if any, is there in "being linked with a single object over a relatively long span of time" (par. 9)? Write a short essay on the subject.

4. Using the textbooks in a course you are taking or have taken as your main source of material, write an essay explaining a thesis related to the topic "The Throw-Away Society."

5. Using reading, interviews, or both as your chief sources of material, write a short essay on disposable clothing, throw-away drink containers, automobile junkyards, garbage dumps, or any other product or by-product of "the throw-away society."

THE PROBLEM THAT HAS NO NAME
Betty Friedan

Betty Friedan, American writer and social reformer, is active in the feminist movement. Her popular **The Feminine Mystique** (1963) helped draw attention to American women's lack of fulfillment as childbearers and housewives.

1   Gradually I came to realize that the problem that has no name was shared by countless women in America. As a magazine writer I often interviewed women about problems with their children, or their marriages, or their houses, or their communities. But after a while I began to recognize the telltale signs of this other problem. I saw the same signs in suburban ranch houses and split-levels on Long Island and in New Jersey and Westchester County; in colonial houses in a small Massachusetts town; on patios in Memphis; in suburban and city apartments; in living rooms in the Midwest. Sometimes I sensed the problem, not as a reporter, but as a suburban housewife, for during this time I was also bringing up my own three children in Rockland County, New York. I heard echoes of the problem in college dormitories and semi-private maternity wards, at PTA meetings and luncheons of the League of Women Voters, at suburban cocktail parties, in station wagons waiting for trains, and in snatches of conversations overheard at Schrafft's. The groping words I heard from other women, on quiet afternoons when children were at school or on quiet evenings when husbands worked late, I think I understood first as a woman long before I understood their larger social and psychological implications.

2   Just what was this problem that has no name? What were the words women used when they tried to express it? Sometimes a woman would say, "I feel empty somehow . . . incomplete." Or she

would say, "I feel as if I don't exist." Sometimes she blotted out the feeling with a tranquilizer. Sometimes she thought the problem was with her husband, or her children, or that what she really needed was to redecorate her house, or move to a better neighborhood, or have an affair, or another baby. Sometimes, she went to a doctor with symptoms she could hardly describe: "A tired feeling . . . I get so angry with the children it scares me . . . I feel like crying without any reason." (A Cleveland doctor called it "the housewife's syndrome.") A number of women told me about great bleeding blisters that break out on their hands and arms. "I call it the housewife's blight," said a family doctor in Pennsylvania. "I see it so often lately in these young women with four, five and six children who bury themselves in their dishpans. But it isn't caused by detergent and it isn't cured by cortisone."

3   Sometimes a woman would tell me that the feeling gets so strong she runs out of the house and walks through the streets. Or she stays inside her house and cries. Or her children tell her a joke, and she doesn't laugh because she doesn't hear it. I talked to women who had spent years on the analyst's couch, working out their "adjustment to the feminine role," their blocks to "fulfillment as a wife and mother." But the desperate tone in these women's voices, and the look in their eyes, was the same as the tone and the look of other women, who were sure they had no problem, even though they did have a strange feeling of desperation.

4   A mother of four who left college at nineteen to get married told me:

> I've tried everything women are supposed to do—hobbies, gardening, pickling, canning, being very social with my neighbors, joining committees, running PTA teas. I can do it all, and I like it, but it doesn't leave you anything to think about—any feeling of who you are. I never had any career ambitions. All I wanted was to get married and have four children. I love the kids and Bob and my home. There's no problem you can even put a name to. But I'm desperate. I begin to feel I have no personality. I'm a server of food and a putter-on of pants and a bedmaker, somebody who can be called on when you want something. But who am I?

5   A twenty-three-year-old mother in blue jeans said:

I ask myself why I'm so dissatisfied. I've got my health, fine children, a lovely new home, enough money. My husband has a real future as an electronics engineer. He doesn't have any of these feelings. He says maybe I need a vacation, let's go to New York for a weekend. But that isn't it. I always had this idea we should do everything together. I can't sit down and read a book alone. If the children are napping and I have one hour to myself I just walk through the house waiting for them to wake up. I don't make a move until I know where the rest of the crowd is going. It's as if ever since you were a little girl, there's always been somebody or something that will take care of your life: your parents, or college, or falling in love, or having a child, or moving to a new house. Then you wake up one morning and there's nothing to look forward to.

6   A young wife in a Long Island development said:

I seem to sleep so much. I don't know why I should be so tired. This house isn't nearly so hard to clean as the cold-water flat we had when I was working. The children are at school all day. It's not the work. I just don't feel alive.

Questions About "Readings and Interviews"

1. How did Friedan find out about "the problem that has no name"?

2. What does the information in paragraph 2 add to what Friedan writes in paragraph 1?

3. Why does the writer include the quotations in paragraphs 2 through 6? Without the quotations, could she have set forth the ideas in those paragraphs as convincingly as she does with them? Explain. How are the paragraphs related to the writer's thesis?

4. Explain whether, and to what extent, your understanding of "the problem" is enhanced by Friedan's explanation of it in this piece.

Questions on Diction and Writing Techniques

1. Define "telltale" (par. 1) and use the word in a sentence.

2. What is the effect on you of the repetition of "problem that has no name" and of "problem" (par. 1)? Does the repetition contribute to the coherence of the selection? Explain.

3. What is Friedan's purpose in writing "Or" in paragraph 2? Find another instance in this essay of her use of this conjunction for the same reason.

For Discussion, Reading, and Writing

1. Friedan's conclusion in this essay is (circle one):

   A. Bringing up her own three children was crucial to Friedan's understanding the problem that has no name.

   B. Of the women interviewed by Friedan, the suburban housewives are the most unfulfilled.

   C. Women in rural America are happier than those elsewhere.

   D. The Equal Rights Amendment is the only solution to the problem that Friedan identifies.

   E. The problem that has no name was shared by countless women in America.

2. Using information in this essay or from other sources, including interviews, explain in a paragraph or two whether the proper place of a woman is in the home.

3. In 1869 John Stuart Mill wrote in "The Subjection of Women" (italics added): "The principle which regulates the existing social relations between the two sexes—the legal subordination of one sex to the other—is wrong in itself, and now one of the chief hindrances to human improvement; . . . *it ought to be replaced by a principle of perfect equality, admitting no power or privilege on the one side, nor disability on the other.*" Using specific details and recommendations, write a short essay that explains clearly your views on the italicized portion of Mill's statement.

4. Using as your main source of material interviews of your mother, aunts, sisters, or any other women you know well, write a short essay that explains the frustration or the success of some woman or women in making their lives interesting, satisfying, purposeful. (You may be able to borrow a tape recorder from the audiovisual department of your college to record your interviews.)

4

Types of
Essays

Narration

THE information that a writer gathers from the various sources of material discussed in Part Three may be used in one or another of four types of essays: narration, description, exposition, and argumentation. (Narration, description, and exposition are discussed in the three sections of Part Four. Argumentation will be treated separately, following Part Five.) Although for convenience we will examine them one at a time, an essay may contain elements of two or more types, in any combination. An expository essay—whose purpose is to explain—might narrate, might describe, and might argue a point to convince readers to accept the writer's beliefs. Langston Hughes' "Salvation" (pages 176–178) is an essay containing elements of more than one type of composition. To be sure, it does tell a story. But it also describes the scene in the church, and it explains why Langston was not really saved.

The placement of selections in this and the next two sections is not inevitable. I have placed each as I have because, in my view, the essay chosen better exemplifies one type of composition than another. What I have just said about the placement of selections in

Part Four also applies to the essays in the other parts of the book. For example, the pieces in Part Three that illustrate the use of personal experience as a source of material are also examples of narration. They tell about events.

We all have stories to tell and the desire to tell them—in conversation, diaries, and letters. Some are about events we have experienced; some have been related to us by others; some may be about imagined occurrences. The type of composition called *narration* gives an account of events or experiences in *time*. (A *description*, in contrast, gives an account of observed details in *space*; see pages 193–212.)

Here are some things to keep in mind when you use the narrative form:

1. *Be sure your story has a point.* If you ask yourself *why* you are telling a story, you are likely to discover that it is because the events seemed significant to you; often they made you more aware of yourself, of others, of your surroundings, and of your thoughts.

    Some beginning writers either see no meaning in their stories or fail to communicate the meaning to their readers. Have you ever heard a story told by a person to whom you felt like saying or did say, "Okay, so what's your point?" It's a valid question because, except for stories told just to entertain, writers tell stories for a reason.

    In some narration, writers make their points explicitly, although usually not quite so explicitly as in this fable—a short tale that teaches a practical lesson:

    In the woods of the Far West there once lived a brown bear who could take it or let it alone. He would go into a bar where they sold mead, a fermented drink made of honey, and he would have just two drinks. Then he would put some money on the bar and say, "See what the bears in the back room will have," and he would go home. But finally he took to drinking by himself most of the day. He would reel home at night, kick over the umbrella stand, knock down the bridge lamps, and ram his elbows through the windows. Then he would collapse on the floor and lie there until he went to sleep. His wife was greatly distressed and his children were very frightened.

At length the bear saw the error of his ways and began to reform. In the end he became a famous teetotaller and a persistent
temperance lecturer. He would tell everybody that came to his
house about the awful effects of drink, and he would boast about
how strong and well he had become since he gave up touching the
stuff. To demonstrate this, he would stand on his head and on his
hands and he would turn cartwheels in the house, kicking over
the umbrella stand, knocking down the bridge lamps, and ram-
ming his elbows through the windows. Then he would lie down
on the floor, tired by his healthful exercise, and go to sleep. His
wife was greatly distressed and his children were very frightened.
  *Moral: You might as well fall flat on your face as lean over too far
backward* [James Thurber, *Fables for Our Time*].

A story will often imply the point the writer wants to
make. This is the method Willie Morris uses in his account
of an accident on the train tracks in upper Manhattan (page
120). But, whether implied or made explicit, the point of
any story included in an essay should be clear to readers.
  See how George Orwell achieves this purpose in "A
Hanging":

It was about forty yards to the gallows. I watched the bare brown
back of the prisoner marching in front of me. He walked clumsily
with his bound arms, but quite steadily, with that bobbing gait of
the Indian who never straightens his knees. At each step his muscles slid neatly into place, the lock of hair on his scalp danced up
and down, his feet printed themselves on the wet gravel. And
once, in spite of the men who gripped him by each shoulder, he
stepped slightly aside to avoid a puddle in the path.
  It is curious; but till that moment I had never realized what it
means to destroy a healthy, conscious man. When I saw the prisoner step aside to avoid the puddle I saw the mystery, the unspeakable wrongness, of cutting a life short when it is in full
tide. . . .

Having had a sudden insight into the wrongness of capital
punishment, Orwell makes a significant generalization
about the events he relates in his essay. This evaluation of
his experience is the point he wants to make in his account

of a hanging. Your evaluation of your experiences—expressing the significance you discover in them—will make your stories more effective too.

2. *Be sure the time sequence is clear.* You can readily impose order on your story by narrating the events in the sequence in which they occurred—by telling the story in *chronological order*. The natural order of events—beginning, middle, and end—is narration's simplest and most-used arrangement. You may choose, however, to start your story at any important point in the sequence of events to be narrated, especially if by doing so you can better arrest the attention of your readers. You can then go back in time—like flashbacks in movies—to tell about the early incidents of your story.

Chronological order can readily be assured by the use of words pertaining to time, as in this passage from John James Audubon's *Ornithological Autobiography* (italics added):

As soon as the Pigeons discover a sufficiency of food to entice them to alight, they fly round in circles, reviewing the country below. *During* their evolutions, *on such occasions,* the dense mass which they form exhibits a beautiful appearance, *as it changes its direction, now* displaying a glistening sheet of azure, *when* the backs of the birds come simultaneously into view, *and anon, suddenly* presenting a mass of rich deep purple. They *then* pass lower, over the woods, and *for a moment* are lost among the foliage, but *again* emerge, and are seen gliding aloft. They *now* alight, but *the next moment,* as if *suddenly* alarmed, they take to wing, producing by the flappings of their wings a noise like the roar of distant thunder, and sweep through the forests to see if danger is near. Hunger, however, *soon* brings them to the ground. *When* alighted, they are seen industriously throwing up the withered leaves in quest of the fallen mast. The rear ranks are continually rising, passing over the main-body, and alighting in front, *in such rapid succession,* that the whole flock seems still on wing. The quantity of ground thus swept is astonishing, and so completely has it been cleared, that the gleaner who might follow in their rear would find his labour completely lost. *Whilst* feeding, their avidity is at times so great that in attempting to swallow a large acorn or nut, they are seen gasping for a *long while,* as if in the agonies of suffocation.

3. *Use dialogue whenever possible.* The reporting of conversation between two or more persons is a useful method of moving a story forward. It also helps to make the story seem more authentic and more immediate. Finally, dialogue is an effective way to characterize persons in a story, as it is in a play. Needless to say, the conversation in your narration should sound natural and be appropriate to the speaker.

4. *Select details carefully.* Good storytelling requires the purposeful selection of details. Some beginning writers include either the wrong details or more details than the effective relating of the events requires. In your narrative writing you should select details that help you to convey to your readers the point of your essay. This is what Orwell did in the passage from "A Hanging" just quoted. The detail of the condemned man avoiding the puddle of water related to Orwell's purpose in telling the story and to the meaning he saw in it.

5. *Choose a point of view.* In everyday usage, "point of view" means an opinion or attitude. In writing, the term has other meanings:

   a. One definition of point of view is the relation of the writer to a story, whether as a participant in the events being narrated, that is, as a first-person narrator, using "I" or "we," or as a reporter of events other people have experienced, using "he," "she," or "they," as in Maya Angelou's "Cotton-picking Time" (pages 220–224).

   b. Point of view also means the physical place from which the writer views the events in a story.

   c. Point of view means, as well, the perception of the observer through whose eyes the events narrated are seen. A parent and child walking in the woods would not view the environment in the same way. The writer has the option of describing the scene as seen by (from the viewpoint of) the child, the parent, or, alternately, both.

To avoid confusing readers, your point of view within a single piece must be consistent.

YUMBO
Andrew Ward

Andrew Ward is a short-story writer and the author of humorous essays that have appeared in a variety of journals.

1   I was sitting at an inn with Kelly Susan, my ten-year-old niece, when she was handed the children's menu. It was printed in gay pastels on construction paper and gave her a choice of a Ferdinand Burger, a Freddie the Fish Stick, or a Porky Pig Sandwich. Like most children's menus, it first anthropomorphized the ingredients and then killed them off. As Kelly read it her eyes grew large, and in them I could see gentle Ferdinand being led away to the stockyard, Freddie gasping at the end of a hook, Porky stuttering his entreaties as the ax descended. Kelly Susan, alone in her family, is a resolute vegetarian and has already faced up to the dread that whispers to us as we slice our steaks. She wound up ordering a cheese sandwich, but the children's menu had ruined her appetite, and she spent the meal picking at her food.

2   Restaurants have always treated children badly. When I was small, my family used to travel a lot, and waitresses were forever calling me "Butch" and pinching my cheeks and making me wear paper bibs with slogans on them. Restaurants still treat children badly; the difference is that restaurants have lately taken to treating us all as if we were children. We are obliged to order an Egg McMuffin when we want breakfast, a Fishamajig when we want a fish sandwich, a Fribble when we want a milkshake, a Whopper when we want a hamburger with all the fixings. Some of these names serve a certain purpose. By calling a milkshake a Fribble, for instance, the management need make no promise that it contains milk, or even that it was shaken.

3   But the primary purpose is to convert an essentially bleak industry, mass-marketed fast foods, into something festive. The burger used to be a culinary last resort; now resorts are being built around it. The patrons in the commercials for burger franchises are all bug-eyed and goofy, be they priests or grandmothers or crane operators, and behave as if it were their patriotic duty, their God-given right, to consume waxy buns, translucent patties, chewy fries, and industrial strength Coca-Cola.

4   Happily, the patrons who actually slump into these places are an entirely different matter. I remember with fond admiration a tidy little man at the local Burger King whom I overheard order a ham and cheese sandwich.

5   "A wha'?" the eruptive girl at the counter asked, pencil poised over her computer card.

6   "I wish to order a ham and cheese sandwich," the man repeated.

7   "I'm sorry, sir," the girl said, "but we don't carry ham and cheese. All we got is what's on the board up there."

8   "Yes, I know," the man politely persisted, "but I believe it is up there. See? The ham and cheese?"

9   The girl gaped at the menu board behind her. "Oh," she finally exclaimed. "You mean a *Yumbo*. You want a *Yumbo*."

10   "The ham and cheese. Yes."

11   "It's called a *Yumbo*, sir," the girl said. "Now, do you want a Yumbo or not?"

12   The man stiffened. "Yes, thank you," he said through his teeth, "the *ham* and *cheese*."

13   "Look," the girl shouted, "I've got to have an order here. You're holding up the line. You want a *Yumbo*, don't you? You want a *Yumbo*!"

14   But the tidy man was not going to say it, and thus were they locked for a few more moments, until at last he stood very straight, put on his hat, and departed intact.

Questions About "Narration"

1. Explain the purpose and the function of the anecdote about Kelly Susan.

2. How does the anecdote relate to the main idea of the essay?

3. Why does Ward tell the story of the tidy little man?

4. Instead of "said" (par. 8), Ward chose "persisted." Find two other examples of his using strong verbs to make his writing vivid and concise.

5. What does dialogue contribute to the impression the story makes on you?

Questions on Diction and Writing Techniques

1. What is the function, in paragraph 2, of sentence 2? Of sentence 4?

2. What, in paragraph 2, does "for instance" signal?

3. Why does Ward begin paragraph 3 with "But"?

For Discussion, Reading, and Writing

1. What, according to Ward, is the difference between the treatment of customers in restaurants lately and when he was small?

2. How, according to Ward, do real patrons differ from the patrons in the commercials for burger franchises?

3. In search of material for an anecdote about a fast-food eatery, go to such a restaurant with a friend and take notes, mental or written, when he or she orders food in the manner of the tidy little man. Compare ideas with your friend and then write jointly an essay based on that experience.

SALVATION
Langston Hughes

Langston Hughes (1902–1967), American writer and poet, was among the first to urge his fellow black artists to use their distinctive experiences as the material for their works.

1   I was saved from sin when I was going on thirteen. But not really saved. It happened like this. There was a big revival at my Auntie Reed's church. Every night for weeks there had been much preaching, singing, praying, and shouting, and some very hardened sinners had been brought to Christ, and the membership of the church had grown by leaps and bounds. Then just before the revival ended, they held a special meeting for children, "to bring the young lambs to the fold." My aunt spoke of it for days ahead. That night I was escorted to the front row and placed on the mourners' bench with all the other young sinners, who had not yet been brought to Jesus.

2   My aunt told me that when you were saved you saw a light, and something happened to you inside! And Jesus came into your life! And God was with you from then on! She said you could see and hear and feel Jesus in your soul. I believed her. I had heard a great many old people say the same thing and it seemed to me they ought to know. So I sat there calmly in the hot, crowded church, waiting for Jesus to come to me.

3   The preacher preached a wonderful rhythmical sermon, all moans and shouts and lonely cries and dire pictures of hell, and then he sang a song about the ninety and nine safe in the fold, but one little lamb was left out in the cold. Then he said: "Won't you come? Won't you come to Jesus? Young lambs, won't you come?" And he held out his arms to all us young sinners there on the

mourners' bench. And the little girls cried. And some of them jumped up and went to Jesus right away. But most of us just sat there.

₄   A great many old people came and knelt around us and prayed, old women with jet-black faces and braided hair, old men with work-gnarled hands. And the church sang a song about the lower lights are burning, some poor sinners to be saved. And the whole building rocked with prayer and song.

₅   Still I kept waiting to *see* Jesus.

₆   Finally all the young people had gone to the altar and were saved, but one boy and me. He was a rounder's son named Westley. Westley and I were surrounded by sisters and deacons praying. It was very hot in the church, and getting late now. Finally Westley said to me in a whisper: "God damn! I'm tired o' sitting here. Let's get up and be saved." So he got up and was saved.

₇   Then I was left all alone on the mourners' bench. My aunt came and knelt at my knees and cried, while prayers and songs swirled all around me in the little church. The whole congregation prayed for me alone, in a mighty wail of moans and voices. And I kept waiting serenely for Jesus, waiting, waiting—but he didn't come. I wanted to see him, but nothing happened to me. Nothing! I wanted something to happen to me, but nothing happened.

₈   I heard the songs and the minister saying: "Why don't you come? My dear child, why don't you come to Jesus? Jesus is waiting for you. He wants you. Why don't you come? Sister Reed, what is this child's name?"

₉   "Langston," my aunt sobbed.

₁₀   "Langston, why don't you come? Why don't you come and be saved? Oh, Lamb of God! Why don't you come?"

₁₁   Now it was really getting late. I began to be ashamed of myself, holding everything up so long. I began to wonder what God thought about Westley, who certainly hadn't seen Jesus either, but who was now sitting proudly on the platform, swinging his knickerbockered legs and grinning down at me, surrounded by deacons and old women on their knees praying. God had not struck Westley dead for taking his name in vain or for lying in the temple. So I decided that maybe to save further trouble, I'd better lie, too, and say that Jesus had come, and get up and be saved.

₁₂   So I got up.

₁₃   Suddenly the whole room broke into a sea of shouting, as they saw me rise. Waves of rejoicing swept the place. Women leaped in the air. My aunt threw her arms around me. The minister took me by the hand and led me to the platform.

14   When things quieted down, in a hushed silence, punctuated by a few ecstatic "Amens," all the new young lambs were blessed in the name of God. Then joyous singing filled the room.

15   That night, for the last time in my life but one—for I was a big boy twelve years old—I cried. I cried, in bed alone, and couldn't stop. I buried my head under the quilts, but my aunt heard me. She woke up and told my uncle I was crying because the Holy Ghost had come into my life, and because I had seen Jesus. But I was really crying because I couldn't bear to tell her that I had lied, that I had deceived everybody in the church, that I hadn't seen Jesus, and that now I didn't believe there was a Jesus any more, since he didn't come to help me.

═══════════════════════════════════

Questions About "Narration"

1. The aunt, by "see," meant "see . . . Jesus in your soul" (par. 2). The boy, however, uses the word literally: "Still I kept waiting to *see* Jesus" (par. 5). What other evidence is there in this essay that Hughes wrote it from the point of view of a twelve-year-old?

2. What does the writer's reporting the boy's reaction in bed to the way he resolved his dilemma in church contribute to the impression on you of the story he relates?

3. In a sentence of not over twenty-five words, state the point Hughes makes in his essay.

4. Make a list of five or more specific details Hughes uses to make his story real and vivid.

Questions on Diction and Writing Techniques

1. How do the first two sentences help paragraph 1 to fulfill the requirements of an introductory paragraph (see pages 29–30)?

2. Why does the writer use "but" in the last sentence of paragraph 3?

3. Why does Hughes make the sentences of paragraphs 5 and 12 separate paragraphs?

4. Are "sea of shouting" and "waves of rejoicing" (par. 13) apt phrases? Explain.

5. What is the effect on you of the short sentences in paragraph 13?

6. By what technique for expanding a sentence (see pages 50–60) does Hughes increase the density of the last sentence of his essay?

For Discussion, Reading, and Writing

1. Fill the blanks in this passage from memory to make it intelligible:

My aunt told me that when you were _____ you saw a

_____, and something _____ to you inside. And Jesus came into your life! And God was with you from then on! She said you could see and hear and _____ Jesus in your soul. I _____ her.

Compare your words with those in paragraph 2.

2. If, as happened to young Langston Hughes, pressures of one kind or another ever forced you to be hypocritical, write in a paragraph or two the story of that experience, making sure to explain to your reader its effect on you.

3. Evoking memories of your childhood, tell in the first person, from the point of view of yourself as a child, the story of an insightful religious experience.

4. In his autobiography, the Irish poet William Butler Yeats said about an early disillusioning experience that it was "the first breaking of the dream of childhood." If you ever were disillusioned similarly, write a short essay showing how, selecting vivid, specific details to convey your story to your reader.

38 WHO SAW MURDER DIDN'T CALL THE POLICE

Martin Gansberg

Martin Gansberg, a reporter and editor of **The New York Times** for many years, is also a contributor to several magazines and a teacher at Fairleigh Dickinson University.

1   For more than half an hour 38 respectable, law-abiding citizens in Queens watched a killer stalk and stab a woman in three separate attacks in Kew Gardens.

2   Twice the sound of their voices and the sudden glow of their bedroom lights interrupted him and frightened him off. Each time he returned, sought her out and stabbed her again. Not one person telephoned the police during the assault; one witness called after the woman was dead.

3   That was two weeks ago today. But Assistant Chief Inspector Frederick M. Lussen, in charge of the borough's detectives and a veteran of 25 years of homicide investigations, is still shocked.

4   He can give a matter-of-fact recitation of many murders. But the Kew Gardens slaying baffles him—not because it is a murder, but because the "good people" failed to call the police.

5   "As we have reconstructed the crime," he said, "the assailant had three chances to kill this woman during a 35-minute period. He returned twice to complete the job. If we had been called when he first attacked, the woman might not be dead now."

6   This is what the police say happened beginning at 3:20 A.M. in the staid, middle-class, tree-lined Austin Street area:

7   Twenty-eight-year-old Catherine Genovese, who was called Kitty by almost everyone in the neighborhood, was returning home from her job as manager of a bar in Hollis. She parked her

red Fiat in a lot adjacent to the Kew Gardens Long Island Rail Road Station, facing Mowbray Place. Like many residents of the neighborhood, she had parked there day after day since her arrival from Connecticut a year ago, although the railroad frowns on the practice.

8   She turned off the lights of her car, locked the door and started to walk the 100 feet to the entrance of her apartment at 82-70 Austin Street, which is in a Tudor building, with stores on the first floor and apartments on the second.

9   The entrance to the apartment is in the rear of the building because the front is rented to retail stores. At night the quiet neighborhood is shrouded in the slumbering darkness that marks most residential areas.

10   Miss Genovese noticed a man at the far end of the lot, near a seven-story apartment house at 82-40 Austin Street. She halted. Then, nervously, she headed up Austin Street toward Lefferts Boulevard, where there is a call box to the 102d Police Precinct in nearby Richmond Hill.

'He Stabbed Me!'

11   She got as far as a street light in front of a bookstore before the man grabbed her. She screamed. Lights went on in the 10-story apartment house at 82-67 Austin Street, which faces the bookstore. Windows slid open and voices punctured the early-morning stillness.

12   Miss Genovese screamed: "Oh, my God, he stabbed me! Please help me! Please help me!"

13   From one of the upper windows in the apartment house, a man called down: "Let that girl alone!"

14   The assailant looked up at him, shrugged and walked down Austin Street toward a white sedan parked a short distance away. Miss Genovese struggled to her feet.

15   Lights went out. The killer returned to Miss Genovese, now trying to make her way around the side of the building by the parking lot to get to her apartment. The assailant stabbed her again.

16   "I'm dying!" she shrieked. "I'm dying!"

A City Bus Passed

17   Windows were opened again, and lights went on in many

apartments. The assailant got into his car and drove away. Miss Genovese staggered to her feet. A city bus, Q-10, the Lefferts Boulevard line to Kennedy International Airport, passed. It was 3:35 A.M.

18   The assailant returned. By then, Miss Genovese had crawled to the back of the building, where the freshly painted brown doors to the apartment house held out hope of safety. The killer tried the first door; she wasn't there. At the second door, 82-62 Austin Street, he saw her slumped on the floor at the foot of the stairs. He stabbed her a third time—fatally.

19   It was 3:50 by the time the police received their first call, from a man who was a neighbor of Miss Genovese. In two minutes they were at the scene. The neighbor, a 70-year-old woman and another woman were the only persons on the street. Nobody else came forward.

20   The man explained that he had called the police after much deliberation. He had phoned a friend in Nassau County for advice and then he had crossed the roof of the building to the apartment of the elderly woman to get her to make the call.

21   "I didn't want to get involved," he sheepishly told the police.

Suspect Is Arrested

22   Six days later, the police arrested Winston Moseley, a 29-year-old business-machine operator, and charged him with the homicide. Moseley had no previous record. He is married, has two children and owns a home at 133-19 Sutter Avenue, South Ozone Park, Queens. On Wednesday, a court committed him to Kings County Hospital for psychiatric observation.

23   When questioned by the police, Moseley also said that he had slain Mrs. Annie May Johnson, 24, of 146-12 133d Avenue, Jamaica, on Feb. 29 and Barbara Kralik, 15, of 174-17 140th Avenue, Springfield Gardens, last July. In the Kralik case, the police are holding Alvin L. Mitchell, who is said to have confessed that slaying.

24   The police stressed how simple it would have been to have gotten in touch with them. "A phone call," said one of the detectives, "would have done it." The police may be reached by dialing "O" for operator or SPring 7-3100.

25   The question of whether the witnesses can be held legally re-

sponsible in any way for failure to report the crime was put to the Police Department's legal bureau. There, a spokesman said:

26   "There is no legal responsibility, with few exceptions, for any citizen to report a crime."

Statutes Explained

27   Under the statutes of the city, he said, a witness to a suspicious or violent death must report it to the medical examiner. Under state law, a witness cannot withhold information in a kidnapping.

28   Today witnesses from the neighborhood, which is made up of one-family homes in the $35,000 to $60,000 range with the exception of the two apartment houses near the railroad station, find it difficult to explain why they didn't call the police.

29   Lieut. Bernard Jacobs, who handled the investigation by the detectives, said:

30   "It is one of the better neighborhoods. There are few reports of crimes. You only get the usual complaints about boys playing or garbage cans being turned over."

31   The police said most persons had told them they had been afraid to call, but had given meaningless answers when asked what they had feared.

32   "We can understand the reticence of people to become involved in an area of violence," Lieutenant Jacobs said, "but where they are in their homes, near phones, why should they be afraid to call the police?"

33   He said his men were able to piece together what happened —and capture the suspect—because the residents furnished all the information when detectives rang doorbells during the days following the slaying.

34   "But why didn't someone call us that night?" he asked unbelievingly.

35   Witnesses—some of them unable to believe what they had allowed to happen—told a reporter why.

36   A housewife, knowingly if quite casual, said, "We thought it was a lover's quarrel." A husband and wife both said, "Frankly, we were afraid." They seemed aware of the fact that events might have been different. A distraught woman, wiping her hands in her apron, said, "I didn't want my husband to get involved."

37   One couple, now willing to talk about that night, said they heard the first screams. The husband looked thoughtfully at the bookstore where the killer first grabbed Miss Genovese.

38   "We went to the window to see what was happening," he said, "but the light from our bedroom made it difficult to see the street." The wife, still apprehensive, added: "I put out the light and we were able to see better."

39   Asked why they hadn't called the police, she shrugged and replied: "I don't know."

40   A man peeked out from a slight opening in the doorway to his apartment and rattled off an account of the killer's second attack. Why hadn't he called the police at the time? "I was tired," he said without emotion. "I went back to bed."

41   It was 4:25 A.M. when the ambulance arrived for the body of Miss Genovese. It drove off. "Then," a solemn police detective said, "the people came out."

Questions About "Narration"

1. What purpose, aside from reciting the story of a murder, does Gansberg have in writing this essay? In your answer make specific reference to your text.

2. What do Gansberg's opening paragraphs contribute to the dominant impression he leaves you with?

3. How else and where in his essay does he reinforce that impression?

4. What does dialogue contribute to the point he makes? To the effectiveness of the narration?

5. To better understand Gansberg's purpose and how he succeeds in making this an effective essay, divide the essay into logical units and explain the function of each.

Questions on Diction and Writing Techniques

1. Gansberg might have written sentence 2 of paragraph 7: "She parked her car near a Long Island Rail Road station." Which version of the sentence is preferable? Why?

2. He might have written the second sentence of paragraph 9: "At night the neighborhood is dark." Why did he write the sentence the way he did?

3. What are Gansberg's sources of material?

4. What do the kind of words, sentences, and paragraphs Gansberg chooses contribute to the readability of his essay?

For Discussion, Reading, and Writing

1. Why was Inspector Lussen shocked?

2. What reasons did people give for not helping Miss Genovese?

3. If you had been one of the thirty-eight citizens, what would you have done?

4. Relate in a short essay an event or series of events that illustrates people's inhumanity toward or love for others. Consider organizing your essay the way Gansberg organized his.

A HANGING
George Orwell

George Orwell (1903–1950), British novelist and essayist, reports in this essay a personal experience in Burma where, as a young man, he served with the Indian imperial police.

1   It was in Burma, a sodden morning of the rains. A sickly light, like yellow tinfoil, was slanting over the high walls into the jail yard. We were waiting outside the condemned cells, a row of sheds fronted with double bars, like small animal cages. Each cell measured about ten feet by ten and was quite bare within except for a plank bed and a pot of drinking water. In some of them brown silent men were squatting at the inner bars, with their blankets draped round them. These were the condemned men, due to be hanged within the next week or two.

2   One prisoner had been brought out of his cell. He was a Hindu, a puny wisp of a man, with a shaven head and vague liquid eyes. He had a thick, sprouting moustache, absurdly too big for his body, rather like the moustache of a comic man on the films. Six tall Indian warders were guarding him and getting him ready for the gallows. Two of them stood by with rifles and fixed bayonets, while the others handcuffed him, passed a chain through his handcuffs and fixed it to their belts, and lashed his arms tight to his sides. They crowded very close about him, with their hands always on him in a careful, caressing grip, as though all the while feeling him to make sure he was there. It was like men handling a fish which is still alive and may jump back into the water. But he stood quite unresisting, yielding his arms limply to the ropes, as though he hardly noticed what was happening.

3   Eight o'clock struck and a bugle call, desolately thin in the wet

air, floated from the distant barracks. The superintendent of the jail, who was standing apart from the rest of us, moodily prodding the gravel with his stick, raised his head at the sound. He was an army doctor, with a grey toothbrush moustache and a gruff voice. "For God's sake hurry up, Francis," he said irritably. "The man ought to have been dead by this time. Aren't you ready yet?"

4   Francis, the head jailer, a fat Dravidian in a white drill suit and gold spectacles, waved his black hand. "Yes sir, yes sir," he bubbled. "All iss satisfactorily prepared. The hangman iss waiting. We shall proceed."

5   "Well, quick march, then. The prisoners can't get their breakfast till this job's over."

6   We set out for the gallows. Two warders marched on either side of the prisoner, with their rifles at the slope; two others marched close against him, gripping him by arm and shoulder, as though at once pushing and supporting him. The rest of us, magistrates and the like, followed behind. Suddenly, when we had gone ten yards, the procession stopped short without any order or warning. A dreadful thing had happened—a dog, come goodness knows whence, had appeared in the yard. It came bounding among us with a loud volley of barks, and leapt round us wagging its whole body, wild with glee at finding so many human beings together. It was a large woolly dog, half Airedale, half pariah. For a moment it pranced round us, and then, before anyone could stop it, it had made a dash for the prisoner, and jumping up tried to lick his face. Everyone stood aghast, too taken aback even to grab at the dog.

7   "Who let that bloody brute in here?" said the superintendent angrily. "Catch it, someone!"

8   A warder, detached from the escort, charged clumsily after the dog, but it danced and gambolled just out of his reach, taking everything as part of the game. A young Eurasian jailer picked up a handful of gravel and tried to stone the dog away, but it dodged the stones and came after us again. Its yaps echoed from the jail walls. The prisoner, in the grasp of the two warders, looked on incuriously, as though this was another formality of the hanging. It was several minutes before someone managed to catch the dog. Then we put my handkerchief through its collar and moved off once more, with the dog still straining and whimpering.

9   It was about forty yards to the gallows. I watched the bare

brown back of the prisoner marching in front of me. He walked clumsily with his bound arms, but quite steadily, with that bobbing gait of the Indian who never straightens his knees. At each step his muscles slid neatly into place, the lock of hair on his scalp danced up and down, his feet printed themselves on the wet gravel. And once, in spite of the men who gripped him by each shoulder, he stepped slightly aside to avoid a puddle on the path.

10   It is curious, but till that moment I had never realised what it means to destroy a healthy, conscious man. When I saw the prisoner step aside to avoid the puddle, I saw the mystery, the unspeakable wrongness, of cutting a life short when it is in full tide. This man was not dying, he was alive just as we were alive. All the organs of his body were working—bowels digesting food, skin renewing itself, nails growing, tissues forming—all toiling away in solemn foolery. His nails would still be growing when he stood on the drop, when he was falling through the air with a tenth of a second to live. His eyes saw the yellow gravel and the grey walls, and his brain still remembered, foresaw, reasoned—reasoned even about puddles. He and we were a party of men walking together, seeing, hearing, feeling, understanding the same world; and in two minutes, with a sudden snap, one of us would be gone—one mind less, one world less.

11   The gallows stood in a small yard, separate from the main grounds of the prison, and overgrown with tall prickly weeds. It was a brick erection like three sides of a shed, with planking on top, and above that two beams and a crossbar with the rope dangling. The hangman, a grey-haired convict in the white uniform of the prison, was waiting beside his machine. He greeted us with a servile crouch as we entered. At a word from Francis the two warders, gripping the prisoner more closely than ever, half led, half pushed him to the gallows and helped him clumsily up the ladder. Then the hangman climbed up and fixed the rope round the prisoner's neck.

12   We stood waiting, five yards away. The warders had formed in a rough circle round the gallows. And then, when the noose was fixed, the prisoner began crying out on his god. It was a high, reiterated cry of "Ram! Ram! Ram! Ram!", not urgent and fearful like a prayer or a cry for help, but steady, rhythmical, almost like the tolling of a bell. The dog answered the sound with a whine. The

hangman, still standing on the gallows, produced a small cotton bag like a flour bag and drew it down over the prisoner's face. But the sound, muffled by the cloth, still persisted, over and over again: "Ram! Ram! Ram! Ram! Ram!"

13 The hangman climbed down and stood ready, holding the lever. Minutes seemed to pass. The steady, muffled crying from the prisoner went on and on, "Ram! Ram! Ram!" never faltering for an instant. The superintendent, his head on his chest, was slowly poking the ground with his stick; perhaps he was counting the cries, allowing the prisoner a fixed number—fifty, perhaps, or a hundred. Everyone had changed colour. The Indians had gone grey like bad coffee, and one or two of the bayonets were wavering. We looked at the lashed, hooded man on the drop, and listened to his cries— each cry another second of life; the same thought was in all our minds: oh, kill him quickly, get it over, stop that abominable noise!

14 Suddenly the superintendent made up his mind. Throwing up his head he made a swift motion with his stick. "Chalo!" he shouted almost fiercely.

15 There was a clanking noise, and then dead silence. The prisoner had vanished, and the rope was twisting on itself. I let go of the dog, and it galloped immediately to the back of the gallows; but when it got there it stopped short, barked, and then retreated into a corner of the yard, where it stood among the weeds, looking timorously out at us. We went round the gallows to inspect the prisoner's body. He was dangling with his toes pointed straight downwards, very slowly revolving, as dead as a stone.

16 The superintendent reached out with his stick and poked the bare body; it oscillated slightly. "*He's* all right," said the superintendent. He backed out from under the gallows, and blew out a deep breath. The moody look had gone out of his face quite suddenly. He glanced at his wrist-watch. "Eight minutes past eight. Well, that's all for this morning, thank God."

17 The warders unfixed bayonets and marched away. The dog, sobered and conscious of having misbehaved itself, slipped after them. We walked out of the gallows yard, past the condemned cells with their waiting prisoners, into the big central yard of the prison. The convicts, under the command of warders armed with lathis, were already receiving their breakfast. They squatted in long rows, each man holding a tin pannikin, while two warders with buckets

marched round ladling out rice; it seemed quite a homely, jolly scene, after the hanging. An enormous relief had come upon us now that the job was done. One felt an impulse to sing, to break into a run, to snigger. All at once everyone began chattering gaily.

18   The Eurasian boy walking beside me nodded towards the way we had come, with a knowing smile: "Do you know, sir, our friend (he meant the dead man), when he heard his appeal had been dismissed, he pissed on the floor of his cell. From fright.—Kindly take one of my cigarettes, sir. Do you not admire my new silver case, sir? From the boxwallah, two rupees eight annas. Classy European style."

19   Several people laughed—at what, nobody seemed certain.

20   Francis was walking by the superintendent, talking garrulously: "Well, sir, all hass passed off with the utmost satisfactoriness. It wass all finished—flick! like that. It iss not always so—oah, no! I have known cases where the doctor wass obliged to go beneath the gallows and pull the prisoner's legs to ensure decease. Most disagreeable!"

21   "Wriggling about, eh? That's bad," said the superintendent.

22   "Ach, sir, it iss worse when they become refractory! One man, I recall, clung to the bars of hiss cage when we went to take him out. You will scarcely credit, sir, that it took six warders to dislodge him, three pulling at each leg. We reasoned with him. 'My dear fellow,' we said, 'think of all the pain and trouble you are causing to us!' But no, he would not listen! Ach, he wass very troublesome!"

23   I found that I was laughing quite loudly. Everyone was laughing. Even the superintendent grinned in a tolerant way. "You'd better all come out and have a drink," he said quite genially. "I've got a bottle of whisky in the car. We could do with it."

24   We went through the big double gates of the prison, into the road. "Pulling at his legs!" exclaimed a Burmese magistrate suddenly, and burst into a loud chuckling. We all began laughing again. At that moment Francis's anecdote seemed extraordinarily funny. We all had a drink together, native and European alike, quite amicably. The dead man was a hundred yards away.

Questions About "Narration"

1. In a paragraph of not over one hundred words, narrate in your own words the sequence of events Orwell reports in this essay.

2. Why did he choose to include in the essay the incident of the dog?

3. What other incident seemed to Orwell to be significant? Why?

4. Is paragraph 10 a digression from Orwell's storytelling? Explain.

Questions on Diction and Writing Techniques

1. Mark in your text those words that, though new to you, you understood from their context. Define them in your own words. Compare your definitions with those in your dictionary. Look up in your dictionary any other words that are new to you. Use the words in both groups in sentences.

2. Identify five or more similes in this essay.

3. Orwell might have written "sounded" instead of "floated" (par. 3). What alternative verbs might he have chosen in lieu of "marched," "bounding," and "pranced" (par. 6)? Which—Orwell's or your alternative words—are more vivid? Explain.

4. In lieu of the last sentence of paragraph 8, Orwell might have written "Then we put my handkerchief through its collar and moved off once more, with the dog still hassling." Which version of the sentence do you prefer? Why?

5. Orwell might have written sentence 4 of paragraph 10 "All the organs of his body were working, all toiling away in solemn foolery." Which version of the sentence conveys more meaning? Explain.

6. Orwell might have written the next-to-last sentence in paragraph 24 "We all had a drink together, quite amicably, native and European alike." How, in the rewritten sentence, is emphasis changed?

7. What does dialogue contribute to Orwell's portrayal of the characters in this essay? To the effectiveness of his storytelling?

8. What is the purpose and the effect of the last sentence in Orwell's essay?

9. Find, in addition to the details listed on pages 117–118, ten or more specific details in this essay that make it evident that Orwell was a careful observer.

For Discussion, Reading, and Writing

1. Making specific reference to the text, explain why the superintendent was impatient.

2. Nowhere in his essay does Orwell tell you what the offense of the prisoner was. Is this omission significant? Why or why not?

3. What went through Orwell's mind when he realized what it means to kill a fellow human being?

4. For the punishment of what crime(s) would you recommend or condone capital punishment?

5. Attend a trial in a criminal court in your area, or any other public event that interests you. In preparation for writing a short essay on the subject, make a list of details—as you observe them and again just before writing your first draft—that will help you to relate the event effectively. In a second draft,

　　replace inapt and general words with words that are appropriate (when in doubt consult your dictionary) and concrete and thus will more clearly tell your story;

　　add as much imagery as may be appropriate to the purpose of your story;

　　revise your sentences, where necessary, to convey more meaning or to shift emphasis to their main ideas; and

　　add dialogue wherever appropriate.

Description

"THE artistic aim when expressing itself in written words must make its appeal through the senses. . . . My task which I am trying to achieve is, by the power of the written word to make you hear, to make you feel—it is, before all, to make you *see*." Although when Joseph Conrad wrote this he had in mind his work as a writer of fiction, what he says applies to the writing of description in nonfiction prose.

The purpose of description is to give an account of observed details in *space*. The aim is to make the reader see. The appeal is to the mind's eye. Photographers reproduce their subjects on photographic paper; painters may do likewise on canvas. Writers, in contrast, must create their subjects in their readers' minds. Their medium is words. Whether the thing to be depicted is as small as a lemon or as extensive as a landscape, through language writers transform the objects of their attention into mental images.

In this context, "see" means to perceive with all our senses— hearing, sight, smell, taste, and touch. Thus it follows that writers of description, in transposing their perceptions into words, will mention details that appeal to one or more of the five senses. Such language is called *sensory diction*. Writers will report that a peach, for example, is a combination of *yellows, pinks,* and *reds*; that its skin feels *velvety*; that it tastes *sweet*. They will write about a campfire that the *moist* logs burn with a *hiss* and a *crackle*, giving off a *piny* odor and casting on the *cold, rough* ground *wavering, black* shadows. Words that refer to sensory experiences evoke sensory images; by reporting as many sensory details as practicable, writers can more readily make their readers see what they saw.

Description is of two kinds: objective or factual and subjective or personal. *Objective description* attempts to represent things as they are, as in the report of a scientist. Writers striving for objectivity exclude their own feelings about their subject; they stay detached, personally uninvolved. *Subjective description* is quite different. The subjective writer reports his or her view of the subject and includes personal feelings and opinions.

Here is an example of objective description:

> Shark, member of a group of almost exclusively marine and predaceous fishes. Sharks are heavy fishes, possessing neither lungs nor swim bladders. Their skeletons are made of cartilage rather than bone, and this, along with large deposits of fat, partially solves their weight problem; nevertheless, most sharks must keep moving in order to breathe and to stay afloat. They are good swimmers; the wide spread of the pectoral fins and the upward curve of the tail fin provide lift, and the sweeping movements of the tail provide drive. Their tough hides are studded with minute, toothlike structures called denticles. Sharks have pointed snouts; their crescent-shaped mouths are set on the underside of the body and contain several rows of sharp, triangular teeth. . . .

This description, from *The New Columbia Encyclopedia*, is scientific, factual, objective. Nowhere in it do the writer's feelings or opinions intrude. Contrast it with this description:

> His entire form is fluid, weaving from side to side; his head moves slightly from left to right, right to left, timed to the rhythm of his motion through the water. Only the eye is fixed, focused on me, circling within the orbit of the head, in order not to lose sight for a fraction of a second of his prey or, perhaps, of his enemy. . . .

There is no threat, no movement of aggression. Only a sort of nonchalant suspicion is apparent in the movements and attitudes of the shark, and yet he generates fear. Amazed and startled, filled with apprehension, circling with movements as slow and silent as possible, I try to keep him constantly in front of me.

There is something of the miraculous in the suddenness of his appearance as well as in his infinite grace; the surface of the water is far above and its absence contributes to the magical quality of the moment. He turns once more, and the sphere he encompasses expands or contracts, in accordance with his own primitive impulses or the subtle changes of the current. His silent circling is a ballet governed by untraceable mechanisms. The blue tranquillity of his form surrounds me with the sensation of a web of murderous and yet beautiful force. I have the feeling that I have accompanied his circular voyage since the beginning of time. His configuration is perfect. Suddenly, the idea that he deserves killing comes to me like a shock and instantly shatters the spell. Murder is the real function of this ideal form, of this icy-blue camouflage, and of that enormous, powerful tail. . . .

The great blue shark continues his approach toward me in the unchanging manner which has been that of his race throughout its existence. He is really a superb animal, almost seven feet in length, and I know, since I have often seen them before, that his jaws are lined with seven rows of teeth, as finely honed as the sharpest razor [Jacques-Yves Cousteau, *The Shark*].

Notice that Cousteau refers to the shark not as "it," but, more personally, as "he." At the outset the writer makes us aware of his presence ("the eye is fixed, focused on *me*"), of his feelings about his subject ("*he generates fear*"), and of his own behavior in response to it ("Amazed and startled, filled with apprehension, *circling with movements as slow and silent as possible, I try to keep him constantly in front of me*").

Cousteau's choice of adjectives also reveals a subjective reaction —an emphasis on the observer and a personal appraisal of his subject: "There is something of the *miraculous* in the suddenness of his appearance"; "*magical* quality of the moment"; "*superb* animal." Moreover, Cousteau doesn't hesitate to state an opinion, with a play on words: "Murder is the *real* function of this *ideal* form. . . ."

Finally, the writer uses figures of speech to call forth visual images: "His silent circling is a *ballet*"; "The blue tranquillity of his form surrounds me with the sensation of *a web* of murderous and yet beautiful force"; "his jaws are lined with seven rows of teeth, *as finely honed as the sharpest razor."*

Unlike the writing in *The New Columbia Encyclopedia*, which focuses exclusively on the shark, Cousteau's description includes himself. It not only reports the writer's responses to the shark; it tries to affect the reader's as well.

Even photography is not purely objective: What a camera records on film is determined by the direction the photographer chooses to aim it, by the operator's choice of lens, composition, aperture stop, speed, film, and by the photographer's purpose and bias. Your observations of the world around you are affected by your background, training, point of view, and sharpness of senses. Other people, with different attributes and experiences, observe the world differently. None of the views, yours or theirs, is purely objective. Each description will reflect dissimilar biases and varying responses.

Your purpose in writing description will be to recreate in the mind of your reader a place, person, or thing that you have seen. Thus the process of description begins with observation.

Here are two suggestions for writing description:

1. *Select details carefully.* Choose details that will best delineate the thing described. These details must be arranged methodically. If you were to describe the place where you are now, you would choose details not at random, but in some logical order, such as from left to right, from one consistent physical point of view. If you were to describe a thing in motion, you could impose order on your subject by describing the sequence of its movements.

2. *Be sure your diction is apt.* To convey clearly what you saw, you must use diction that is specific (words that refer to individual things) rather than general language (words that include all of a group or a class). Specific words convey to readers a precise mental picture (see the discussion of specific and general words on pages 76–78).

The ultimate effect of successful description is to make on the reader a harmonious, vivid impression, as Mark Twain does in this descriptive passage from *Roughing It*:

As the sun was going down, we saw the first specimen of an animal known familiarly over two thousand miles of mountain and desert—from Kansas clear to the Pacific Ocean—as the "jackass rabbit." He is well named. He is just like any other rabbit, except that he is from one-third to twice as large, has longer legs in proportion to his size, and has the most preposterous ears that ever were mounted on any creature *but* a jackass. When he is sitting quiet, thinking about his sins, or is absent minded or unapprehen sive of danger, his majestic ears project above him conspicuously; but the breaking of a twig will scare him nearly to death, and then he tilts his ears back gently and starts for home. All you can see, then, for the next minute, is his long gray form stretched out straight and "streaking it" through the low sage-brush, head erect, eyes right, and ears just canted a little to the rear, but showing you where the animal is, all the time, the same as if he carried a jib. Now and then he makes a marvelous spring with his long legs, high over the stunted sage-brush, and scores a leap that would make a horse envious. Presently, he comes down to a long, graceful "lope," and shortly he mysteriously disappears. He has crouched behind a sage-brush, and will sit there and listen and tremble until you get within six feet of him, when he will get under way again. But one must shoot at this creature once, if he wishes to see him throw his heart into his heels, and do the best he knows how. He is frightened clear through, now, and he lays his long ears down on his back, straightens himself out like a yardstick every spring he makes, and scatters miles behind him with an easy indifference that is enchanting.

THE OPIUM DEN
W. Somerset Maugham

W. Somerset Maugham (1874–1965) was an English playwright,
novelist, short-story writer, and essayist. His best-known works
are the novels **Of Human Bondage** (1915) and
The Moon and Sixpence (1919).

On the stage it makes a very effective set. It is dimly lit. The
room is low and squalid. In one corner a lamp burns mysteriously
before a hideous image and incense fills the theatre with its exotic
scent. A pig-tailed Chinaman wanders to and fro, aloof and saturnine, while on wretched pallets lie stupefied the victims of the drug.
Now and then one of them breaks into frantic raving. There is a
highly dramatic scene where some poor creature, unable to pay for
the satisfaction of his craving, with prayers and curses begs the vil-
lainous proprietor for a pipe to still his anguish. I have read also in
novels descriptions which made my blood run cold. And when I
was taken to an opium den by a smooth-spoken Eurasian the narrow, winding stairway up which he led me prepared me sufficiently
to receive the thrill I expected. I was introduced into a neat enough
room, brightly lit, divided into cubicles the raised floor of which,
covered with clean matting, formed a convenient couch. In one an
elderly gentleman, with a grey head and very beautiful hands, was
quietly reading a newspaper, with his long pipe by his side. In another two coolies were lying, with a pipe between them, which
they alternately prepared and smoked. They were young men, of a
hearty appearance, and they smiled at me in a friendly way. One of
them offered me a smoke. In a third four men squatted over a
chess-board, and a little farther on a man was dandling a baby (the
inscrutable Oriental has a passion for children) while the baby's

From *The Travel Books of W. Somerset Maugham* (London: William Heinemann,
1955), p. 37. Reprinted by permission of the Estate of Somerset Maugham.

mother, whom I took to be the landlord's wife, a plump, pleasant-faced woman, watched him with a broad smile on her lips. It was a cheerful spot, comfortable, home-like, and cosy. It reminded me somewhat of the little intimate beer-houses of Berlin where the tired working man could go in the evening and spend a peaceful hour. Fiction is stranger than fact.

Questions About "Description"

1. In his description of the scene on the stage, Maugham first gives a general impression: "The room is low and squalid." What does he then report?

2. Does the order of his description of the real opium den parallel that of the stage set?

3. List the sensory details Maugham singles out to make the scene on the stage vivid to you.

4. What specific details about the opium den does he report to warrant the conclusion: "It was a cheerful spot, comfortable, home-like, and cosy"?

5. Is the description in the essay objective, subjective, or both? Explain, making specific reference to the text.

Questions on Diction and Writing Techniques

1. Define the following words and write sentences using each of them appropriately: saturnine, inscrutable.

2. In lieu of "dandling," what other words might Maugham have used? Is "dandling" a precise choice of word? Explain.

3. To describe the landlord's wife, Maugham might have chosen, instead of "plump," "portly," "fleshy," "fat," or "stout." What does each of these words connote?

4. Explain the purpose and the effect of the next-to-last sentence.

5. What is the writer's purpose in concluding with "Fiction is stranger than fact"?

6. Comment on Maugham's use of description to help fulfill that purpose.

For Discussion, Reading, and Writing

1. What does Maugham imply by "the inscrutable Oriental"?

2. Do you think that Westerners look inscrutable to Orientals?

3. Write a one-paragraph detailed description of any group of people assembled anywhere in your college.

4. Taking a pencil and notebook with you, visit a place such as an ice-cream parlor, a doughnut shop, a chess club, a pool hall, a diner, or a saloon and record what you see. Then, using specific details, write a one-paragraph descriptive essay based on your observations of the place and the people in it.

=======================================

A WALK ON THE TOWPATH
Berton Roueché

Berton Roueché, formerly a reporter on various newspapers, contributes often to **The New Yorker** magazine. He is especially well known for his narratives of medical detection.

———————

₁ It had rained in the night, and the lane was awash with thin red mud, and puddles stood in the ruts and potholes. It was steep, wet, slippery walking. And cold. Under the trees the morning air had a bite. It felt more like fall than spring. But from what I could see of the sky overhead, the clouds were beginning to break and

lift, and there was a hint of a watery sun. I slid down the lane to
the foot of the ridge. A coterie of chickadees burst up from a thicket
and scattered like a handful of gravel. The lane cut sharply to the
left and emerged in a little meadow. At the edge of the meadow
stretched the canal. Some fifty feet wide, the color of mud, and
flanked by head-high banks, it looked like a sunken road. The towpath followed the farther bank, and beyond it, through a heavy
screen of trees, I caught a distant glimpse and murmur of the river.
The Canal lay as still as a pond. I found a pebble and tossed it in. It
sank with a throaty plunk. I guessed the water to be five or six feet
deep. About a hundred yards downstream, the canal funneled into
a kind of open culvert, which was bridged by a railed catwalk. Facing it, on the towpath side, sat a small white-washed stone house
with two stone chimneys and a pitched roof of corrugated iron.
That would have been the lock tender's house. The culvert was the
lock.

₂   I walked out on the bridge and looked down at the lock. The
canal flowed into the lock through a sprung wooden gate just under
the bridge. It ran between two narrowly confining walls for about a
hundred feet. Then, with a sudden boil and bubble, it broke against
another gate, spilled through, and resumed its sluggish course. The
walls of the lock were faced with big blocks of rust-red sandstone.
Some of the stones were so huge they could have been hoisted into
place only with a block and tackle. It was beautiful stone, and it
had been beautifully finished and fitted. Time had merely softened
it. Here and there along the courses I could even make out the remains of a mason's mark. One device was quite distinct—a double-
headed arrow. Another appeared to be two overlapping equilateral
triangles. I went on across the bridge to the house. The windows
were shuttered and boarded up, and the door was locked. No matter. It was enough just to stand and look at it. It was a lovely house,
as beautifully made as the lock, and as firmly designed for function.
It gave me a pang to think that there had once been a time when even
a lock tender could have so handsome a house. A phoebe called
from a sweet-gum tree in the dooryard. Far away, somewhere
down by the river, a mourning dove gave an answering sigh. I
looked at my watch. It was ten minutes after ten. I started up the
towpath.

₃   The sun was still no more than a promise, but the air had lost

its chill. It was going to be a spring day after all. The signs of it
abounded. Most of the trees that lined the path—sycamore, dog-
wood, sweet gum, hickory, elm—were coming into bud. Only the
oaks still had the wrought-iron look of winter. Some creeping vine
—Virginia creeper or honeysuckle—was even in leaf. And everywhere there were birds in sight or sound. Robins hopped and stood
and listened at intervals along the way. A woodpecker drummed. A
blue jay raced from tree to tree, screaming a wild alarm. There was
a flash of cardinal red across the canal. I turned—but too late. It was
gone. And so were the lock and the house. They had vanished
around a bend. There was nothing behind me but water and
woods. It gave me a curious sensation. I felt for the first time completely alone, but I didn't feel lonely. It was an exhilarating loneliness. It was solitude. I took a deep breath and lighted a cigarette. I
felt at peace with the world.

4   But peace was mine alone. Every step I took spread panic.
The sentinel jay was joined by a dozen agitated crows. A terrified
rabbit sprang out from behind a fallen tree and ran for its life up the
path. I had no choice but to follow it. It erupted again almost under
my feet. This time, more sensibly, it took to the woods. I watched
it bounding through the brush, changing its course with every
bound, and finished my cigarette. I pitched the butt into the canal.
There was a tiny splash near the water's edge. I stepped to the bank
and looked down and around. Nothing moved but the drifting cigarette. A long minute passed. Then, a foot or two off the opposite
shore, the water just perceptibly stirred. The top of a little black
head appeared, and then two bright eyes—a muskrat. We exchanged an inscrutable glance. I moved up a step for a better look.
The muskrat disappeared without a ripple.

Questions About "Description"

1. What is Roueché's purpose in this piece?

2. How do the modifying adjectives in "It was steep, wet, slippery
    walking" (par. 1) help the writer to achieve his purpose?

3. What does the visual image evoked by the simile (see pages 78–79) in paragraph 1 contribute to this description?

4. Instead of writing the third-from-last sentence in paragraph 1 as he did, Roueché might have written, "Facing it, on the towpath side, sat a house with chimneys and a roof." Which sentence conveys more clearly to you what he saw? Why?

5. Point out examples of Roueché's use of specific words (see pages 76–78) in his description of the "sandstone" (par. 2).

6. What details does the writer choose to show that "It was going to be a spring day after all" (par. 3)?

7. "And everywhere there were birds in sight or sound" (par. 3). Find examples of the writer's use of sensory diction in his description of the birds.

Questions on Diction and Writing Techniques

1. Define "coterie" (par. 1) and use it aptly in a sentence.

2. What is the effect of the sentence fragments in paragraphs 1 and 2?

3. What purpose is served by "but" in paragraph 1? Find elsewhere in the essay an instance where Roueché uses "but" with a similar purpose.

4. What verbs might Roueché have chosen instead of "funneled" (par. 1)? Which do you prefer? Why? Find in paragraph 3 examples of his use of strong, active verbs.

5. "But peace was mine alone. Every step I took spread panic" (par. 4). How does the writer support these statements?

For Discussion, Reading, and Writing

1. Fill the blanks in this passage from memory to make it intelligible:

   But _____ was mine alone. Every step I took spread _____.

The sentinel jay was joined by a dozen _____ crows. A
_____ rabbit sprang out from behind a fallen tree and ran for
_____ up the path.

Compare your words with those in paragraph 4.

2. Write a paragraph beginning with, "It was going to be a sum-
    mer (or winter or fall) day after all."

3. With a pencil and notebook in hand, take a walk anywhere,
    jotting down details you observe. Choosing the details that best
    serve your purpose, write a paragraph or two describing what
    you saw.

4. Take a short trip anywhere—to a park, a beach, a nearby
    town, a large city, a national landmark, a museum. Then, using
    specific and sensory diction, write a descriptive essay about the
    place or any portion of it, trying to convey to your readers
    what you observed.

EMPEROR NORTON I
Joan Parker

Joan Parker is a freelance writer who has a special interest in
memorabilia of the American West. Her articles have appeared
in various journals.

1   During the Gold Rush of 1849 and the years that followed,
San Francisco attracted more than any city's fair share of eccentrics.
But among all the deluded and affected that spilled through the

Golden Gate in those early years, one man rose to become perhaps the most successful eccentric in American history: Norton I, Emperor of the United States and Protector of Mexico.

2 Joshua Abraham Norton, an English Jew, arrived in San Francisco on the steamer *Franzika* in 1849 from Algoa Bay, Cape of Good Hope, with $40,000. With that stake, he proceeded to make a fortune. He was an astute agent for several mercantile houses, a broker, and an energetic land speculator. In a few years Norton had become a respected citizen worth a quarter of a million dollars. But in 1853 he overextended himself in one grand effort to corner every grain of rice already in the city or on its way there. When unexpected shiploads sailed into port, prices crashed, and with them toppled the fortunes of Norton and several friends who had trusted his advice. During the long, excruciating lawsuit resulting from default on his contract, Norton's fine mind began to warp. Ruined, he dropped from the city's life — only to emerge a few years later in the guise of an emperor.

3 In September of 1859 a dignified, stocky man appeared in the offices of the San Francisco *Evening Bulletin* and solemnly submitted a proclamation that began: "At the peremptory request and desire of a large majority of the citizens of these United States, I, Joshua Norton . . . declare and proclaim myself Emperor of these United States. . . ." Amused by this unusual feature story, the editor ran it without comment, but few people in the busy boom town paid much attention — even when the subsequent proclamations abolished Congress and the state supreme court for fraud and corruption. However, when Norton began appearing in the streets in a gaudy uniform given him by the commander of the Presidio, San Francisco's army garrison, the citizenry began to take notice. There was, of course, some jeering, and rival newspapers ridiculed the Emperor. He riposted in the *Bulletin*, which he now used as his official publication, against "certain scurrilous and untrue articles attacking our right and propriety . . . in one or two insignificant papers . . . and the portions of a community whose taste can be pampered by low and improper articles," and decreed that the "good sense and honesty of purpose of the nations . . . not be insulted by such trash."

4 Resplendent in his large gold epaulets, garrison cap, and saber, Norton applied himself to the business of being an emperor as dili-

gently as he had to being an entrepreneur. He joined the prome-
nade along Montgomery and Kearney streets to show himself to his
people, and accepted the ironic bows of his subjects with the seren-
ity befitting his new profession. He faithfully attended public gath-
erings of all kinds and continued to issue proclamations for the
progress and justice of his empire.

5   His unfeigned concern for his people, his inherent dignity,
and his tact (he never stayed long enough during his many calls to
be considered a bore) soon won over the city completely. For
twenty years the citizens of San Francisco cheerfully supported him
in his delusion. His imperial bonds—usually issued in the amount
of fifty cents—were honored, and the modest taxes he levied were
paid. He ate and drank free at the best restaurants and saloons and
was invited to speak at political rallies. When the state legislature
met, a large upholstered chair was always reserved for him. The city
directory listed him as "Norton, Joshua, Emperor." And when the
genuine Emperor Dom Pedro II of Brazil visited the city in 1876,
San Francisco proudly presented its own to him with fitting pomp
and circumstance.

6   When Norton's uniform wore out, a public subscription
bought him a new one. On a similar occasion the board of supervi-
sors voted city funds. Tailors who made and contributed uniforms
proudly announced themselves on window cards "by appointment
to His Majesty." His loyal subjects gave him a variety of hats, a
magnificent walking stick, and a big tricolored Chinese umbrella to
keep his imperial self dry on rainy days. When an inevitable do-
gooder attempted to have him committed, the judge dismissed the
inquiry into the Emperor's sanity with the curt remark that Norton
was "just about the best going in the king line."

7   Norton I, Emperor of the United States (he had earlier shed
his original title of Protector of Mexico, declaring it impossible to
protect such an unsettled nation), died in January, 1880. As he lay
in the morgue, a crowd began to gather. "The general interest felt
in the deceased was soon manifest," reported the San Francisco
Chronicle in an article headed "LE ROI EST MORT." By noon the crush
was so large that the police were called. All classes were represented, from "capitalist to pauper, clergyman, pickpocket, well-
dressed ladies and social outcasts, the aged and children." "He is
dead," mourned the *Morning Call,* "and no citizen of San Francisco

could have been taken away who would be more generally missed."
A kind of innocence had been taken away, and would indeed be
missed.

8   A reported thirty thousand San Franciscans attended his first
funeral. But more than fifty years later, there was another. In 1934,
when the still growing city engulfed the Masonic Cemetery, the
Emperor's remains were dug up and reburied at Woodlawn. Norton remained so alive in the imagination of his city even then that
Mayor Angelo J. Rossi placed a wreath on the grave, the municipal
band played, and the Third Batallion, 159th Infantry, fired three
volleys. A fine granite monument was set in place; it read: NORTON I,
EMPEROR OF THE UNITED STATES, PROTECTOR OF MEXICO, JOSHUA A.
NORTON 1819–1880. And as one historian has noted, there were no
quotation marks around the inscription.

Questions About "Description"

1. Mark in your text the specific details that Parker reports to
   make clear to you the eccentricity of Norton. Indicate with an
   A or a B which of these details relate to Norton's appearance,
   which to his behavior.

2. Does Parker explain sufficiently and clearly how Norton became an eccentric and how the citizens of San Francisco supported him in his delusion? Explain, making specific reference
   to your text.

Questions on Diction and Writing Techniques

1. Underline in your text those words that are new to you, but
   whose meaning you inferred from their context. Define them
   in your own words. Compare your definitions with those in
   your dictionary. Look up in your dictionary any other words
   that are new to you. Use the words in both groups in sentences.

2. Did paragraph 1 engage your attention and thereby make you
   want to read on? Why or why not?

3. Parker might have written "came" or "sailed" instead of "spilled" (par. 1). Why did she choose the verb she did?

4. Why did Parker write "perhaps" (par. 1)?

5. Sentence 1 of paragraph 5 is an example of the joining of grammatical elements of identical construction in pairs or series — coordination. To better understand what this means, consider this diagram of the sentence (omitting, to simplify, the portion of the sentence in parentheses):

    His unfeigned concern for his people,
    his inherent dignity, and
    his tact

                                    soon won over the
                                    city completely.

    The coordinate elements are the nouns *concern*, *dignity*, and *tact*. There is, in paragraph 6, another sentence with coordinate elements. Find the sentence and diagram it.

For Discussion, Reading, and Writing

1. How old was Norton when he arrived in San Francisco?

2. Fill the blanks in this passage from memory to make it intelligible:

    During the _____ _____ of 1849 and the _____ that followed, San Francisco attracted more than any city's fair share

    of _____. But among all the deluded and affected that

    _____ through the Golden Gate in those early years, one

    _____ rose to become perhaps the most successful _____ in

    American history: Norton I, _____ of the United States and

    Protector of _____.

3. In a short essay, describe an eccentric or any other person you know, using narration to round out your portrayal.

THE SANTA ANA
Joan Didion

Joan Didion is a novelist and the author of two collections of essays, **Slouching Towards Bethlehem** (1968) and **The White Album** (1979).

1   There is something uneasy in the Los Angeles air this afternoon, some unnatural stillness, some tension. What it means is that tonight a Santa Ana will begin to blow, a hot wind from the northeast whining down through the Cajon and San Gorgonio Passes, blowing up sandstorms out along Route 66, drying the hills and the nerves to the flash point. For a few days now we will see smoke back in the canyons, and hear sirens in the night. I have neither heard nor read that a Santa Ana is due, but I know it, and almost everyone I have seen today knows it too. We know it because we feel it. The baby frets. The maid sulks. I rekindle a waning argument with the telephone company, then cut my losses and lie down, given over to whatever it is in the air. To live with the Santa Ana is to accept, consciously or unconsciously, a deeply mechanistic view of human behavior.

2   I recall being told, when I first moved to Los Angeles and was living on an isolated beach, that the Indians would throw themselves into the sea when the bad wind blew. I could see why. The Pacific turned ominously glossy during a Santa Ana period, and one woke in the night troubled not only by the peacocks screaming in the olive trees but by the eerie absence of surf. The heat was surreal. The sky had a yellow cast, the kind of light sometimes called "earthquake weather." My only neighbor would not come out of her house for days, and there were no lights at night, and her husband roamed the place with a machete. One day he would tell me that he had heard a trespasser, the next a rattlesnake.

3   "On nights like that," Raymond Chandler once wrote about
the Santa Ana, "every booze party ends in a fight. Meek little wives
feel the edge of the carving knife and study their husbands' necks.
Anything can happen." That was the kind of wind it was. I did not
know then that there was any basis for the effect it had on all of us,
but it turns out to be another of those cases in which science bears
out folk wisdom. The Santa Ana, which is named for one of the
canyons it rushes through, is a *foehn* wind, like the *foehn* of Austria
and Switzerland and the *hamsin* of Israel. There are a number of
persistent malevolent winds, perhaps the best known of which are
the mistral of France and the Mediterranean sirocco, but a *foehn*
wind has distinct characteristics: it occurs on the leeward slope of a
mountain range and, although the air begins as a cold mass, it is
warmed as it comes down the mountain and appears finally as a hot
dry wind. Whenever and wherever a *foehn* blows, doctors hear
about headaches and nausea and allergies, about "nervousness,"
about "depression." In Los Angeles some teachers do not attempt to
conduct formal classes during a Santa Ana, because the children become unmanageable. In Switzerland the suicide rate goes up during
the *foehn*, and in the courts of some Swiss cantons the wind is considered a mitigating circumstance for crime. Surgeons are said to
watch the wind, because blood does not clot normally during a *foehn*.
A few years ago an Israeli physicist discovered that not only during
such winds, but for the ten or twelve hours which precede them,
the air carries an unusually high ratio of positive to negative ions.
No one seems to know exactly why that should be; some talk about
friction and others suggest solar disturbances. In any case the positive ions are there, and what an excess of positive ions does, in the
simplest terms, is make people unhappy. One cannot get much
more mechanistic than that.

4   Easterns commonly complain that there is no "weather" at all in
Southern California, that the days and the seasons slip by relent-
lessly, numbingly bland. That is quite misleading. In fact the climate
is characterized by infrequent but violent extremes: two periods of
torrential subtropical rains which continue for weeks and wash out
the hills and send subdivisions sliding toward the sea; about twenty
scattered days a year of the Santa Ana, which, with its incendiary
dryness, invariably means fire. At the first prediction of a Santa Ana,
the Forest Service flies men and equipment from northern California

into the southern forests, and the Los Angeles Fire Department cancels its ordinary nonfirefighting routines. The Santa Ana caused Malibu to burn the way it did in 1956, and Bel Air in 1961, and Santa Barbara in 1964. In the winter of 1966–67 eleven men were killed fighting a Santa Ana fire that spread through the San Gabriel Mountains.

₅   Just to watch the front-page news out of Los Angeles during a Santa Ana is to get very close to what it is about the place. The longest single Santa Ana period in recent years was in 1957, and it lasted not the usual three or four days but fourteen days, from November 21 until December 4. On the first day 25,000 acres of the San Gabriel Mountains were burning, with gusts reaching 100 miles an hour. In town, the wind reached Force 12, or hurricane force, on the Beaufort Scale; oil derricks were toppled and people ordered off the downtown streets to avoid injury from flying objects. On November 22 the fire in the San Gabriels was out of control. On November 24 six people were killed in automobile accidents, and by the end of the week the Los Angeles *Times* was keeping a box score of traffic deaths. On November 26 a prominent Pasadena attorney, depressed about money, shot and killed his wife, their two sons, and himself. On November 27 a South Gate divorcee, twenty-two, was murdered and thrown from a moving car. On November 30 the San Gabriel fire was still out of control, and the wind in town was blowing eighty miles an hour. On the first day of December four people died violently, and on the third the wind began to break.

₆   It is hard for people who have not lived in Los Angeles to realize how radically the Santa Ana figures in the local imagination. The city burning is Los Angeles's deepest image of itself: Nathanael West perceived that, in *The Day of the Locust*; and at the time of the 1965 Watts riots what struck the imagination most indelibly were the fires. For days one could drive the Harbor Freeway and see the city on fire, just as we had always known it would be in the end. Los Angeles weather is the weather of catastrophe, of apocalypse, and, just as the reliably long and bitter winters of New England determine the way life is lived there, so the violence and the unpredictability of the Santa Ana affect the entire quality of life in Los Angeles, accentuate its impermanence, its unreliability. The wind shows us how close to the edge we are.

Questions About "Description"

1. List the sensory details that Didion chooses in paragraph 1 to describe the Santa Ana and its physical effects. What other kind of effect does it have? What examples of this effect does Didion give in paragraph 1?

2. What does the information in paragraph 2 add to Didion's description of the Santa Ana?

3. How, in paragraph 3, does Didion tell you what kind of wind the Santa Ana is?

4. What characteristic of the Santa Ana is stressed in paragraph 4?

5. Explain the purpose and effect of the information in paragraph 5.

Questions on Diction and Writing Techniques

1. Mark in your text those words that are new to you, but whose meaning you inferred from their context. Define them in your own words. Compare your definitions with those in your dictionary. Look up in your dictionary any other words that are new to you. Use the words in both groups in sentences.

2. What is Didion's purpose in making the comparison with New England weather?

For Discussion, Reading, and Writing

1. How does Didion know that a Santa Ana will begin to blow?

2. How does Didion come to believe what she was told about the Indians?

3. How long is the usual Santa Ana period? What was the longest single Santa Ana period in recent years?

4. Recall and jot down bits of information about a phenomenon of nature that you have experienced. Using both objective and subjective description, write a short essay about your experience and its significance.

Exposition

"EXPOSITION" means explanation. It is the type of composition you probably will write most often in college—in reports, term papers, research papers, critical essays, exams.

The main objective of narration is to tell a story, and the main objective of description is to create vivid images. The main objective of exposition is to expose—to set forth and explain—information and ideas. This is not to say that expository writing may not utilize the techniques of narration, description, and argumentation to achieve its goal. We will examine exposition separately, as we do the others, for convenience merely.

This introduction to exposition is itself exposition—a setting forth of information college students will need to know to write expository essays. How I present this information depends on my audience—you, your classmates, and other students like you. Were my readers different—high school freshmen, graduate students, teachers of composition—my choice of material, my arrangement of it, and the extent of my explanation would be different. My purpose with each group would be the same: to present sufficient information to allow my readers to understand how to write exposition. But my writing would vary, in that I might—depending on the group—set forth different material, more or less information, simpler or more complex, shorter or more extensive explanations. There is a connection between purpose and audience. By "purpose" I mean the result a writer intends to achieve with a given group of readers. The purpose in writing exposition is to communicate to readers what they need to know to understand a subject. Keeping them in mind helps the writer to choose appropriate material and to arrange it effectively.

Since knowing how a writer explains a subject to readers may be useful to you when you write, let's consider an expository paragraph:

Watch your grip on the handle closely when you are learning to saw. It should be held firm but not tight. The saw should run freely. A tight grip prevents the free running of the saw and tends to swerve the blade away from the line. The thumb should be against the left side of the handle. Keep the index finger extended along the right side of the handle to help guide the blade. If the blade starts to cut into the marked line or to move too far away from it, twist the handle slightly in order to draw it back to the correct position [Alfred P. Morgan, *Tools and How to Use Them*].

This paragraph is a response to the question: How do you use a handsaw?

Any expository paragraph or essay gives answers to questions: What? Where? When? Who? How? Why? Most of the essays in this text (though in different sections to illustrate a variety of subjects) are expository, as some of their titles indicate:

"What I Have Lived For," in which Bertrand Russell explains *what* his personal philosophy is

"Who Killed Benny Paret?" in which Norman Cousins explains *who* should be blamed for deaths in professional boxing

"An Ugly New Footprint in the Sand," in which A. B. C. Whipple explains *how* humans are polluting even remote islands

"Jailbreak Marriage," in which Gail Sheehy explains *why* some young women marry

You will find it helpful to consider an expository essay as the answer to a question.

Let's assume that you want to write an essay about women in America. Instead of this general subject you would turn your attention to restricted subjects (see pages 2–9) such as day-care centers for the children of working mothers, battered women, or the Equal Rights Amendment. These and related ideas for an essay could be put in the form of questions:

> *How* do day-care centers help working mothers to be independent?
>
> *What* legal remedies are there for battered women?
>
> *Why* should the Equal Rights Amendment be adopted?
>
> *Why* should male-oriented words be revised?
>
> *Who* was Margaret Fuller?
>
> *Why* were the women in America granted suffrage?
>
> *What* is male chauvinism?
>
> *Why* are there relatively few women medical doctors in the United States?

Asking What? Where? When? Who? How? or Why? has several advantages. The question you ask will emphasize the need for an explanation that will satisfy your readers. If the question is specific, it will restrict your broad subject and narrow the search for information required to convince your readers of the validity of your thesis.

Here are a few additional things to keep in mind when you write expository prose:

1. *Choose your sources of material carefully.* What sources you use will depend on your subject. In an essay with a restricted subject you might find all the information you need in your personal experience, in your observations of others,

or in notes in your diary. Or you might seek it in reading or interviews. Whatever your sources of material (see Part Three), you will want to know as much about your topic as its nature demands and time will permit.

2. *Know your purpose.* Keep your readers in mind when assembling your material so that you will be able to communicate to them what they need to know to understand your explanation of your restricted subject. The ultimate question about the success of an expository essay is: "Did the writer, having engaged the readers' attention, make them understand?"

3. *Organize your material to achieve your purpose.* Beginning writers generally find exposition more difficult to write than narration and description. In narration, a sequence of events suggests a proper arrangement of the writer's material. In description, order can be achieved by arranging details methodically, from a consistent physical point of view. In exposition, quite often, a method of organization is less immediately apparent. In Part Five, we will examine in detail techniques for imposing order on expository paragraphs and essays—illustration, comparison and contrast, definition, division and classification, process, and causal analysis.

ELIXIRS OF DEATH
Rachel Carson

Rachel Carson writes here in specific terms and in detail on the general subject "A Fable for Tomorrow" (see pages 46–47).

1   For the first time in the history of the world, every human being is now subjected to contact with dangerous chemicals, from the

moment of conception until death. In the less than two decades of their use, the synthetic pesticides have been so thoroughly distributed throughout the animate and inanimate world that they occur virtually everywhere. They have been recovered from most of the major river systems and even from streams of groundwater flowing unseen through the earth. Residues of these chemicals linger in soil to which they may have been applied a dozen years before. They have entered and lodged in the bodies of fish, birds, reptiles, and domestic and wild animals so universally that scientists carrying on animal experiments find it almost impossible to locate subjects free from such contamination. They have been found in fish in remote mountain lakes, in earthworms burrowing in soil, in the eggs of birds —and in man himself. For these chemicals are now stored in the bodies of the vast majority of human beings, regardless of age. They occur in the mother's milk, and probably in the tissues of the unborn child.

₂   All this has come about because of the sudden rise and prodigious growth of an industry for the production of man-made or synthetic chemicals with insecticidal properties. This industry is a child of the Second World War. In the course of developing agents of chemical warfare, some of the chemicals created in the laboratory were found to be lethal to insects. The discovery did not come by chance: insects were widely used to test chemicals as agents of death for man.

₃   The result has been a seemingly endless stream of synthetic insecticides. In being man-made—by ingenious laboratory manipulation of the molecules, substituting atoms, altering their arrangement —they differ sharply from the simpler inorganic insecticides of prewar days. These were derived from naturally occurring minerals and plant products—compounds of arsenic, copper, lead, manganese, zinc, and other minerals, pyrethrum from the dried flowers of chrysanthemums, nicotine sulphate from some of the relatives of tobacco, and rotenone from leguminous plants of the East Indies.

₄   What sets the new synthetic insecticides apart is their enormous biological potency. They have immense power not merely to poison but to enter into the most vital processes of the body and change them in sinister and often deadly ways. Thus, as we shall see, they destroy the very enzymes whose function is to protect the body from harm, they block the oxidation processes from which the body receives its energy, they prevent the normal functioning of various organs, and they may initiate in certain cells the slow and irreversible change that leads to malignancy.

₅ Yet new and more deadly chemicals are added to the list each year and new uses are devised so that contact with these materials has become practically worldwide. The production of synthetic pesticides in the United States soared from 124,259,000 pounds in 1947 to 637,666,000 pounds in 1960—more than a five-fold increase. The wholesale value of these products was well over a quarter of a billion dollars. But in the plans and hopes of the industry this enormous production is only a beginning.

₆ A Who's Who of pesticides is therefore of concern to us all. If we are going to live so intimately with these chemicals—eating and drinking them, taking them into the very marrow of our bones—we had better know something about their nature and their power.

Questions About "Exposition"

1. What facts does Carson present to support her statement that "synthetic pesticides . . . occur virtually everywhere" (par. 1)? Are they significant enough and sufficient in number to convince you of the truth of her judgment? Why or why not?

2. Does Carson make clear to you how "all this has come about" (par. 2)? Explain.

3. How do the statistics Carson gives in paragraph 5 serve her purpose in writing this piece?

4. Jot down, in a phrase or a short sentence, the main idea of each paragraph. Are the main ideas related one to another? Is their sequence logical? Using Carson's words as much as you please, write a one-paragraph summary of this essay. Be prepared to comment in class on whether she adequately explains to you why "we had better know something about [the] nature and [the] power" (par. 6) of pesticides.

Questions on Diction and Writing Techniques

1. Define the following words and write sentences using each of them appropriately: synthetic (par. 1), pesticides (par. 1), lethal (par. 2), ingenious (par. 3), inorganic (par. 3), leguminous (par. 3), enzymes (par. 4).

2. By what means does the writer achieve coherence (see pages 27–28) in paragraph 1?

3. By what means does Carson achieve coherence elsewhere in her essay?

4. Here is an example of coordination: "They have been found in fish in remote mountain lakes, in earthworms burrowing in the soil, in the eggs of birds—and in man himself" (par. 1). Find in paragraph 4 another example of this method of expanding a sentence (see page 50).

5. Is "Elixirs of Death" an appropriate title? Explain.

For Discussion, Reading, and Writing

1. Carson's conclusion in "Elixirs of Death" is (circle one):

    A. Every human being is now subjected to contact with dangerous chemicals.

    B. There has been a seemingly endless stream of synthetic insecticides.

    C. What sets the new synthetic insecticides apart is their enormous biological potency.

    D. New and more deadly chemicals are added to the list of insecticides every year.

    E. A Who's Who of insecticides is of concern to us all.

2. In 1962, when *Silent Spring,* the source of this selection, was published, Carson was criticized severely by some for being an alarmist. Does she seem so to you? Can you add other "elixirs of death" to the pesticides that prompted her concern then?

3. If your answer to the previous question is Yes, write a short essay explaining in a logical sequence of coherent paragraphs why you are concerned about one of the "elixirs of death" you listed.

4. After seeking information from newspapers, magazines, and other sources to supplement your own experiences and observations, write an expository essay on a topic such as

    How to Garden Organically

    How Oil Spills at Sea Affect Marine Ecology

    Why Nuclear Power Plants Should (or Should Not) Be Installed in or Near Your Town or City

    Where Nuclear Waste Should Be Disposed Of

    What Is the Risk of Nuclear Fallout From the Sky

    Why the Surgeon General's Warning on Cigarette Packs Should Be Observed

    How Smoking in Public Should Be Controlled

    How the Pollution of Inland Waters Can Be Avoided

    What Is the Effect on One's Health of Medical X-rays

    Why Nitrates and Nitrites Are Used as Food Preservatives

COTTON-PICKING TIME
Maya Angelou

Maya Angelou is a poet and also the author of three autobiographical works based on her experience as a black woman in America.

---

1   Each year I watched the field across from the Store turn caterpillar green, then gradually frosty white. I knew exactly how long it

would be before the big wagons would pull into the front yard and load on the cotton pickers at daybreak to carry them to the remains of slavery's plantations.

2 During the picking season my grandmother would get out of bed at four o'clock (she never used an alarm clock) and creak down to her knees and chant in a sleep-filled voice, "Our Father, thank you for letting me see this New Day. Thank you that you didn't allow the bed I lay on last night to be my cooling board, nor my blanket my winding sheet. Guide my feet this day along the straight and narrow, and help me to put a bridle on my tongue. Bless this house, and everybody in it. Thank you, in the name of your Son, Jesus Christ, Amen."

3 Before she had quite arisen, she called our names and issued orders, and pushed her large feet into homemade slippers and across the bare lye-washed wooden floor to light the coal-oil lamp.

4 The lamplight in the Store gave a soft make-believe feeling to our world which made me want to whisper and walk about on tiptoe. The odors of onions and oranges and kerosene had been mixing all night and wouldn't be disturbed until the wooden slat was removed from the door and the early morning air forced its way in with the bodies of people who had walked miles to reach the pickup place.

5 "Sister, I'll have two cans of sardines."

6 "I'm gonna work so fast today I'm gonna make you look like you standing still."

7 "Lemme have a hunk uh cheese and some sody crackers."

8 "Just gimme a coupla them fat peanut paddies." That would be from a picker who was taking his lunch. The greasy brown paper sack was stuck behind the bib of his overalls. He'd use the candy as a snack before the noon sun called the workers to rest.

9 In those tender mornings the Store was full of laughing, joking, boasting and bragging. One man was going to pick two hundred pounds of cotton, and another three hundred. Even the children were promising to bring home fo' bits and six bits.

10 The champion picker of the day before was the hero of the dawn. If he prophesied that the cotton in today's field was going to be sparse and stick to the bolls like glue, every listener would grunt a hearty agreement.

11 The sound of the empty cotton sacks dragging over the floor

and the murmurs of waking people were sliced by the cash register
as we rang up the five-cent sales.

12   If the morning sounds and smells were touched with the su-
pernatural, the late afternoon had all the features of the normal Arkansas life. In the dying sunlight the people dragged, rather than
their empty cotton sacks.

13   Brought back to the Store, the pickers would step out of the
backs of trucks and fold down, dirt-disappointed, to the ground.
No matter how much they had picked, it wasn't enough. Their
wages wouldn't even get them out of debt to my grandmother, not
to mention the staggering bill that waited on them at the white
commissary downtown.

14   The sounds of the new morning had been replaced with
grumbles about cheating houses, weighted scales, snakes, skimpy
cotton and dusty rows. In later years I was to confront the stereo-
typed picture of gay song-singing cotton pickers with such inordi-
nate rage that I was told even by fellow Blacks that my paranoia
was embarrassing. But I had seen the fingers cut by the mean little
cotton bolls, and I had witnessed the backs and shoulders and arms
and legs resisting any further demands.

15   Some of the workers would leave their sacks at the Store to
be picked up the following morning, but a few had to take them
home for repairs. I winced to picture them sewing the coarse material under a coal-oil lamp with fingers stiffening from the day's
work. In too few hours they would have to walk back to Sister
Henderson's Store, get vittles and load, again, onto the trucks.
Then they would face another day of trying to earn enough for the
whole year with the heavy knowledge that they were going to end
the season as they started it. Without the money or credit necessary to sustain a family for three months. In cotton-picking time
the late afternoons revealed the harshness of Black Southern life,
which in the early morning had been softened by nature's blessing
of grogginess, forgetfulness and the soft lamplight.

Questions About "Exposition"

1.   What is Angelou's purpose in this essay?

2. Does Angelou make clear to you why "the pickers were dirt-disappointed" (par. 13)? Explain, making specific reference to the text.

3. What does description contribute to Angelou's explanation of her thesis?

Questions on Diction and Writing Techniques

1. Why does Angelou write "*caterpillar* green" and "*frosty* white" (par. 1)

2. Why does Angelou choose to write "the remains of slavery's plantations" (par. 1)? Is the diction apt?

3. What significant details does the writer choose to portray her grandmother?

4. Contrast the second half of the sentence that constitutes paragraph 3 with this alternate: ". . . pushed her feet into slippers and across the floor to light the lamp."

5. Is the description in paragraph 4 objective or subjective?

6. Comment on the effectiveness of Angelou's use of dialogue in portraying the cotton pickers in the morning.

7. What does "like glue" contribute to the meaning of the second sentence of paragraph 10?

8. Cite examples of Angelou's use of sensory diction (see pages 193–194).

For Discussion, Reading, and Writing

1. "Cotton-picking Time" is mainly about (circle one):

   A. cotton pickers.

   B. Angelou's grandmother's store.

   C. a day on a cotton farm.

   D. how to pick cotton.

   E. the harshness of black Southern life.

2. Do you agree with Thoreau that "There is no such thing as pure objective observation"? (See the passage from his *Journal*, page 119.) Can any description be altogether objective? Support your answer with specific reference to this essay or any other in this text.

3. Incorporating description, write a paragraph or two that explains the harshness (or pleasantness) of any job you have ever had.

4. The explanation of Angelou's thesis (see pages 5–9) in this essay depends in part on a comparison between the way the farm hands felt and acted at the beginning and at the end of the day. Considering any day that was especially meaningful to you, imitate Angelou's strategy to explain that day's significance.

WHAT UNDERDEVELOPMENT MEANS
Robert L. Heilbroner

Robert L. Heilbroner, an eminent economist and teacher, is the author of numerous books and articles on economics and social affairs, including **The Great Ascent: The Struggle for Economic Development in Our Time** (1963).

1   To begin to understand economic development we must have a picture of the problem with which it contends. We must conjure up in our mind's eye what underdevelopment means for the two billion human beings for whom it is not a statistic but a living experience of daily life. Unless we can see the Great Ascent from the vantage point of those who must make the climb, we cannot hope to understand the difficulties of the march.

2   It is not easy to make this mental jump. But let us attempt it by imagining how a typical American family, living in a small sub-

urban house on an income of six or seven thousand dollars, could be transformed into an equally typical family of the underdeveloped world.

₃   We begin by invading the house of our imaginary American family to strip it of its furniture. Everything goes: beds, chairs, tables, television set, lamps. We will leave the family with a few old blankets, a kitchen table, a wooden chair. Along with the bureaus go the clothes. Each member of the family may keep in his "wardrobe" his oldest suit or dress, a shirt or blouse. We will permit a pair of shoes to the head of the family, but none for the wife or children.

₄   We move into the kitchen. The appliances have already been taken out, so we turn to the cupboards and larder. The box of matches may stay, a small bag of flour, some sugar and salt. A few moldy potatoes, already in the garbage can, must be hastily rescued, for they will provide much of tonight's meal. We will leave a handful of onions, and a dish of dried beans. All the rest we take away: the meat, the fresh vegetables, the canned goods, the crackers, the candy.

₅   Now we have stripped the house: the bathroom has been dismantled, the running water shut off, the electric wires taken out. Next we take away the house. The family can move to the toolshed. It is crowded, but much better than the situation in Hong Kong, where (a United Nations report tells us) "it is not uncommon for a family of four or more to live in a bedspace, that is, on a bunk bed and the space it occupies—sometimes in two or three tiers—their only privacy provided by curtains."

₆   But we have only begun. All the other houses in the neighborhood have also been removed; our suburb has become a shantytown. Still, our family is fortunate to have a shelter; 250,000 people in Calcutta have none at all and simply live in the streets. Our family is now about on a par with the city of Cali in Colombia, where, an official of the World Bank writes, "on one hillside alone, the slum population is estimated at 40,000—without water, sanitation, or electric light. And not all the poor of Cali are as fortunate as that. Others have built their shacks near the city on land which lies beneath the flood mark. To these people the immediate environment is the open sewer of the city, a sewer which flows through their huts when the river rises."

7   And still we have not reduced our American family to the level at which life is lived in the greatest part of the globe. Communication must go next. No more newspapers, magazines, books — not that they are missed, since we must take away our family's literacy as well. Instead, in our shantytown we will allow one radio. In India the national average of radio ownership is one per 250 people, but since the majority of radios is owned by city dwellers, our allowance is fairly generous.

8   Now government services must go. No more postman, no more fireman. There is a school, but it is three miles away and consists of two classrooms. They are not too overcrowded since only half the children in the neighborhood go to school. There are, of course, no hospitals or doctors nearby. The nearest clinic is ten miles away and is tended by a midwife. It can be reached by bicycle, provided that the family has a bicycle, which is unlikely. Or one can go by bus — not always inside, but there is usually room on top.

9   Finally, money. We will allow our family a cash hoard of five dollars. This will prevent our breadwinner from experiencing the tragedy of an Iranian peasant who went blind because he could not raise the $3.94 which he mistakenly thought he needed to secure admission to a hospital where he could have been cured.

10   Meanwhile the head of our family must earn his keep. As a peasant cultivator with three acres to tend, he may raise the equivalent of $100 to $300 worth of crops a year. If he is a tenant farmer, which is more than likely, a third or so of his crop will go to his landlord, and probably another 10 percent to the local moneylender. But there will be enough to eat. Or almost enough. The human body requires an input of at least 2,000 calories to replenish the energy consumed by its living cells. If our displaced American fares no better than an Indian peasant, he will average a replenishment of no more than 1,700–1,900 calories. His body, like any insufficiently fueled machine, will run down. That is one reason why life expectancy at birth in India today averages less than forty years.

11   But the children may help. If they are fortunate, they may find work and thus earn some cash to supplement the family's income. For example, they may be employed as are children in Hyderabad, Pakistan, sealing the ends of bangles over a small kerosene flame, a simple task which can be done at home. To be sure, the pay is small: eight annas — about ten cents — for sealing bangles. That

is, eight annas per *gross* of bangles. And if they cannot find work?
Well, they can scavenge, as do the children in Iran who in times of
hunger search for the undigested oats in the droppings of horses.

12   And so we have brought our typical American family down
to the very bottom of the human scale. It is, however, a bottom in
which we can find, give or take a hundred million souls, at least a
billion people.* Of the remaining billion in the backward areas,
most are slightly better off, but not much so; a few are comfortable;
a handful rich.

13   Of course, this is only an impression of life in the underdeveloped lands. It is not life itself. There is still lacking the things that
underdevelopment gives as well as those it takes away: the urinous
smell of poverty, the display of disease, the flies, the open sewers.
And there is lacking, too, a softening sense of familiarity. Even in a
charnel house life has its passions and pleasures. A tableau, shocking
to American eyes, is less shocking to eyes that have never known
any other. But it gives one a general idea. It begins to add pictures
of reality to the statistics by which underdevelopment is ordinarily
measured. When we are told that half the world's population enjoys a standard of living "less than $100 a year," this is what the
figures mean.

* Such an estimate is, of necessity, highly conjectural. It takes in only 300 million
of India's population and 50 million of Pakistan's, a charitable figure. It includes 50
million Arabs and 100 million Africans, a large underestimate. From South and
Central America's poverty it adds in but another 50 millions. The remainder of the
billion can be made up from mainland China alone. And we have kept as a statistical reserve the Afghans, Burmese, Indonesians, Koreans, Vietnamese — nearly 200
million in all, among whom is to be found some of the worst poverty on the face
of the globe.

====================

Questions About "Exposition"

1. What does Heilbroner try to explain to you?

2. Why does he choose the method of explanation that he does?

3. Does he make abundantly clear to you what it means to live on
    less than one hundred dollars a year? Explain.

Questions on Diction and Writing Techniques

1. Mark in your text those words that are new to you, but whose meaning you inferred from their context. Define them in your own words. Compare your definitions with those in your dictionary. Look up in your dictionary any other words that are new to you. Use the words in both groups in sentences.

2. What does coherence within and between paragraphs contribute toward ease of reading? By what means does Heilbroner achieve this coherence?

3. What is Heilbroner's source(s) of material?

4. Making specific reference to the text, comment on the effect of Heilbroner's use of detailed information.

For Discussion, Reading, and Writing

1. Mark and number in your text the steps by which Heilbroner transforms a typical American family into an equally typical family of the underdeveloped world.

2. Why, according to Heilbroner, is the life expectancy at birth in India what it is?

3. Fill the blanks in this passage from memory to make it intelligible:

To begin to _____ economic development we must have a picture of the _____ with which it contends. We must conjure up in our mind's eye what _____ means for the two billion human beings for whom it is not a _____ but a living _____ of daily life. Unless we can see the Great Ascent from the _____ point of those who must make the _____, we cannot hope to understand the _____ of the march.

Compare your words with those in paragraph 1 of this essay.

4. Consider the probable benefits or disadvantages of your being stripped of a possession such as a car, a hi-fi, a TV set, a pocket computer, an electric hair dryer. Write a short essay on the subject, making sure to explain your ideas with sufficient detail and clarity to convince a reader of the validity of your thesis.

5. To support your ideas in a short expository essay on a subject with which you are familiar, include in it apt quotations from the writing of one or more experts.

OUSTING THE STRANGER FROM THE HOUSE
Colman McCarthy

Coleman McCarthy is a journalist and freelance writer whose wide-ranging interests are evident in articles published in diverse journals.

1   When I turned off the television for the last time about a year ago and dumped the set for good, some friends, relatives and un-asked advisers on the block predicted I would not last long without it. Few disputed the common gripe that TV is a wasteland, with irrigation offered only by the rare trickle of a quality program. Instead, they doubted that the addiction of some twenty years before the tube could be stilled by this sudden break with the past. It is true that an addiction had me, my veins eased only by a fix of 30 to 35 hours a week; my wife's dosage was similar, and our children—three boys under 7—already listened more to the television than to us.

2   Now, a year later—a family living as cultural cave men, says an anthropologist friend—the decision we made was one of the wisest

of our married life. The ratings—our private Nielsens—during this year of setlessness have been high, suggesting that such common acts as talking with one's children, sharing ideas with one's wife, walking to the neighborhood library on a Saturday morning, quiet evenings of reading books and magazines aloud to each other, or eating supper as a family offer more intellectual and emotional stimulation than anything on television.

3   The severity of an addiction to TV is not that it reduces the victim to passivity while watching it but that it demands he be a compulsive activist to get in front of it. If I arrived home at 6, for example, and dinner was ready at 6:25—my wife's afternoon movie had run late, so dinner was late—I would shove down the food in five minutes. The deadline, falling like a guillotine, was at 6:30. Chancellor came on then, Cronkite at 7; if CBS was dull, Smith and Reasoner were on ABC. If I hadn't finished dinner, I would sprint back to the table during the commercials for short-order gulps, then back to cool John, Uncle Walter or wry Harry. My wife, desperate Mav, was left at the table to control the bedlam of the kids, caused by my in-and-out sprints. The chaos I heard coming from the dining room was fitting: it was matched by the chaos in the world reported on the evening news, except the latter, in the vague "out there," was easier to handle.

4   With the set gone, these compulsions and in-turnings have gone too. We eat dinner in leisure and peace now. We stay at the playground until the children have had enough fun, not when I need to rush home to watch the 4 P.M. golf. Occasionally, my wife and I have the exotic experience of spending an evening in relaxed conversation, not the little half-stops of talk we once made in a forced march to Marital Communication. In those days, we would turn off the set in midevening and be immediately oppressed by the silence.

5   What had been happening all those years of watching television, I see now, was not only an addiction but also, on a deeper level, an adjustment. All of us had become adjusted to living with a stranger in the house. Is there any more basic definition of a television set than that? More, the stranger in the house was not there to entertain us, a notion the televisers would like to serve. The stranger was present to sell us products. The person before a set may think he is a viewer but the sponsors who pay for broadcasts know

better: he is a buyer. It is a commercial arrangement, with the TV
set a salesman permanently assigned to one house, and often two or
three salesmen working different rooms. It is a myth that TV is free
entertainment.

6   I was not only paying personally for the stranger-salesman in
my house but he was often manipulating or lying to my children. I
saw the effects in such places as the supermarket aisles, when the
boys would loudly demand a sugared cereal, junk-snack or six pack
of soda, all of these items only high-priced garbage that helps rot
the teeth and keeps children from fruit and other nutritious food.
My kids had been conditioned well by the sellers on TV, predatory
strangers as menacing in one way as street predators are in another.
But, someone told me, that's only commercial television, suggesting
that programs like "Sesame Street" and its mimics are different.
They are, perhaps, but no more worthy.

7   If the televisers want to teach my children something, I suggest such subjects as obedience to parents, sharing toys with brothers and sisters, kindness to animals, respect for grandparents. These
kinds of lessons were strangely missing from the "quality" childrens'
shows I looked in on. It is true that these concepts must be taught
by the parents but it is insufferable to note the preachings of the
"Sesame"-type producers, hearing them blat about how they care
for children. I see their programs as a moral hustle, conning parents
into thinking it's a high educational experience to dump the kids before the tube. In the end, the yammering about letters, shapes,
numbers does not liberate the child's imagination. It captures it, a
quick-action lariat that ropes in the child's most precious resource,
his creativity.

8   Occasionally I have feelings that I may be missing an event of
special value, a feeling that the televised truth goes marching on
without me. But in my straggler status I have never failed to catch
up eventually with the essence of what I missed, mostly by reading
the newspapers or magazines—say a Presidential press conference
or the Watergate testimony.

9   The stranger is gone now. Our lives are fuller and richer. Cold
turkey worked. The kids don't run to neighbors' houses to watch
TV, as I had feared. As for whether we ever invite the stranger back
to our house, it isn't likely unless the industry learns new manners.

10   A first sign of the kind of manners I'm thinking about would

be revealed if, say, some evening this announcement was beamed into the 97 per cent of America's electrically wired homes that have TV's: "Ladies and gentlemen, until further notice we are ceasing our broadcasts. The programs we had planned are now seen to be dull, banal, pointless, not worth your time and not ours. Don't turn to another channel, because you will only be insulted there too — insulted by the programs and by the corporate advertisers who want to gull you into buying products you can live well, even better, without.

11   "Come forward and turn off your set. When the die-out dot appears, get up and take a walk to the library and get a book. Or turn to your husband and wife and surprise them with a conversation. Or call a neighbor you haven't spoken with in months. Write a letter to a friend who has lost track of you. Turn off your set now. When we devise some worthwhile programing, we'll be back on the air. Meanwhile, you'll be missing almost nothing."

Questions About "Exposition"

1. Does McCarthy adequately explain why he defines TV the way he does? Explain, making specific reference to the text.

2. Be prepared to discuss in class whether he sufficiently explains why he banned TV.

3. Does he explain, to your satisfaction, how the quality of the life of the McCarthy family has changed since the stranger he refers to has gone?

Questions on Diction and Writing Techniques

1. Mark in your text those words that are new to you, but whose meaning you inferred from their context. Define them in your own words. Compare your definitions with those in your dictionary. Look up in your dictionary any other words that are new to you. Use the words in both groups in sentences.

2. Does McCarthy's choice of the words "wasteland" and "addiction" help to fulfill his expository purpose? Explain.

3. Rewrite sentence 2 of paragraph 2 to make all members of its series of coordinate elements of the same kind.

4. What is McCarthy's purpose in writing "for example" (par. 3)?

5. McCarthy might have written, in paragraph 3, "I would go back to the table." Why did he choose the verb he did?

6. State, in a sentence of not over twenty-five words, the main idea of this essay.

7. Summarize the essay in a paragraph of not over one hundred words.

For Discussion, Reading, and Writing

1. What, according to McCarthy, is "the severity of an addiction to TV"?

2. "It is a myth that TV is free entertainment." Do you agree? Explain.

3. Would you add to or subtract from the list of subjects that McCarthy suggests to televisers who want to teach children something? Explain.

4. Make a list of TV programs that you find beneficial and another of those you find useless. Prepare to defend your choices in class. Explain your choices in a short essay.

5. Explain in a short essay—with specific examples from your own experience—your opinion regarding any point McCarthy makes in his essay.

5

Patterns of Organization

Illustration

THERE are a number of techniques for imposing order on and for organizing the material in expository writing. We will examine six of them—illustration, comparison and contrast, definition, division and classification, process, and causal analysis.

The simplest and most common pattern is illustration—giving examples. If you wanted to show that some doctors see their patients not merely as cases of appendicitis, measles, or athlete's foot but as whole persons, you might cite as examples humane doctors you know or have heard about. If you wanted to show that Doc Jones is considerate of his patients, you might explain what you mean with examples: He doesn't keep his patients waiting in his office; he listens attentively to their complaints; he doesn't interpose a telephone answering service between himself and them; he makes house calls. Illustration makes a generality concrete, more intelligible, and more interesting.

Illustration can be used in a sentence, a paragraph, or an essay. Consider this sentence:

Illustration 237

I had such wonderful toys: a real steam engine, a magic lantern, and a collection of soldiers already nearly a thousand strong [Winston Churchill, *My Early Life*].

Winston Churchill makes clear what he means by the vague generalization "I had such wonderful toys" with illustration—by giving examples.

Here is an example of illustration in a paragraph:

Even the most productive writers are expert dawdlers, doers of unnecessary errands, seekers of interruptions—trials to their wives or husbands, associates, and themselves. They sharpen well-pointed pencils and go out to buy more blank paper, rearrange offices, wander through libraries and bookstores, chop wood, walk, drive, make unnecessary calls, nap, daydream, and try not "consciously" to think about what they are going to write so they can think subconsciously about it [Donald M. Murray, "Write Before Writing"].

Without the examples given in the second sentence, would you know as well as you do what the writer meant by "expert dawdlers, doers of unnecessary errands, seekers of interruptions"?

Illustration is a means of explaining, with specific information, a generalization that might otherwise be obscure:

Most research in ecology over the past thirty years has been concerned with the growth of populations or, more specifically, with environmental factors that prevent unchecked growth of a population. Usually natural populations are under the control of various environmental factors such as weather, food supply, parasites, and predators, and so maintain an equilibrium. When this steady state is altered by a significant change in one factor, a population may increase to the point of catastrophe.

A classic example was provided on the Kaibab Plateau in Arizona. The area had been set aside as a game preserve, and to protect the deer population, their natural predators, mountain lions, wolves, and coyotes, were exterminated. The deer population increased beyond the carrying capacity of the environment, and an estimated 80,000 animals died of starvation. Even then the popu-

lation continued to decline because forage plants had been dam-
aged and could not regenerate quickly enough to support the remaining animals. With fewer plants to hold the soil, erosion took
place, permanently damaging the area's productivity.

Here the specific example, in the second paragraph, of the game
preserve on the Kaibab Plateau in Arizona clarifies the generalization that the writer makes in the first paragraph.

   Here is an instructive instance of the use of illustration. Its
author starts a paragraph with

   There is a rule of economy in the endowments with which nature
   equips her creatures. For each one, there is the gift of this or that
   kind of competence to achieve living effectiveness; but, such competence being assured, there are not commonly given gifts beyond
   that necessary measure. Each possession of an endowment implies, so to speak, the sacrifice—or at any rate the lack—of others
   [Alan Devoe, "Snapping Turtle"].

Notice that Devoe, after making a generalization in the first sentence, gives variations of it in the second and third. Then, to explain further what he means, he adds

   It is given to a rat to be canny and quick; and a rat's body, com-
   pensatingly, is vulnerable. A porcupine is dim and slow; it has the
   gift of a protecting armament. A hare can outrun its foes; it has
   not the genius of outfighting them. A mole can outburrow its
   enemies; it has not the gift of outthinking them. Natural economy disallows that any creature shall have at once agility, armor,
   fighting tools, keen senses, and shrewd wits.

The writer's four examples—a rat, a porcupine, a hare, and a mole
—make plain to the reader what otherwise might not be clear about
nature's "rule of economy."

   To better understand what I mean when I call illustration a
pattern of organization, consider the structure of Devoe's paragraph. First is the topic sentence:

   There is a rule of economy in the endowments with which nature
   equips her creatures.

Illustration 239

The second and third sentences clarify, expand, restate, and make more specific the topic sentence:

> For each one, there is the gift of this or that kind of competence to achieve living effectiveness; but, such competence being assured, there are not commonly given gifts beyond that necessary measure. Each possession of an endowment implies, so to speak, the sacrifice—or at any rate the lack—of others.

Each of the next four sentences is a specific example of the generalization made in the topic sentence:

> It is given to a rat to be canny and quick; and a rat's body, compensatingly, is vulnerable. A porcupine is dim and slow; it has the gift of a protecting armament. A hare can outrun its foes; it has not the genius of outfighting them. A mole can outburrow its enemies; it has not the gift of outthinking them.

The final sentence summarizes the paragraph:

> Natural economy disallows that any creature shall have at once agility, armor, fighting tools, keen senses, and shrewd wits.

Devoe's illustration of nature's "rule of economy" not only explains his topic sentence; it also supports it—that is, it demonstrates its validity. By means of his four examples the writer makes acceptable to his readers the generalization in his topic sentence. At the same time he is also developing his paragraph. This is what I mean when I call illustration a pattern of organization.

Recall how the author of "Menial Jobs Taught Me a Lot" (pages 31–35) developed the first paragraph in the body of his essay, paragraph 2. After stating in his topic sentence the main idea of the paragraph, "jobs available to a teenager without special training do not pay well," he illustrates that idea. He gives five examples of poorly paying jobs: mowing lawns, waiting on tables, packaging groceries, tending a machine in a factory, and working as a laborer on a construction project. These examples—in explanation of his topic sentence—supply the details needed to develop the topic sentence, make out of an unsupported statement (a mere assertion) a statement with reasons, and, in addition, make the paragraph complete and its main idea convincing.

The author of "Menial Jobs Taught Me a Lot" also develops paragraph 3 with illustration, this time with two examples. The first —in support of the main idea of the paragraph, "my jobs . . . soon became boring"—is an extended example, which takes up most of the paragraph. The second, in the last two sentences of the paragraph, also in support of the paragraph's thesis, is relatively short. Paragraph 4 in the body of the essay is also developed by illustration in support of its main idea: "none of the jobs I had was fulfilling." Each of these paragraphs constitutes in itself an example of the lessons learned by the author from his menial jobs. "Menial Jobs Taught Me a Lot" is a good example of the use of illustration to develop an essay.

THE MAGIC OF SHEEP DRESSING
E. B. White

E. B. White, a witty observer and reporter of American mores, is one of the country's best essayists and a master of the informal essay whose first purpose is to entertain. This piece, from **One Man's Meat** (1942), illustrates his celebrated literary style.

1   Last fall I hauled rockweed up from the shore and spread it to a depth of five or six inches on the dirt floor of the sheep shed and covered it with straw. Now the sheep droppings are accumulating on this rockweed base and forming a rich dressing for the land. There is no doubt about it, the basic satisfaction in farming is manure, which always suggests that life can be cyclic and chemically perfect and aromatic and continuous.

₂   A brilliant testimonial to the magic of sheep dressing is written in the leaves of my New York City rubber plant, which has lately been receiving an occasional shot of liquid tonic made of a barnyard mixture which I prepare in old Scotch-whisky bottles and keep handy for use on house plants. This rubber plant is one I bought thirteen years ago on West Eighth Street and it has been my companion ever since. As rubber plants go it has been a success and I am attached to it in a curious sort of way, as a man does get attached to anything that manages to last thirteen years under the same roof with him. Its growth has been erratic and inconsistent and it has not always enjoyed good health. Some of its leaves are large and shiny and well-formed. Others I try not to think about. One leaf is barely two inches long—mute reminder of a hard winter when the plague spread over everything in our apartment. And dotting its trunk and branches are scars of one miasmic summer when I loaned the plant to an obscure biographer named Henry Pringle and it lost all its leaves but two, and a white milky fluid oozed from every wound. That summer finally ended. Pringle went on to win the Pulitzer prize, and I went on to nursing a rubber plant back to health.

₃   Essentially, rubber plants are city plants. They often do better in dark hallways in gloomy city apartments than in the sunny south windows of country homes. For a while after we came here I kept my rubber plant in the sun, as an experiment, but it began to sicken and the leaves would turn yellow and drop off. So I removed it to a north location and it improved. But one day, more as a gag than anything else, I poured a little of the liquid sheep manure on the plant. I say more as a gag—I had always had a notion that a rubber plant drew its nourishment not so much from the ball of exhausted earth surrounding its roots as from the people it lived with and the conversations it overheard. This theory of mine was wrong. The effect of the manure was instantaneous. The plant sent out enormous red leaf spears three times the size of anything it had ever produced before, and these unrolled into leaves of magnificent proportions, so that the plant as a whole looked like a monstrosity, as though the old part didn't belong to the new. It was a startling experience, and for a while I flirted with the idea of getting rich quick by selling bottled strength to city people who harbored rubber plants. But when I figured out how much Scotch I should have to drink in order to have enough empty bottles I got cold feet and the idea blew up.

Questions About "Illustration"

1. What is the generalization that, based on his personal experience with sheep droppings, White makes?

2. With what word(s) does White announce that he is going to develop that idea with illustration?

Questions on Diction and Writing Techniques

1. Mark in your text those words that are new to you, but whose meaning you inferred from the context. Define them in your own words. Compare your definitions with those in your dictionary. Look up in your dictionary any other words that are new to you. Use the words in both groups in sentences.

2. By what means does White achieve coherence within paragraph 2?

3. If you find this essay easy to read and to comprehend, list the reasons that you find it so.

For Discussion, Reading, and Writing

1. What theory of White's proved to be wrong?

2. What was the effect of the treatment he gave to his ailing rubber plant?

3. What is the tone of the essay? Support your judgment with specific reference to the text.

4. Find in your personal experience simple material that can be used to illustrate a meaningful generalization. Embody this information in a short essay.

ALUMINUM, THE MAGIC METAL
Thomas Y. Canby

Thomas Y. Canby, senior editor of **National Geographic**, explains in this excerpt from an article in that magazine why this era may be called the Aluminum Age.

1   It is 1942: A Nazi U-boat surfaces in foggy darkness off a lonely Long Island beach and four invaders land stealthily. Armed with sophisticated explosives, the saboteurs seek to cripple America's burgeoning air armada. Among their targets—aluminum smelters in New York and Tennessee. Their plan—destroy the cables that carry electricity for processing the aluminum. Long before power can be restored, the molten metal will solidify in the furnaces so that only blasting can remove it, knocking out the smelters for months.

2   Before the enemy agents can strike, the FBI scoops them up. But the lesson is clear. The light, shiny metal that began its working life as kitchen pots and pans has emerged as a sinew of industrial society.

3   Discovered a mere 150 years ago and manufactured commercially just half that long, aluminum today ranks behind only iron and steel among metals serving mankind. The key is incredible versatility.

4   The same filmy metal that makes our kitchen foil (last year we unrolled 20 billion square feet of it) serves as armor for Uncle Sam's battlefield tanks. The stuff of lawn chairs and Little League baseball bats also forms the vitals of our air and space vehicles—most of their skeletons, their skins, even the rivets that bind them together.

5   Versatile? Spread less than an ounce of aluminum over a thin Mylar sheet and it keeps a sleeping camper snugly warm; spread just a few ounces over an asbestos suit and it keeps a fire fighter

"cool." Mix pulverized aluminum in a liquid medium and it forms a durable paint; reduce it to powder and it becomes rocket fuel and a high explosive.

6   Look around. The magic metal clads trucks, trains, houses, skyscrapers. Look seaward. Aluminum ships in swelling squadrons cleave the waves, from trawlers to pleasure craft; five of the seven yachts fighting for the 1977 *America's* Cup raced on aluminum hulls.

7   Glance overhead. A vast web of aluminum transmission cables feeds the nation's vital electric power grids.

8   Indeed, just as earlier ages of human development have taken their names from the distinctive material that nurtured them — Stone, Bronze, Iron — there are those who believe our era may be called the Aluminum Age. Cultural analyst Lewis Mumford observes that just as the industrial revolution transmuted "clumsy wooden machines into stronger and more accurate iron ones," a task of today is "to translate heavy iron forms into lighter aluminum ones."

9   Behind aluminum's versatility lie properties so diverse they almost seem to belong to several different metals.

10   For example, in pure form aluminum is soft enough to whittle. Yet its alloys can possess the strength of steel, though only a third the weight. Thus when sculptor Alexander Calder designed his last mobile — a soaring creation 80 feet long — his choice of aluminum over steel slashed two tons from its weight. Aluminum also assures the masterpiece virtual immortality: The instant the metal is exposed to air its surface acquires a transparent film of "rust" that seals the interior against further corrosion.

11   Consider a few more of aluminum's useful properties. Farmers throughout the South and the Southwest, knowing that cows give more milk when cool, nail heat-reflecting aluminum roofs on their dairy barns. Homeowners cherish aluminum siding and gutters, whose durable surfaces can keep paintbrushes on the shelf 15 years or more. Food and beverage packagers revel in a metal so chemically stable that it doesn't react with most foods.

12   No other metal so obligingly takes the myriad shapes that meet our everyday needs. You can roll aluminum and forge it, saw, slit, and shear it, and shape it by extruding — forcing it through a die of almost any shape, much as you squeeze toothpaste through a

tube. By drawing aluminum, you can wind a wire so spiderweb thin that a strand weighing only a few hundred pounds could stretch around the world.

Questions About "Illustration"

1. Making specific reference to the text, show how Canby explains the versatility of aluminum.

2. How does he explain that aluminum has "properties so diverse they almost seem to belong to several different metals"? That "its alloys can possess the strength of steel, though only a third the weight"?

3. How does Canby develop the paragraph that begins "Consider a few more of aluminum's useful properties"? The paragraph that begins "No other metal so obligingly takes the myriad shapes that meet our everyday needs"?

Questions on Diction and Writing Techniques

1. Mark in your text those words that are new to you, but whose meaning you inferred from their context. Define them in your own words. Compare your definitions with those in your dictionary. Look up in your dictionary any other words that are new to you. Use the words in both groups in sentences.

2. Comment on the usefulness of narration in making paragraph 1 an effective opening paragraph.

3. What is Canby's purpose in using the present tense in paragraphs 1 and 2?

4. Sentence 2 of paragraph 1 is an example of subordination. Canby could have expressed the ideas in that sentence thus:

   They are armed with sophisticated explosives. The saboteurs seek to cripple America's burgeoning air armada.

Write two sentences with related ideas, for example:

Mary is the best swimmer in college. She comes in first in every intramural swimming contest.

Then, subordinating one idea to the other, combine the sentences, thus:

Mary, the best swimmer in college, comes in first in every intramural swimming contest.

5. What is Canby's purpose in writing "indeed" (par. 8)?

6. What transitional words does Canby use in paragraph 10 to help make it coherent?

7. What do quotation marks contribute to the meaning of the first complete sentence in paragraph 5? To the meaning of the last sentence of paragraph 10?

8. Is the main idea of paragraph 10 expressed or implied? If expressed, say where; if implied, state it in your own words.

9. Does Canby make clear the meaning of "extruding" (par. 12)? Explain.

10. Does Canby succeed in convincing you that aluminum is indeed a "magic metal"? Is the title of his essay apt? Explain.

For Discussion, Reading, and Writing

1. Fill the blanks in this passage from memory to make it intelligible:

Consider a few more of aluminum's useful _____. Farmers throughout the South and the Southwest, knowing that cows give more milk when _____, nail _____ aluminum roofs on their _____ barns. Homeowners cherish aluminum _____ and gutters, whose _____ surfaces can keep _____ on the shelf 15 years or more. Food and _____ packagers revel in a metal so chemically _____ that it doesn't _____ with most foods.

Compare your words with those in paragraph 11.

2. Why, according to Canby, might our era be termed the Aluminum Age?

3. Why, according to Canby, does aluminum assure the "virtual immortality" of the sculptor Calder's last mobile?

4. How many useful properties of aluminum does Canby mention?

5. List some of the uses of aluminum, other than those mentioned by Canby, that you have observed or are familiar with.

6. Despite the merits of aluminum, wood remains a much-used material. Giving sufficient examples to make clear to your readers the merits of wood (or of any other material you are familiar with), write a short essay explaining its usefulness.

ITALIAN GESTURES
Luigi Barzini

Luigi Barzini, after completing his education at Columbia University and writing for two New York newspapers, returned to his native land to continue to write there. In **The Italians** (1965), he wrote discerningly about the manners and morals of the men and women of his country.

———

1   Italian gestures are justly famous. Indeed Italians use them more abundantly, efficiently, and imaginatively than other people.

They employ them to emphasize or clarify whatever is said, to suggest words and meanings it is not prudent to express with words, sometimes simply to convey a message at great distance, where the voice could not carry. In the hurried world of today gestures are also employed more and more as time-saving devices. Motorists no longer slow down and waste precious seconds to shout intelligible and elaborate insults to each other or to pedestrians, as they used to do but a few years ago. Now they merely extend one hand in the general direction of the person to whom they want to address the message; a hand with all fingers folded except the forefinger and the little finger. It conveys the suggestion that the other man does, should or will shortly wear horns, in other words be cuckolded by his wife, fiancée or mistress. A few gestures are as arbitrary and conventional as the deaf and dumb alphabet or the sign language of American Indians. Most of them, however, are based on natural and instinctive movements, common to the majority of men, certainly common to all Western men, elaborated, intensified, stylized, sharpened, made into art. Like all great traditional arts, this one too can generally be understood by the inexperienced at first sight.

2   The mimicry is not, as many think, always exaggerated and dramatic, emphatic contortions of arms and body, rolling of eyes, convulsive agitation of hands and fingers. Probably the acting of opera singers, directly derived from the Italians' natural mimicry, spread this erroneous impression. The best gestures are often so economical as to be almost imperceptible. Sicilians, for instance, are known to convey a vast range of grave and sometimes mortal messages practically without stirring a muscle of their faces or moving their hands. For them, a slowly raised chin means "I don't know" or, more often, "Perhaps I know but I will not tell you." It is the answer policemen always get when questioning possible witnesses of a Mafia killing which took place in front of hundreds of people in a busy market square. It is also the answer a harmless stranger gets from diffident Sicilian peasants when he asks the way to the nearest village.

3   The extended fingers of one hand moving slowly back and forth under the raised chin means: "I couldn't care less. It's no business of mine. Count me out." This is the gesture made in 1860 by the grandfather of Signor O.O. of Messina as an answer to Garibaldi. The general, who had conquered Sicily with his volunteers

and was moving on to the mainland, had seen him, a robust youth at the time, dozing on a little stone wall, in the shadow of a carob tree, along a country lane. He reined in his horse and asked him: "Young man, will you not join us in our fight to free our brothers in Southern Italy from the bloody tyranny of the Bourbon kings? How can you sleep when your country needs you? Awake and to arms!" The young man silently made the gesture. Garibaldi spurred his horse on.

4   The lifting of one single eyebrow means, "I'm ready to take what decisions are necessary." The slow closing of both eyes in an otherwise immobile and expressionless face signifies resignation in front of the inevitable, acceptance of a difficult and unpleasant duty, as, for instance: "We warned him again and again. The man is stubborn. He does not want to listen to reason. We will do our duty."

5   One of the most economical and eloquent of Sicilian gestures I saw one day in the lobby of the Hotel des Palmes, in Palermo. A man entered from the street. He obviously wanted everybody to know immediately, beyond doubt, that he was a gentleman, *un gran signore*, a man of means and authority, accustomed to being attended on. He looked around as if searching for a friend among the people loitering in the room, took off his overcoat, held it at arm's length for a fraction of a second, and, without bothering to see whether a servant was at his side, dropped it. A real *signore* always has somebody ready to receive his coat when he takes it off. He never needs to check. The coat, of course, did not drop to the floor. A bell-boy was there to catch it. . . .

6   Often enough, a simple gesture, accompanied by suitable facial expressions, takes the place not of a few words but of a whole and eloquent speech. This, for instance: imagine two gentlemen sitting at a café table. The first is explaining at great length some intricate question which interests him, perhaps how the world will shortly be changed for the better by some new and impending development. He may be saying: "This continent of ours, Europe, old, decrepit Europe, all divided into different nations, each nation subdivided into provinces, each nation and each province living its own petty life, speaking its incomprehensible dialect, nurturing its ideas, prejudices, defects, hatreds. . . . Each of us gloating over the memories of the defeats inflicted by us on our neighbours and completely oblivious of the defeats our neighbours inflicted on us. . . .

How easy life would become if we were to fuse into one whole, Europa, the Christendom of old, the dream of Charlemagne, of Metternich, of many great men, and why not? the dream of Hitler too. . . ." The second gentleman is listening patiently, looking intently at the first's face. At a certain moment, as if overwhelmed by the abundance of his friend's arguments or the facility of his optimism, he slowly lifts one hand, perpendicularly, in a straight line, from the table, as far as it will go, higher than his head. Meanwhile he utters only one sound, a prolonged "eeeeeeh," like a sigh. His eyes never leave the other credulous. The mimicry means: "How quickly you rush to conclusions, my friend, how complicated your reasoning, how unreasonable your hopes, when we all know the world has always been the same and all bright solutions to our problems have in turn produced more and different problems, more serious and unbearable problems than the ones we were accustomed to."

Questions About "Illustration"

1. How does Barzini support his statement that gestures are "employed more and more as time-saving devices" (par. 1)?

2. "The best gestures are often so economical as to be almost imperceptible" (par. 2). Does the writer try to convince you that this is so? How? What is the function of "for instance" in paragraph 2? Find another example of its use in this essay for a similar purpose.

3. What is Barzini's purpose in writing paragraphs 3, 4, and 5?

4. What does paragraph 6 add to Barzini's explanation of Italian gestures?

5. After reading this essay, are you convinced of the truth of Barzini's generalization that Italians use gestures "abundantly, efficiently, and imaginatively" (par. 1)? Explain, making specific reference to the text.

Questions on Diction and Writing Techniques

1. What does "also" signal in paragraph 1? Find, elsewhere in this essay, the use of this word for the same purpose.

2. Find another transition word in paragraph 1. Why does Barzini use it?

3. What is the derivation of *"signore"* (par. 5)?

4. How does your dictionary define "mimicry" (par. 6)?

5. Is this essay unified (see pages 24–27)? Does the writer at any point digress? Explain.

For Discussion, Reading, and Writing

1. Make a list of and be prepared to demonstrate in class the gestures you use or have observed others use. Write a paragraph about them.

2. After watching people in conversation in a classroom, sports arena, museum, park, or any other public place, write a paragraph about gestures—with apt examples—based on your observations.

3. Develop a paragraph by illustrating a topic sentence based on your observations of the gestures of one of the following:

Ballet dancers

A character in a silent movie

A policeman directing traffic

An orchestra conductor

Umpires or referees in sports events such as baseball, football, hockey

4. Restrict one of the following subjects to a topic suitable for a brief essay:

Greek music

Scandinavian movies

Japanese poetry

Spanish proverbs

Irish folklore

Russian dances

Black English

Yiddish idioms

Chinese cooking

Danish pastry

Then write an essay, using illustrations and signaling with appropriate transition words the examples you use to support your thesis.

MAN IS THE DOG'S WORST FRIEND
James Thurber

James Thurber (1894–1961), American author and cartoonist, is noted especially for his whimsical commentary on the foibles of humankind.

---

1   Leafing through Plutarch's *Lives*, on a winter's day, I came upon the story of Xanthippus and his dog. It seems that the old Greek, fleeing Athens one time by ship, left his dog behind—or thought he left him behind. To his amazement and delight, the dog, in the finest whither-thou-goest tradition known to the animal kingdom, plunged into the sea and swam after the galley all the way to Salamis, a feat of which even a seal might well be proud. When the dog died, Xanthippus built a conspicuous tomb for it, high on a windy cliff, that men, infirm of purpose, weak of heart,

might be reminded of the miracles which can be wrought by courage, loyalty, and resolution.

2   Man first gained superiority over the other animals not because of his mind, but because of his fingers. He could pick up rocks and throw them, and he could wield a club. Later he developed the spear and the bow and arrow. It is my theory that the other animals, realizing they were as good as cooked if they came within range of Man's weapons, decided to make friends with him. He probably tried to make a pet and companion out of each species in turn. (It never occurred to him, in those days, to play or go hunting with Woman, a peculiarity which has persisted down to the present time.)

3   It did not take Man long—probably not more than a hundred centuries—to discover that all the animals except the dog were impossible around the house.[1] One has but to spend a few days with an aardvark or a llama, command a water buffalo to sit up and beg, or try to housebreak a moose, to perceive how wisely Man set about his process of elimination and selection. When the first man brought the first dog to his cave (no doubt over and above his wife's protests), there began an association by which Man has enormously profited. It is conceivable that the primordial male held the female, as mate or mother, in no aspect of esteem whatsoever, and that the introduction of the dog into the family circle first infected him with that benign disease known as love. Certain it is that the American male of today, in that remarkable period between infancy and adolescence, goes through a phase, arguably atavistic, during which he views mother, sister, and the little girl next door with cold indifference, if not, indeed, outspoken disdain, the while he lavishes wholehearted affection on Rex or Rover. In his grief over the loss of a dog, a little boy stands for the first time on tiptoe, peering into the rueful morrow of manhood. After this most inconsolable of sorrows, there is nothing life can do to him that he will not be able somehow to bear.

4   If Man has benefited immeasurably by his association with the dog, what, you may ask, has the dog got out of it? His scroll has, of course, been heavily charged with punishments: he has known the

---

[1] There is no deliberate intention here to offend admirers of the cat, although I don't really much care whether I do or not.

muzzle, the leash, and the tether; he has suffered the indignities of the show bench, the tin can on the tail, the ribbon in the hair; his love life with the other sex of his species has been regulated by the frigid hand of authority, his digestion ruined by the macaroons and marshmallows of doting women. The list of his woes could be continued indefinitely. But he has also had his fun, for he has been privileged to live with and study at close range the only creature with reason, the most unreasonable of creatures.

5   The dog has got more fun out of Man than Man has got out of the dog, for the clearly demonstrable reason that Man is the more laughable of the two animals. The dog has long been bemused by the singular activities and the curious practices of men, cocking his head inquiringly to one side, intently watching and listening to the strangest goings-on in the world. He has seen men sing together and fight one another in the same evening. He has watched them go to bed when it is time to get up, and get up when it is time to go to bed. He has observed them destroying the soil in vast areas, and nurturing it in small patches. He has stood by while men built strong and solid houses for rest and quiet, and then filled them with lights and bells and machinery. His sensitive nose, which can detect what's cooking in the next township, has caught at one and the same time the bewildering smells of the hospital and the munitions factory. He has seen men raise up great cities to heaven and then blow them to hell.

6   The effect upon the dog of his life with Man is discernible in his eyes, which frequently are capable of a greater range of expression than Man's. The eyes of the sensitive French poodle, for example, can shine with such an unalloyed glee and darken with so profound a gravity as to disconcert the masters of the earth, who have lost the key to so many of the simpler magics. Man has practiced for such a long time to mask his feelings and to regiment his emotions that some basic quality of naturalness has gone out of both his gaiety and his solemnity.

7   The dog is aware of this, I think. You can see it in his eyes sometimes when he lies and looks at you with a long, rueful gaze. He knows that the bare foot of Man has been too long away from the living earth, that he has been too busy with the construction of engines, which are, of all the things on earth, the farthest removed from the shape and intention of nature. I once owned a wise old

poodle who used to try to acquaint me with the real facts of living. It was too late, though. I would hastily turn on the radio or run out and take a ride in the car.

8   The dog has seldom been successful in pulling Man up to its level of sagacity, but Man has frequently dragged the dog down to his. He has instructed it in sloth, pride, and envy; he has made it, in some instances, neurotic; he has even taught it to drink. There once lived in Columbus, Ohio, on Franklin Avenue, a dog named Barge. He was an average kind of dog, medium in size and weight, ordinary in markings. His master and mistress and their two children made up a respectable middle-class family. Some of the young men in the neighborhood, however, pool-shooting, motorcycle-riding bravos, lured Barge into a saloon one day and set before him a saucer of beer. He lapped it up and liked it. From there it was but an easy step to whisky.

9   Barge was terribly funny, the boys thought, when he got stiff. He would bump into things, hiccup, grin foolishly, and even raise his muzzle on high in what passed for "Sweet Adeline." Barge's coat became shabby, his gait uncertain, and his eyes misty. He took to staying out in the town all night, raising hell. His duties as watchdog in the home of his owners were completely neglected. One night, when Barge was off on one of his protracted bats, burglars broke in and made off with his mistress' best silver and cut glass.

10   Barge, staggering home around noon of the next day, sniffed disaster when he was still a block away. His owners were waiting for him grimly on the front porch. They had not straightened up after the burglars. The sideboard drawers were pulled out, the floor littered with napkins and napkin rings. Barge's ears, chops, and tail fell as he was led sternly into the house to behold the result of his wicked way of life. He took one long, sad look around, and the cloudiness cleared from his head. He realized that he was not only a ne'er-do-well but a wrongo. One must guard the house at night, warn the family of fire, pull drowning infants out of the lake. These were the sacred trusts, the inviolable laws. Man had dragged Barge very far down, but there was still a spark of doghood left in him. He ran quickly and quietly upstairs, jumped out of an open window, and killed himself. This is a true and solemn legend of Franklin Avenue.

Questions About "Illustration"

1. What point does Thurber illustrate with the anecdote in paragraph 1?

2. How does he try to convince you that "Man first gained superiority over the other animals not because of his mind, but because of his fingers"?

3. What is Thurber's primary way of explaining in paragraph 4 what the dog has gotten out of his association with man?

4. How does he develop the idea in the first sentence of paragraph 5?

5. What is Thurber's purpose in introducing "the sensitive French poodle"?

6. What generalization does Thurber support by introducing the story of Barge?

Questions on Diction and Writing Techniques

1. Mark in your text those words that are new to you, but whose meaning you inferred from their context. Define them in your own words. Compare your definitions with those in your dictionary. Look up in your dictionary any other words that are new to you. Use the words in both groups in sentences.

2. What is the allusion in "whither-thou-goest" (par. 1)?

3. Underline the main or independent clause of sentence 3 of paragraph 1. Write a main clause. Then amplify it, as Thurber did his, by adding information in subordinate clauses.

4. What is the topic sentence of paragraph 4?

5. What is the function of "But" in paragraph 4?

6. To what word in paragraph 5 does "He" refer? What other pronoun refers to that word? Write a paragraph in which you use pronoun reference as a means of achieving coherence.

7. Instead of "bravos" (par. 8), Thurber might have written "men," "guys," or "fellows." Why did he choose the word he did?

8. Thurber might have written the first sentence of paragraph 9 "Barge was terribly funny when he got stiff, the boys thought." Which version do you prefer? Why?

9. Thurber uses slang in paragraph 9. Find two or more examples of it elsewhere in this essay. Are the words consistent with the diction of the rest of the essay? With the tone of the essay?

For Discussion, Reading, and Writing

1. Add one or more items to Thurber's list of the dog's woes.

2. Write a paragraph in which you illustrate people's treatment, good or bad, of any animal you are familiar with.

3. Using ample appropriate examples to explain your main idea, write a short essay about two people's treatment of one another.

4. If the idea appeals to you as the subject of a short essay, write about "the only creature with reason, the most unreasonable of creatures." Be sure to include ample examples to support your generalization(s).

Comparison and Contrast

"I can hit a ball as far as you can."
　"My brother can run as fast as your brother."
　"My sister is smarter than your sister."
　"I'm taller than you are."
　Almost from the time that children begin to talk they compare, show similarities, and contrast, point out differences. (Since "to compare" means to examine for the purpose of noting similarities *and* differences, I will from time to time use "comparison" to denote comparison *and* contrast.)

　When you bought a blue nylon long-sleeved shirt instead of a brown cotton short-sleeved one, when you decided to watch TV instead of going to a movie, when you elected to attend college A instead of college B—you used comparison. Your comparisons drew your attention to details and helped you to discover characteristics of things compared that you might not otherwise have been aware of. Your appreciation of one shirt was enhanced by comparing it with the other. Your decision to watch TV was made easier by comparing the benefits of doing so with those of attending a movie. And the virtues of college A became apparent only when you compared its facilities and opportunities with those of college B.

In your expository writing in college, you might use comparison to explain to your reader something unfamiliar by comparing it with something familiar, as, for example, George Orwell does in "Shooting an Elephant":

> It was a serious matter to shoot a working elephant—it is comparable to destroying a large and costly piece of machinery—and obviously one ought not to do it if it can possibly be avoided.

You might want to make clear what a kibbutz is by comparing it with a commune, or what a commune is by comparing it with a family. In doing so, you are likely to give your reader a better understanding of each of the things in your comparison.

You might also use comparison to help to make evident the superiority of one thing over another. You might want to show that a white-collar job is better paying than a blue-collar job, that being a teacher is more fulfilling than being a tax collector, or that the Democrats' plan for tax reform is more helpful to wage-earners in the lower income tax brackets than is that of the Republicans.

Still another purpose might be to arrive at a general principle, idea, or theme shared by the things compared. This would be the case if you were to examine the subjects known as the humanities to see what they have in common.

Regardless of your purpose, your choice of items to compare and to contrast should comply with the following formulas. Items to be contrasted may be ones with unlike characteristics; for example, you may contrast a plant to an animal. Items to be compared should be of the same general type and in a similar area of interest. A rickshaw and an Indy 500 racing car are both vehicles, but their purposes are so different that a useful comparison could hardly be made between them. One might, however, because the comparison would be illuminating and thus useful, compare a rickshaw with a horse and buggy and an Indy 500 racing car with a stock racing car competing on a track at a county fair.

Like illustration, comparison and contrast is a helpful method of organizing exposition, as you saw in Maya Angelou's "Cotton-picking Time" (pages 220–222). It can be used separately or together with one or more patterns of organization. In "Menial Jobs Taught Me a Lot" (pages 31–35), for example, although illustration is the predominant method of development, in the three paragraphs in the body of the essay the writer shows how his jobs were similar — "poorly paying, boring, and unfulfilling"—and is thus using comparison, along with illustration, to explain his thesis.

Observe how another writer uses contrast to develop the first half of a paragraph:

> Lenin, with whom I had a long conversation in Moscow in 1920, was, superficially, very unlike Gladstone, and yet, allowing for the difference of time and place and creed, the two men had much in common. To begin with the differences: Lenin was cruel, which Gladstone was not; Lenin had no respect for tradition, whereas Gladstone had a great deal; Lenin considered all means legitimate for securing the victory of his party, whereas for Gladstone politics was a game with certain rules that must be observed [Bertrand Russell, *Unpopular Essays*].

Notice, first of all, that Russell announces his method of paragraph development in his first, the topic, sentence. He proposes, he tells us, first to contrast: "Lenin . . . was . . . very unlike Gladstone"; then to compare: "the two men had much in common." In the second sentence, he contrasts the two men point by point, listing three points of dissimilarity: cruelty, respect for tradition, attitude toward politics. (Notice the use of "whereas" to signal one of the differences.)

Instead of contrasting point by point (sometimes called an alternating pattern), Russell might have first listed all the qualities of one man and then all the qualities of the other (sometimes called a divided or subject by subject pattern). This way of organizing the comparison requires the reader to remember or reread Lenin's qualities in order to compare them with Gladstone's:

> Lenin was cruel; he had no respect for tradition; he considered all means legitimate for securing the victory of his party. In contrast, Gladstone was not cruel; he had a great deal of respect for tradition; for him politics was a game with certain rules that must be observed.

Notice, in this version, the transitional expression "in contrast." Other expressions used to signal contrast are "on the other hand," "on the contrary," and "however." Some other transition words used to signal comparison are "likewise," "similarly," and "in a like manner."

Here is a full paragraph that is developed by use of contrast:

> As I pored over scouting reports and interviewed players and coaches from numerous NFL teams, it became clear that offensive football players like structure and discipline. They want to maintain the status quo. They tend to be conservative as people, and as football players they take comfort in repetitious practice of well-planned and well-executed plays. The defensive players, just as clearly, can't stand structure; their attitudes, their behavior, and their life-styles bear this out. They operate as though they've been put out of the tribe and are trying to show people that tribal structure is worthless anyway. Ostracism does not bother them; it serves as a source of fuel for their destructive energies. Rules or regulations put forward by anybody, anyplace, are to be challenged. Coaches find defensive players notably more difficult to control than their offensive teammates [Arnold J. Mandell, from *Saturday Review*, October 5, 1974].

Mandell first says all he has to say about offensive football players and then all he has to say about defensive players. Using this tactic, he reveals the qualities of one group by means of the qualities of the other just as Russell, using the point by point method, reveals the qualities of Lenin and Gladstone. In each case, comparison and contrast help us understand better the items the writer is trying to explain.

Here is a series of paragraphs that uses comparison *and* contrast effectively to explain the traits of two great Civil War generals:

> So Grant and Lee were in complete contrast, representing two diametrically opposed elements in American life. Grant was the modern man emerging; beyond him, ready to come on the stage, was the great age of steel and machinery, of crowded cities and a restless, burgeoning vitality. Lee might have ridden down from the old age of chivalry, lance in hand, silken banner fluttering over his head. Each man was the perfect champion of his cause, drawing both his strengths and his weaknesses from the people he led.

Yet it was not all contrast, after all. Different as they were—in background, in personality, in underlying aspiration—these two great soldiers had much in common. Under everything else, they were marvelous fighters. Furthermore, their fighting qualities were really very much alike.

Each man had, to begin with, the great virtue of utter tenacity and fidelity. Grant fought his way down the Mississippi Valley in spite of acute personal discouragement and profound military handicaps. Lee hung on in the trenches at Petersburg after hope itself had died. In each man there was an indomitable quality . . . the born fighter's refusal to give up as long as he can still remain on his feet and lift his two fists.

Daring and resourcefulness they had, too; the ability to think faster and move faster than the enemy. These were the qualities which gave Lee the dazzling campaigns of Second Manassas and Chancellorsville and won Vicksburg for Grant.

Lastly, and perhaps greatest of all, there was the ability, at the end, to turn quickly from war to peace once the fighting was over [Bruce Catton, "Grant and Lee: A Study in Contrasts"].

Like illustration and the other methods of organizing exposition to be considered farther on, comparison and contrast is a convenient way to order material in a paragraph or an essay.

THE DOG AND THE CAT
Konrad Z. Lorenz

Konrad Z. Lorenz, Austrian zoologist, reveals in **Man Meets Dog** (1953)—the source of this excerpt—the dedication to the study of animal behavior that won him the Nobel Prize for Physiology and Medicine in 1973, as well as the ability to report his findings simply and clearly.

Only two animals have entered the human household otherwise than as prisoners and become domesticated by other means than those of enforced servitude: the dog and the cat. Two things they have in common, namely, that both belong to the order of carnivores and both serve man in their capacity of hunters. In all other characteristics, above all in the manner of their association with man, they are as different as the night from the day. There is no domestic animal which has so rapidly altered its whole way of living, indeed its whole sphere of interests, that has become domestic in so true a sense as the dog: and there is no animal that, in the course of its century-old association with man, has altered so little as the cat. There is some truth in the assertion that the cat, with the exception of a few luxury breeds, such as Angoras, Persians and Siamese, is no domestic animal but a completely wild being. Maintaining its full independence it has taken up its abode in the houses and outhouses of man, for the simple reason that there are more mice there than elsewhere. The whole charm of the dog lies in the depth of the friendship and the strength of the spiritual ties with which he has bound himself to man, but the appeal of the cat lies in the very fact that she has formed no close bond with him, that she has the uncompromising independence of a tiger or a leopard while she is hunting in his stables and barns; that she still remains mysterious and remote when she is rubbing herself gently against the legs of her mistress or purring contentedly in front of the fire. The purring cat is, for me, a symbol of the hearthside and the hidden security which it stands for. I should no more like to be without a cat in my home than to be without the dog that trots behind me in field or street. Since my earliest youth I have always had dogs and cats about me, and it is about them that I shall talk in this book. Business-like friends have advised me to write a dog-book and a cat-book separately, because dog-lovers often dislike cats and cat-lovers frequently abhor dogs. But I consider it the finest test of genuine love and understanding of animals if a person has sympathies for both these creatures, and can appreciate in each its own special virtues.

Questions About "Comparison and Contrast"

1.   How, according to Lorenz, are the dog and the cat alike?

2. How, according to Lorenz, do dogs and cats differ?

3. Do comparison and contrast help Lorenz to explain to you each animal's features? If so, how?

Questions on Diction and Writing Techniques

1. Lorenz might have written his first sentence like this: "Only two animals, the dog and the cat, have entered the human household otherwise than as prisoners and become domesticated by other means than those of enforced servitude." Why did he write the sentence as he did?

2. What does "namely" signal?

3. How does your dictionary define "carnivores"?

4. In the sentence beginning "The whole charm of the dog," what is the function of "but"?

5. What is the connotation (see page 74) of "hearthside" to Lorenz?

6. Lorenz might have used "characteristics" in lieu of "virtues." How do the words differ in meaning? Use each in a sentence.

For Discussion, Reading, and Writing

1. Fill the blanks in this passage from memory to make it intelligible:

   Only two animals have entered the human household other-wise than as _____ and become _____ by other means than those of enforced _____: the dog and the cat. Two things they have in common, namely, that both belong to the order of carnivores and both _____ man in their capacity of

   _____.

   Compare your words with those in Lorenz's paragraph.

2. Use comparison and contrast in a paragraph to explain the characteristics of any two animals or plants that you are familiar with.

3. Write a paragraph or two comparing and contrasting things such as two

Cars

Musical instruments

Athletes

TV shows

Beverages

Rock groups

===

A GLIMPSE OF WHAT IT WAS
Charles Kuralt

Charles Kuralt is an award-winning CBS News reporter and author of its **On the Road** and **Dateline America** series.

---

1   That irrepressible old tourist, Mark Twain, walked up the mountain from Carson City carrying an ax and a couple of blankets to take a look at Lake Tahoe and found it worth the climb.

2   "As it lay there," he wrote, "with the shadows of the mountains brilliantly photographed upon its still surface, I thought it must surely be the fairest picture the whole earth affords."

3   That was 115 years ago. Today there is smog about the lake.

4   "So singularly clear was the water," Mark Twain wrote, "that even where it was 80 feet deep, the bottom was perfectly distinct. . . . The water was not merely transparent, but dazzlingly, brilliantly so."

5   Today brown smudges muddy the water hundreds of yards out into the lake, the runoff from the towns on shore.

6   "Three miles away," Mark Twain wrote, "was a sawmill and some workmen, but there were not 15 other human beings throughout the wide circumference of the lake. . . . We did not see a human being but ourselves."

7   This afternoon fifteen people can be found at any crap table at Lake Tahoe. There is no such thing as solitude here, and never again will there be.

8   "We liked the appearance of the place," Mark Twain wrote, "and so we claimed some three hundred acres of it and stuck our notices on a tree. We were landowners now."

9   Here is an ad from this week's *San Francisco Chronicle*: "3.7 acres on Lake Tahoe, 4-bedroom house, 2-car garage, 200 feet lake frontage, $525,000."

10   Looking at what Lake Tahoe has become makes you want to turn back to Mark Twain for a glimpse of what it was.

11   "Lake Tahoe," he wrote, "would restore an Egyptian mummy to his pristine vigor and give him an appetite like an alligator. I do not mean the oldest and driest mummies, of course, but the fresher ones. The air up there in the clouds is very pure and fine, bracing and delicious. And why shouldn't it be?—it is the same the angels breathe."

12   Ah, Mark, the angels have moved. The condominium salesmen have taken their place.

Questions About "Comparison and Contrast"

1. Where, in this essay, does Kuralt first make clear to you what his main pattern of organization will be?

2. Show how Kuralt's choice of comparison and contrast relates to his expository purpose. What other patterns of organization does he use?

3. Does Kuralt succeed in his purpose? Explain, making specific reference to the text.

Questions on Diction and Writing Techniques

1. Explain whether paragraph 12 is a fitting conclusion to this essay.

2. State in your own words, in a sentence of not over twenty-five words, the point that Kuralt is trying to get across to you.

For Discussion, Reading, and Writing

1. For the benefit of a friend, contrast, in a short essay, the best place and the worst place to vacation you know of.

2. Compare and contrast, in a short essay, a walk in a place such as a large city with a walk in a place such as a state or national park.

TRAVELLING IN WHITE MAN'S STYLE
Farley Mowat

Farley Mowat, Canadian author, has written many books about the lands, seas, and peoples of the Far North. **People of the Deer** (1952), the source of this passage, tells of his experiences with and observation of the Ihalmiut, a nearly extinct group of Eskimos.

1   Summer, which follows spring so closely that the two are almost one, was upon us before it was possible to travel to the shores of Ootek's Lake and meet the People. I had arranged with Franz to take me there while Hans and the children were to remain at Windy Bay to feed the dogs we left behind, and to care for the camp.

₂   As Franz and I prepared for the journey north, I was excited and at the same time depressed. Much as I wished to meet the Ihalmiut in their own land, the fragmentary glimpses of their lives that I had from Franz had left me with a strong feeling of unease at the prospect of meeting them face to face. I wondered if they would have any conception as to how much of their tragedy they owed to men of my color, and I wondered if, like the northern Indians, they would be a morose and sullen lot, resentful of my presence, suspicious and uncommunicative.

₃   Even if they welcomed me into their homes, I was still afraid of my own reactions. The prospect of seeing and living with a people who knew starvation as intimately as I knew plenty, the idea of seeing with my own eyes this disintegrating remnant of a dying race, left me with a sensation closely akin to fear.

₄   We could not make the journey northward by canoe, for the raging streams which had cut across the Barrens only a few weeks before were now reduced to tiny creeks whose courses were interrupted by jumbled barriers of rock. No major rivers flowed the way we wished to go, and so the water routes were useless to us. Since the only alternative was a trek overland, we prepared to go on foot, as the Ihalmiut do.

₅   But there was a difference. The Ihalmiut travel light, and a man of the People crossing the open plains in summer carries little more than his knife, a pipe, and perhaps a spare pair of skin boots called *kamik*. He eats when he finds something to eat. There are usually suckers in the shrunken streams, and these can sometimes be caught with the hands. Or if the suckers are too hard to find, the traveller can take a length of rawhide line and snare the orange-colored ground squirrels on the sandy esker slopes. In early summer there are always eggs, or flightless birds, and if the eggs are nearly at the hatching point, so much the better.

₆   Franz and I, on the other hand, travelled in white man's style. We were accompanied by five dogs and to each dog we fastened a miniature Indian travois — two long thin poles that stretched behind to support a foot-square platform on which we could load nearly thirty pounds of gear that included bedrolls, ammunition, cooking tools, and presents of flour and tobacco for the Eskimos. With this equipment we were also able to carry a little tent, and food for the dogs and ourselves: deer meat for them, and flour, tea, and baking

powder for us. We had more than the bare essentials, but we had
to pay a stiff price for them.

7   Equipped with pack dogs, it took us better than a week to
cover the same sixty miles that the Ihalmiut cross in two days and a
night. I shall not soon forget the tortures of that march. While the
sun shone, the heat was as intense as it is in the tropics, for the clarity of the Arctic air does nothing to soften the sun's rays. Yet we
were forced to wear sweaters and even caribou skin jackets. The flies
did that to us. They rose from the lichens at our feet until they
hung like a malevolent mist about us and took on the appearance of
a low-lying cloud. *Milugia* (black flies) and *kiktoriak* (mosquitoes)
came in such numbers that their presence actually gave me a feeling
of physical terror. There was simply no evading them. The bleak
Barrens stretched into emptiness on every side, and offered no escape and no surcease. To stop for food was torture and to continue
the march in the overwhelming summer heat was worse. At times a
kind of insanity would seize us and we would drop everything and
run wildly in any direction until we were exhausted. But the pursuing hordes stayed with us and we got nothing from our frantic
efforts except a wave of sweat that seemed to attract even more
mosquitoes.

8   From behind our ears, from beneath our chins, a steady dribble
of blood matted into our clothing and trapped the insatiable flies until we both wore black collars composed of their struggling bodies.
The flies worked down under our shirts until our belts stopped
them. Then they fed about our waists until the clothing stuck to us
with drying blood.

9   The land we were passing over offered no easy routes to com-
pensate for the agonies the flies inflicted upon us. It was rolling
country, and across our path ran a succession of mounding hills
whose sides and crests were strewn with angular rocks and with
broken fragments filling the interstices between the bigger boulders.
On these our boots were cut and split and our feet bruised until it
was agony to walk at all. But at that the hills were better walking
than the broad wet valleys which lay in between.

10   Each valley had its own stream flowing down its center.
Though those streams were often less than five feet in width, they
seemed to be never less than five feet in depth. The valley floors
were one continuous mattress of wet moss into which we sank up

to our knees until our feet found the perpetual ice that lay underneath. Wading and stumbling through the icy waters of the muskegs, floundering across streams or around the countless ponds (all of whose banks were undercut and offered no gradual descent), we would become numbed from the waist down, while our upper bodies were bathed in sweat. If, as happened for three solid days, it rained, then we lived a sodden nightmare as we crossed those endless bogs.

11   I am not detailing the conditions of summer travel in order to emphasize my own discomforts but to illustrate the perfectly amazing capacity of the Ihalmiut as travellers. Over sixty miles of such country, the People could move with ease, yes, and with comfort, bridging the distance in less than two days of actual walking. And they, mind you, wore only paper-thin boots of caribou skin on their feet. It is not that they are naturally impervious to discomfort, but simply that they have adjusted their physical reactions to meet the conditions they must face. They have bridged the barriers of their land not by levelling them, as we would try to do, but by conforming to them. It is like the difference between a sailing vessel and one under power, when you compare an Ihalmio and a white traveller, in the Barrens. The white man, driven by his machine instincts, always lives at odds with his environment; like a motor vessel he bucks the winds and the seas and he is successful only while the intricate apparatus built about him functions perfectly. But the Barrens People are an integral part of *their* environment. Like sailing ships, they learn to move with wind and water; to mold themselves to the rhythm of the elements and so accomplish gently and without strain the things that must be done.

Questions About "Comparison and Contrast"

1. What is Mowat's purpose in "detailing the conditions of summer travel" in the Far North?

2. By what means does he signal to you that he intends to contrast the style of travel of a man of the People with that of the white man?

3. What phrase in paragraph 6 does Mowat use to signal a contrast?

4. How does Mowat's contrast of a sailing vessel with one under power (par. 11) relate to his purpose?

5. Does Mowat convince you of the adaptability of the Barrens People to their environment? Explain.

Questions on Diction and Writing Techniques

1. Underline in your text those words that are new to you, but whose meaning you inferred from their context. Define them in your own words. Compare your definitions with those in your dictionary. Look up in your dictionary any other words that are new to you. Use the words in both groups in sentences.

2. Why does Mowat tell you the meaning of "travois" (par. 6)?

3. What is Mowat's purpose in writing the five-word sentence in paragraph 5? What effect does it have on you?

For Discussion, Reading, and Writing

1. Which of the following, according to Mowat, are true (T), which false (F)?

    A. _____ As he prepared for the journey he was excited and at the same time depressed.

    B. _____ Mowat and Franz couldn't make the journey northward by canoe because the major rivers were reduced to tiny creeks.

    C. _____ It took the white men three or four times as long as it did the Ihalmiut to cover the same sixty miles.

    D. _____ The Barrens People are an integral part of their environment.

    E. _____ The People are naturally impervious to discomfort.

2. Compare and contrast, in a short essay, any two modes of traveling that you are familiar with.

SMALL KICKS IN SUPERLAND
Russell Baker

Russell Baker's keen, wide-ranging, humorous commentary
on humankind and its institutions, regular features in his
"Observer" column in **The New York Times**, where this essay
first appeared, have earned him the George Polk and Pulitzer
prizes.

1   I often go to the supermarket for the pure fun of it, and I suspect a lot of other people do too. The supermarket fills some of the
same needs the neighborhood saloon used to satisfy. There you can
mix with neighbors when you are lonely, or feeling claustrophobic
with family, or when you simply feel the urge to get out and be
part of the busy, interesting world.

2   As in the old neighborhood saloon, something is being sold,
and this helps clothe the visit in wholesome material purpose. The
national character tends to fear acts performed solely for pleasure;
even our sexual hedonists usually justify themselves with the
thought that they are doing a higher duty to social reform or mental hygiene.

3   It is hard to define the precise pleasures of the supermarket.
Unlike the saloon, it does not hold out promise of drugged senses
commonly considered basic to pleasure.

4   There is, to be sure, the brilliant color of the fruit-and-vegetable
department to lift the spirit out of gray January's wearies, provided
you do not look at the prices.

5   There are fantastic riches of pointless variety to make the
mind delight in the excess that is America. In my neighborhood
supermarket, for example, there are twenty or thirty yards of nothing but paper towels of varying colors, patterns and thicknesses.

6   What an amazing country that can make it so hard for a man

to choose among things designed for the purpose of being thrown away!

7   The people, however, are the real lure. As in the traditional saloon, there are many who seem determined to leave nothing for anybody else. These sources prowl the aisles with carts overflowing with excesses of consumption. Twenty pounds of red meat, back-breaking cartons of powdered soap, onions wrapped lovingly in molded plastic, peanut butter by the hundredweight, cake mixes, sugar, oils, whole pineapples, wheels of cheese, candied watermelon rind, preserved camel humps from Persia . . .

8   Groaning and sweating, they heave their tonnage up to the checker, see it packaged in a forest's worth of paper bags and, the whole now reassembled as a tower of bags pyramided on another cart, they stagger off to their cars, drained of their wealth but filled with pride in their awesome capacity for consumption.

9   At times, seeing such a customer trying to buy up the whole supermarket, one is tempted to say, "Come now, my good woman, you've had enough for the day." Unfortunately, the ambience of supermarkets does not encourage verbal exchanges. In this it is inferior to the saloon.

10   Urban people, of course, are terribly scared nowadays. They may yearn for society, but it is risky to go around talking to strangers, for a lot of reasons, one being that people are so accustomed not to have many human contacts that they are afraid they may find out they really prefer life that way.

11   Whatever the reason, they go to the supermarket to be with people, but not to talk with people. The rule seems to be, you can look but you can't speak. Ah, well, most days there is a good bit to see. The other day in my own supermarket, for example, there was a woman who was sneakily lifting the cardboard lids on Sara Lee frozen coffee cakes and peeking under, eyeball to coffee cake, to see if—what?

12   Could she have misplaced something? Did she suspect that the contents were not as advertised? Whatever her purpose, she didn't buy.

13   Another woman was kneading a long package of white bread with her fingertips, rather like a doctor going over an abdomen for a yelp of pain that might confirm appendicitis. I had seen those silly women in the television commercial squeeze toilet paper, and so

was prepared for almost anything, but this medical examination of the bread was startling.

14   The woman, incidentally, did not buy. She left the store without a single purchase. This may have been because she looked at the "express checkout" line, saw that it would take forty-five minutes to pay for her bread and decided bread was not worth the wait.

15   (I am making a study of how supermarkets invariably manage to make the "express checkout" line the slowest in the store, and will report when interviews are completed.)

16   I suspect that woman who left empty-handed never intended to buy. I think she had simply become lonely sitting alone in her flat, or had begun to feel claustrophobic perhaps with her family, and had decided to go out to the supermarket and knead a loaf of white bread for the pure fun of feeling herself part of the great busy world.

Questions About "Comparison and Contrast"

1. What is the question to which Baker's essay purports to be an answer?

2. In how many ways, according to Baker, are the saloon and the supermarket alike? How do they differ?

3. Explain how Baker's comparison and contrast of the one with the other serves his expository purpose.

Questions on Diction and Writing Techniques

1. Underline in your text those words that are new to you, but whose meaning you inferred from their context. Define them in your own words. Compare your definitions with those in your dictionary. Look up in your dictionary any other words that are new to you. Use the words in both groups in sentences.

2. Why does Baker write "prowl" (par. 7) and "stagger" (par. 8)? What other verbs might he have chosen? Which do you prefer? Why?

3. There is one simile in this essay. What is its function?

4. What does the word "however" (par. 7) signal to you?

5. In paragraph 5, Baker writes "for example." Where else in the essay does Baker use the words for a similar reason?

6. What language that Baker uses in paragraph 1 does he repeat in paragraph 16?

7. Do you find this essay easy to read and to understand? Why?

For Discussion, Reading, and Writing

1. What are the needs that the neighborhood saloon used to satisfy?

2. What in the supermarket, according to Baker, does not encourage verbal exchanges?

3. Fill the blanks in this passage from memory to make it intelligible:

    Whatever the reason, they go to the supermarket to _____ with people, but not to _____ with people. The rule seems to be, you can _____ but you can't _____. Ah, well, most days there is a good bit to _____. The other day in my own supermarket, for example, there was a woman who was sneakily _____ the cardboard lids on Sara Lee frozen coffee cakes and _____ under, eyeball to coffee cake, to see if—what?

    Compare your words with those in paragraph 11.

Definition

TO communicate with a reader, a writer must choose language that clearly conveys what he or she is trying to say. To use words that are vague and words that are ambiguous is to risk putting meaning in doubt. When a word might mean one thing to the writer and another to the reader, it is useful for the writer to explain what he or she means.

To avoid misunderstanding between you and your readers, you may find it necessary to explain what you mean by words you use. "Liberal" and "conservative" have no commonly accepted definition because different people use the terms to convey different ideas. Thus if you were to write an essay on the topic "Is Ronald Reagan a Liberal or a Conservative?" you would do well to make sure that you explain to your readers what you mean by "liberal" and "conservative." You would want to define these terms early in your essay, and clearly.

Such an essay might be organized in this way:

1. *Opening paragraph:* A statement of your purpose—to deter-

mine whether the President might properly be termed "liberal" or "conservative."

2. *Paragraph 2:* A definition of "liberal," using as many methods as seem necessary to make your meaning clear.

3. *Paragraph 3:* A definition of "conservative."

4. *Paragraphs 4 and 5:* Examples of Mr. Reagan's acts that convince you that one or the other of the two terms would more appropriately be applicable to him.

5. *Concluding paragraph:* Summary and conclusion. Thesis: "The President is a liberal"; or "The President is a conservative."

Defining "liberal" and "conservative" and classifying the President's acts in those categories would be the focus of your writing effort. The words would dictate the pattern of your studies and the area and extent of your research. They would lead you to a discovery of your thesis. They would also indicate a likely manner of arranging your information to best achieve your ultimate purpose: a clear explanation of the main idea.

One obvious advantage of explaining vague words, words that cannot be understood in a clear and specific way, and ambiguous words, words that can be understood in more than one sense, is to facilitate communication. There is another benefit. You may not be fully aware that your understanding of a term is fuzzy, even though it is. In the process of defining it for your readers' sake, you will make it clear to yourself as well.

You know from your studies with what precision terms in mathematics and the sciences are defined:

Triangle: a closed plane figure having three sides and three angles.

Test tube: a hollow cylinder of thin glass with one end closed, used in chemical and biological laboratories.

Other words can be defined precisely, in the same way:

Aquatics: sports practiced on or in water.

Wax: a solid, yellowish substance secreted by bees.

Blue jeans: a garment made of stout twilled cotton fabric.

These are known as *formal definitions.* In each instance the term defined was put in a general class and then differentiated from other members of the class, as in these illustrations:

TERM	CLASS	DIFFERENTIATION
Dime	is a silver coin	of the U.S., the 10th part of a dollar, equal to 10 cents.
Dike	is an embankment	for controlling the waters of the sea or a river.
House	is a building	in which people live.

When, to clarify the meaning of a term you use in your writing, you find it useful to give a formal definition, you should follow the procedure in the examples of formal definition just given.

Sometimes a writer may assume that readers have some knowledge of a term and thus may define the term by naming *examples* of it that they may be expected to be familiar with:

Contact sports such as ice hockey and football . . .

A felony, for example, burglary . . .

A Gothic novel like Ann Radcliffe's *The Mysteries of Udolfo* . . .

Another way to define a term is by the use of a *synonym,* a word having the same or nearly the same meaning:

Pal: a companion, a chum

Film: a motion picture, a movie

Lexicon: a word book, a dictionary

Another way still to define a term is by giving its *etymology,* or derivation, which is found in a dictionary, as in this instance where the writer had an appropriate occasion and audience for using this method:

I believe a liberal education is an education in the root meaning of "liberal" — "liber" — "free" — the liberty of the mind free to explore itself, to draw itself out, to connect with other minds and spirits in the quest for truth. Its goal is to train the whole person to be at once intellectually discerning and humanly flexible, tough-minded and open-hearted; to be responsive to the new and responsible for values that make us civilized. It is to teach us to meet what is new and different with reasoned judgment and humanity. A liberal education is an education for freedom, the freedom to assert the liberty of the mind to make itself new for the others it cherishes.

The audience was the incoming class of freshmen, Yale '85; the writer, A. Bartlett Giamatti, president of Yale University.

Extended definition, whose essential characteristic is its relative elaborateness, is an important means of developing a paragraph or an entire essay. It is especially useful in explaining an uncommon term — whether newly coined or not — or an abstract term. Gail Sheehy uses extended definition to make clear what she means by the expression "jailbreak marriage" (pages 153–154).

John Kenneth Galbraith, in this example of a relatively short extended definition, explains the meaning of a phrase he coined, which has since come into widespread use:

Because familiarity is such an important test of acceptability, the acceptable ideas have great stability. They are highly predictable. It will be convenient to have a name for the ideas which are esteemed at any time for their acceptability. I shall refer to these ideas henceforth as *the conventional wisdom* [John Kenneth Galbraith, *The Affluent Society*].

Having explained what he meant by the term, Galbraith was free to and in fact did use "the conventional wisdom" often in his book without confusing his readers.

Here is an example of the use of extended definition to explain an abstract term, "erotic love":

Brotherly love is love among equals; motherly love is love for the helpless. Different as they are from each other, they have in common that they are by their very nature not restricted to one person. If I love my brother, I love all my brothers; if I love my child, I love all my children; no, beyond that, I love all children, all that are in need of my help. In contrast to both types of love is *erotic love*; it is the craving for complete fusion, for union with one other person. It is by its very nature exclusive and not universal; it is also perhaps the most deceptive form of love there is [Erich Fromm, *The Art of Loving*].

The writer first explains what erotic love is by *differentiation*, showing what it is *not*; it is, he says, *different* from brotherly love and motherly love. In the next-to-last sentence, he gives a formal definition of his term. In the concluding sentence, Fromm elaborates on the definition and on the rest of the paragraph.

The kinds of words that you are most likely to find in need of definition are:

General words: democracy, freedom, human rights

Newly coined terms: black power, common market, hard hat

Words that imply an opinion: free society, happy marriage, beautiful people

Language peculiar to a particular trade, profession, or group: binary fission, differential gear, write-off, meltdown

Metaphorical phrases: bamboo curtain, spring fever

Even terms whose meanings we assume are clear to ourselves and our readers may usefully be explained, as in the first paragraph of the first chapter of *This Fascinating Animal World* by Alan Devoe:

Perhaps the easiest way to put it, in a rough nontechnical fashion, is to say that animals are all of earth's living creatures that are not plants. An animal is a being able to make locomotor movements and perform actions that appear to be what we call voluntary. It shows a certain quickness and "aliveness" in its responses to stimulation. It ingests and digests foods consisting of other animals or plants, and it doesn't contain chlorophyll or perform photosynthesis. Not every animal need meet every one of the requirements; but in a general way this is the stuff of the definition.

In the first sentence Devoe gives a formal definition; he puts the term to be defined ("animals") into a class ("earth's living creatures") and then differentiates ("that are not plants"). In the rest of the paragraph, to further clarify his meaning, he amplifies how animals differ from plants.

In the second paragraph, Devoe extends his definition further:

> Where the higher animals are concerned—a deer, say, or a raccoon or a squirrel—an animals' animality of course seems abundantly obvious, and a need for definition may appear a little absurd. But the kingdom of the animals runs right down to the roots of things. There are animals that consist of only a single cell. There are animals in which there is scarcely discoverable any distinct nervous system; and there are plant forms that look, at least to casual observation, a good deal livelier than these developed animals. Down in the very lowest life levels, in the elementary ooze, so to speak, of the creation, animals and plants are so almost indistinguishably alike that it seems hardly possible that the one line leads to oaks and redwoods and the other one to rabbits and foxes.

Here Devoe adds to his clarification of the meaning of "animal" by adding to his formal definition examples of the term as well as by comparing and contrasting "animal" with "plant."

Each of the methods of defining may be combined with one or more other methods. Recall the definition of "inference" on page 119. Now read it in the complete passage as originally written by Hayakawa in *Language in Thought and Action:*

> An inference, as we shall use the term, is a statement about the unknown made on the basis of the known. We may infer from the material and cut of a woman's clothes her wealth or social position; we may infer from the character of the ruins the origin of the fire that destroyed the building; we may infer from a man's calloused hands the nature of his occupation; we may infer from a senator's vote on an armaments bill his attitude toward Russia; we may infer from the structure of the land the path of a prehistoric glacier; we may infer from a halo on an unexposed photographic plate its past proximity to radioactive materials; we may infer from the sound of an engine the condition of its connecting rods.

Inferences may be carefully or carelessly made. They may be made on the basis of a broad background of previous experience with the subject matter or with no experience at all. For example, the inferences a good mechanic can make about the internal condition of a motor by listening to it are often startlingly accurate, while the inferences made by an amateur (if he tries to make any) may be entirely wrong. But the common characteristic of inferences is that they are statements about matters which are not directly known, made on the basis of what has been observed.

Hayakawa uses formal definition and examples to make the meaning of "inference" abundantly clear.

HOW INTELLIGENT IS ROVER?

Felicia Ames

Felicia Ames is the pseudonym of Jean Burden, author, editor, award-winning poet, and lecturer on poetry at numerous universities.

1   Mr. and Mrs. Isenberg will never forget that day in Scarsdale, New York, and the intelligence of their three-year-old beagle, Snooper. They had gone shopping and had locked the dog in the car. Returning from the store, all heaven broke loose on them and they found themselves at the mercy of a torrential rain. It was then that they discovered they had locked more than Snooper in the car; they had no keys. The dog went to work and, with very little coaxing from the drenched pair, lifted the door lock with his teeth.

2   "How intelligent are dogs?" is a frequent question. Many

owners believe absolutely that Rover or Fido or Schroeder has to be the smartest animal this side of a primate and there are some who won't stop there. On the other hand, quite a number of authorities feel that what passes for intelligence in canines is nothing more than cleverness, an ability to learn by rote or imitation.

3 We have to agree that cleverness is a better word for dogs who can stand on one leg or bow-wow to ninety. We are oversaturated with pictures of dogs swimming, diving, climbing trees and catching anything from fly balls to frisbees. Clever are those pets, too, who pose with cigar in mouth, nautical hat atop head and spectacles over eyes. And, of course, all those dogs who can roll over, play dead or jump through a flaming hoop.

4 Something other than cleverness, though, must account for dogs who have been known to find their way across strange and rugged miles, back to a house whence they roamed or were removed, often long before. This trait—not all dogs reveal it—is mostly labeled the homing instinct or built-in radar, but no one has ever been able to explain it.

5 There is also the dog who, finding himself lost, determines to stay by a bit of his owner's clothing, often for days, apparently knowing that there is a chance of the owner's return.

6 Judgment reflects intelligence and many dogs are capable of making decisions. For example, consider any seeing-eye dog. If he stopped when the light turned red and moved on green, it might be possible to assume, first that he was trained to react to light changes and, secondly, that he wasn't color blind. But we have yet to observe any of these dogs who allow the light to be their only cue for action. Invariably, the dog will watch the traffic, in all directions, as well as any pedestrians nearby, before determining whether to wait or lead his master across the intersection.

7 A story involving an English seeing-eye dog and his master really does much to prove that dogs possess keen intelligence. The dog, named Kim, was taken suddenly ill while walking with his master in the city. Deliberately disobeying his master's pressures on the lead—the man was en route to an appointment—the dog went, instead, to a veterinarian whom he knew to have an office nearby. After the doctor had treated him for a severe stomach distress, he went on to help his master keep the appointment.

8 Another story we like involved another English guide dog.

Simba was her name and she was a three-year-old Alsatian. Every day, in her house in Kent, she led Minky downstairs and then opened the door to let her outside. Minky was a seven-year-old spaniel. The owner of the two dogs, Esme Bidlake, said: "As soon as Minky went blind, Simba seemed to sense it and, with no training from me, started guiding the little spaniel about the house. She even leads Minky to her feeding bowl and sits beside her while she has her meal." When the dogs went out for a walk, Simba held onto Minky's ear, waited for traffic to pass, then gently escorted her across the road, still holding her ear.

9   Dogs have long been respected for their ability to hear and smell. But it also required some intelligence for a dog named Schmutz to rescue a man buried under an avalanche in the Swiss Alps. The man reported later that he could hear his would-be rescuers digging with their shovels. He screamed to them to keep digging, but they didn't hear him. The dog did hear him and went on digging after the men had abandoned the search. Fourteen others were eventually rescued from the same avalanche, thanks to the hearing of a dog and his intelligence to sense danger.

10   Another dog with a sense of danger and the intelligence to act was Spooky, a two-year-old pit bull terrier. The dog observed an injured sea gull struggling about a hundred yards offshore of Hutchinson Island, Florida. The dog's owner watched as the dog climbed down a bridge construction site, swam the distance, grabbed the gull in his mouth and brought it to shore without ruffling a feather. The owner freed a fishing lure that had been hooked from the beak of the bird to its wing, and the gull was able to fly away.

11   For clinching arguments, though, there are Prince, a four-year-old Cockapoo in Los Angeles and a moonshine dog in McNairy County, West Tennessee. The owner of the latter used to operate a still and was in the habit of hiding his product. Since he was either drunk when he hid the stuff or drunk when he went to find it, the poor man never knew quite where to go. But the dog did. Confronted with a sale, the moonshiner would indicate with his fingers how many pint bottles the transaction required and the dog would do the rest. There was one problem. The man would become very ugly and offensive with too much to drink. When this happened, the dog would leave home and stay away until his boss was sober. This never lasted too long, of course, because the boss could never

remember where he stashed the hootch. We never did find out if the dog took a drink, but we presume he was too smart for that.

12   As for Prince, the Los Angeles cocker and poodle cross, his thing is cigarettes. He hates them with such abandon that his owner wonders whether he might be of some use to the American Cancer Society. We're not sure how many people have given up smoking because of Prince, but we know that there isn't one smoker who dares practice his habit in the dog's presence. Ever since he was a pup, says his owner, Margaret Eiden, he's been curling his lip whenever he sees a cigarette being lit. If the lighter of the weed persists and takes a drag, Prince emits a low, horrifying snarl. If the dragger drags on, the dog goes into a crouch that can only spell kill. No one, needless to say, pushes at that point for another puff.

13   A dog with a cause, and more intelligent than many of us, it seems.

Questions About "Definition"

1. Why is it necessary for Ames to explain what she means by intelligence in dogs?

2. What purpose is served by Ames' explanation of what she means by cleverness in dogs? What method(s) does she use to define the term?

3. What method(s) of definition does she use to make clear to you what she means by intelligence in dogs?

4. Does Ames fulfill her purpose in writing this essay? Explain.

Questions on Diction and Writing Techniques

1. Match each item in Column A with the word closest in meaning to it in Column B:

Column A	Column B
torrential	soaked
by rote	rumpling

Column A	Column B
saturated	from memory
avalanche	violent
ruffling	snowslide

Use in a sentence each word or term in Column A.

2. How useful to Ames' purpose is paragraph 1?

3. What does "on the other hand" (par. 2) signal? Find two or more other examples of Ames' use of transition words. Explain in each instance her reason for using the word(s).

4. As an alternative to paragraph 13, write your own concluding paragraph for this essay.

For Discussion, Reading, and Writing

1. Which of these statements, according to Ames, are true (T), which false (F)?

    A. _____ Snooper is clever.

    B. _____ Quite a number of authorities feel that what passes for cleverness in canines is nothing more than intelligence.

    C. _____ An example of intelligence in dogs is the ability to catch frisbees.

    D. _____ No one has been able to explain dogs' homing in- stinct or built-in radar.

    E. _____ Judgment reflects intelligence.

    F. _____ Kim, taken ill suddenly, disobeyed his master's pres- sures on the lead but, nonetheless, after going to a veterinarian for treatment, went on to help his master keep an appointment.

    G. _____ A dog named Schmutz dug out a man buried in an avalanche in the Swiss Alps.

    H. _____ Spooky brought a gull to shore without a feather.

I. _____ Prince's thing is cigarettes.

J. _____ The moonshine dog would leave home and stay away until his boss was sober.

2. Find a term that best fits a characteristic of any animals, including persons, you are familiar with—for example, the curiosity of cats. Write a short essay in which you make clear to your reader the appropriateness of applying the term to them.

GETTING PERSONAL: AD HOMINEM
Stuart Chase

Stuart Chase has written on a variety of subjects, most frequently on economics and matters relating to it. He is the author of **The Tyranny of Words** (1938), chiefly concerned with the misuse of language, and **Guides to Straight Thinking** (1956), the source of this excerpt.

1   The classic example of this fallacy is a scene in a British court of law. As the attorney for the defense takes the floor, his partner hands him a note: "No case. Abuse the plaintiff's attorney."

2   If you can't shake the argument, abuse the person who advances it, and so discredit it through the back door. Go from facing the issue, which jurists call *ad rem*, to the man, *ad hominem*.

3   A story is told about Lincoln as a young lawyer. In one of his first jury cases, he showed his political shrewdness by an adroit and quite non-malicious use of *ad hominem*. His opponent was an experienced trial lawyer, who also had most of the fine legal points on his side. The day was warm and Lincoln slumped in his chair as the case went against him. When the orator took off his coat and vest,

however, Lincoln sat up with a gleam in his eye. His opponent was wearing one of the new city-slicker shirts of the 1840's, which buttoned up the back.

4   Lincoln knew the reactions of frontiersmen, who made up the jury. When his turn came, his plea was brief: "Gentlemen of the jury, because I have justice on my side, I am sure you will not be influenced by this gentleman's pretended knowledge of the law. Why, he doesn't even know which side of his shirt ought to be in front!"

5   Lincoln's *ad hominem* is said to have won the case.

6   This fallacy, like over-generalizing, has been around for a long time. The Sophists must have used it freely, and I suspect it goes back to the dawn of the race.

7   *First cave man:* "Heard the latest on old man Fist Ax? He's putting feathers on his arrows. Says they go straighter."

8   *Second cave man:* "Forget it. Nobody who's such a wife-stealer could come up with a decent idea."

9   Not every personal attack, however, can be classed as faulty logic. When the scandal of Grover Cleveland's illegitimate son was used against him in the presidential campaign, the argument had some point. Did Americans want a President of such a character? (The sovereign voters decided that his virtues overrode his defects.) If, however, Cleveland's enemies had introduced the natural son as an argument against his tariff policy, then a true *ad hominem* would appear. In the first case, Cleveland himself was the issue; in the second the tariff was the issue. When a man is running for office, or being chosen for any position in government or elsewhere, his personal behavior is always relevant. A corporation would naturally hesitate to hire as treasurer a man who had been convicted of embezzlement.

10   The health of President Eisenhower was an important consideration in the nominations of 1956. Was he well enough to serve out another four years in the toughest job in the world? Similarly with Franklin Roosevelt in 1944. But when the enemies of Roosevelt charged that a given government policy was wrong because it originated with "that cripple in the White House," they were practicing a particularly vicious kind of *ad hominem*.

Questions About "Definition"

1. How does your dictionary define "*ad hominem*" (par. 2)? What is the derivation of the term?

2. Which methods of defining does Chase use?

3. What does Chase's extended definition add to the dictionary definition?

4. After reading this selection, do you have a clear idea of what "*ad hominem*" means? Explain.

Questions on Diction and Writing Techniques

1. Does paragraph 1 fulfill the requirements of an opening paragraph? (See pages 29–30.) Explain.

2. What methods of definition does your dictionary use to define "city-slicker" (par. 3)?

3. Define "Sophists" (par. 6). List two or three words derived from "sophist."

4. What is Chase's purpose in writing paragraphs 7 and 8?

5. Why does Chase choose to use "however" in paragraph 9?

For Discussion, Reading, and Writing

1. Chase says that Lincoln's tactic was "non-malicious" (par. 3). Do you agree? In view of the result, does it matter whether the tactic was malicious or not? What risk did Lincoln take by using *ad hominem*? If you had been an opposing lawyer, how might you have countered Lincoln's move?

2. Using a combination of two or more methods, define in a paragraph one of these terms:

   Anchor man

   Lonesome end

   Back-seat driver

   Feminist

   Male chauvinist

3. In a short essay, write an extended definition of one of these terms:

Hypocrisy

Romantic love

Ideal marriage

Population explosion

Maternal overprotection

APPETITE

Laurie Lee

Laurie Lee, British author, has written books of poetry, travel, and autobiography. This selection is from **I Can't Stay Long** (1976), a collection of his essays.

1   One of the major pleasures in life is appetite, and one of our major duties should be to preserve it. Appetite is the keenness of living; it is one of the senses that tells you that you are still curious to exist, that you still have an edge on your longings and want to bite into the world and taste its multitudinous flavours and juices.

2   By appetite, of course, I don't mean just the lust for food, but any condition of unsatisfied desire, any burning in the blood that proves you want more than you've got, and that you haven't yet used up your life. Wilde said he felt sorry for those who never got their heart's desire, but sorrier still for those who did. I got mine once only, and it nearly killed me, and I've always preferred wanting to having since.

3   For appetite, to me, is this state of wanting, which keeps one's expectations alive. I remember learning this lesson long ago as a

child, when treats and orgies were few, and when I discovered that
the greatest pitch of happiness was not in actually eating a toffee
but in gazing at it beforehand. True, the first bite was delicious, but
once the toffee was gone one was left with nothing, neither toffee
nor lust. Besides, the whole toffeeness of toffees was imperceptibly
diminished by the gross act of having eaten it. No, the best was in
wanting it, in sitting and looking at it, when one tasted an inex-
haustible treasure-house of flavours.

₄   So, for me, one of the keenest pleasures of appetite remains in
the wanting, not the satisfaction. In wanting a peach, or a whisky,
or a particular texture or sound, or to be with a particular friend.
For in this condition, of course, I know that the object of desire is
always at its most flawlessly perfect. Which is why I would carry
the preservation of appetite to the extent of deliberate fasting, simply because I think that appetite is too good to lose, too precious to
be bludgeoned into insensibility by satiation and over-doing it.

₅   For that matter, I don't really want three square meals a day —
I want one huge, delicious, orgiastic, table-groaning blow-out, say
every four days, and then not be too sure where the next one is
coming from. A day of fasting is not for me just a puritanical device
for denying oneself a pleasure, but rather a way of anticipating a
rarer moment of supreme indulgence.

₆   Fasting is an act of homage to the majesty of appetite. So I
think we should arrange to give up our pleasures regularly — our
food, our friends, our lovers — in order to preserve their intensity,
and the moment of coming back to them. For this is the moment that
renews and refreshes both oneself and the thing one loves. Sailors
and travellers enjoyed this once, and so did hunters, I suppose. Part
of the weariness of modern life may be that we live too much on
top of each other, and are entertained and fed too regularly. Once
we were separated by hunger both from our food and families, and
then we learned to value both. The men went off hunting, and the
dogs went with them; the women and children waved goodbye.
The cave was empty of men for days on end; nobody ate, or knew
what to do. The women crouched by the fire, the wet smoke in
their eyes; the children wailed; everybody was hungry. Then one
night there were shouts and the barking of dogs from the hills, and
the men came back loaded with meat. This was the great reunion,
and everybody gorged themselves silly, and appetite came into its

own; the long-awaited meal became a feast to remember and an almost sacred celebration of life. Now we go off to the office and come home in the evenings to cheap chicken and frozen peas. Very nice, but too much of it, too easy and regular, served up without effort or wanting. We eat, we are lucky, our faces are shining with fat, but we don't know the pleasure of being hungry any more.

7   Too much of anything—too much music, entertainment, happy snacks, or time spent with one's friends—creates a kind of impotence of living by which one can no longer hear, or taste, or see, or love, or remember. Life is short and precious, and appetite is one of its guardians, and loss of appetite is a sort of death. So if we are to enjoy this short life we should respect the divinity of appetite, and keep it eager and not too much blunted.

8   It is a long time now since I knew that acute moment of bliss that comes from putting parched lips to a cup of cold water. The springs are still there to be enjoyed—all one needs is the original thirst.

Questions About "Definition"

1. How does Lee's definition agree with or differ from your dictionary's definition of "appetite"?

2. Making specific reference to the text, say what methods Lee uses to define "appetite."

3. What is Lee's thesis (see pages 5–9)? Comment on whether he could have explained it intelligibly without making clear to you the sense in which he used "appetite."

Questions on Diction and Writing Techniques

1. Why does Lee choose to write, "bite into the world and taste its multitudinous flavours and juices" (par. 1)? What does this diction contribute to your understanding of his definition?

2. Is "lust" (par. 2) an apt word? What other words might the writer have used? In the context of this essay, which word do you prefer?

3. Does Lee use personal experience to good effect? Explain.

4. Which paragraph does Lee develop by means of comparison and contrast (see pages 258–262)? What does this pattern of organization contribute to the clarification of the paragraph's main idea?

For Discussion, Reading, and Writing

1. Laurie Lee's conclusion in "Appetite" is (circle one):

   A. Appetite is the keenness of living.

   B. Appetite is the lust for food.

   C. One of the major pleasures in life is appetite.

   D. One of the keenest pleasures of appetite is in the wanting, not the satisfaction.

   E. Nowadays we don't know the pleasure of being hungry.

2. According to Lee, "One of the keenest pleasures of appetite remains in the wanting, not the satisfaction" (par. 4). Do you agree? Cite examples from your own experience to support your view.

3. Explaining the terms you use with definitions, write a paragraph or two of comment on the statement just quoted.

4. Giving specific examples from your personal experience and observations of others, write a paragraph defining one of these terms:

   Boredom

   Gamesmanship

   Generation gap

   Happiness

   Guilt

5. Write an extended definition of one of these terms:

Ripoff

Cool cat

Gravy train

Weirdo

No sweat

Vibes

Spaced out

THE ANIMALS SLEEP
Alan Devoe

Alan Devoe (1909–1955), American naturalist and writer, is
the author of many articles and books on nature, such as
Lives Around Us (1942), in which this essay appears.

1   Not many creatures of earth are visible now in the frozen
woods and fields. A walker there can see only the few thick-furred
gray squirrels and hares and deer that are pelted for cold weather,
and can hear no livelier bird-music than the small call-notes of hardy
nuthatches and chickadees. In December the populace of wild
things has a meager look. But could a man see underneath the surface of the frozen earth and below the icy mud of brook-beds, he
would be aware of the presence of a tremendous number of beasts.
Only a very few of the denizens of outdoors removed to other cli-
mates when the autumn cold came. Some of the summer birds departed, to be sure, and some of the insects died. But innumerable
animals only retired to hidden places and went to sleep. By thou-

sands, when the first frosts were felt, they subsided into that lethargy called hibernation.

₂   Indians spoke of hibernation as the Long Sleep, but it is rather more than that. It is profound oblivion midway between sleep and death. It is an unknowing and unfeeling more deep and lasting than can be induced in man by the most powerful drugs, a suspension of life processes more thorough and protracted than even the "frozen slumber" which doctors have lately devised as a palliative of cancer. It is a phenomenon unique in nature, and though we are wiser about it than we were in those cradle-days of biology when Dr Johnson thought that swallows passed the winter asleep in the mud at the bottom of the Thames, it remains a riddle still.

₃   The season of hibernating begins quite early for some of the creatures of outdoors. It is not alone the cold which causes it; there are a multiplicity of other factors—diminishing food supply; increased darkness as the fall days shorten; silence—frequently decisive. Any or all of these may be the signal for entrance into the Long Sleep, depending upon the habits and make-up of the particular creature. Among the skunks, it is usually the coming of the cold that sends them, torpid, to their root-lined underground burrows; but many other mammals (for instance, ground squirrels) begin to grow drowsy when the fall sun is still warm on their furry backs and the food supply is not at all diminished. This ground-squirrel kind of hibernating, independent of the weather and the food supply, may be an old race habit, an instinctual behavior pattern like the unaccountable migrations of certain birds. Weather, food, inheritance, darkness—all of these obscurely play their parts in bringing on the annual subsidence into what one biologist has called "the little death." Investigation of the causes will need a good many years before they can be understood, for in captivity, where observation is more easy than in the wild, the hibernators often do not sleep at all.

₄   The preparations for hibernation begin in early fall, and they are various. The insects—such as survive the winters in adult form—make ready by a drastic dehydration. Their bodies lose the moisture which they have in summer, and which would make them liable to fatal freezing, and become desiccated and brittle. Their reactions to the stimulus of light become, in most cases, the reverse of normal: beetles ordinarily attracted toward the light are violently repelled by it after dehydration. They creep to dark places. Some of them, like the May beetles, repair to deep sub-frostline tunnels in the earth; some of them seek out crannies under the loose bark of trees and interstices in stumps. With all their body tissues radically dried, and all their responses to stimuli slowed and dulled, they lapse into immobility. Their bodies are stiff and straight, wings and legs held parallel. They are ready to remain unmoving and foodless until the spring thaws come. They are ready to undergo the experience, common enough among the surface-hibernating insects, of being chilled to well below 32 degrees, Fahrenheit, without suffering injury.

5   The frogs, in making ready, betake themselves to the deep, soft mud of the brook-bottoms and the shelter of flat underwater stones. The toads, their soft bodies equipped with curious many-fingered lumps of fat to serve as food supply, burrow on cool September days into sandy garden soil or into the banks of their breeding streams, and with arched backs and indrawn legs grow motionless. The snails cease feeding, bury themselves among the moss and leaves, and secrete a covering over the openings of their shells. The trout swim leisurely upstream and grow quiet and unhungry; the spiders that have not perished in the first cold weather withdraw into burrows or spin themselves cocoons.

6   Most striking is the Long Sleep of the mammals. Raccoons, chipmunks, bats, bears, woodchucks—all these make ready in the autumn for a greater or lesser period of dormancy. They are all animals with imprecisely regulated body temperatures, these mammalian hibernators; during normal summer-time activity their temperatures often fluctuate by ten or fifteen degrees. They do not have a wholly static temperature, independent of the warmth of the outer air, as does a man or a wood-mouse or a winter-active deer. They can survive the months of northern cold and snow only by lapsing into a quiescence hardly distinguishable from death. Some of them sleep more deeply than others, some for the whole winter and some for only a part of it. The commonest of them, the woodchuck, serves as a fair exemplar.

7   The woodchuck's hibernation usually starts about the middle of September. For weeks he has been foraging with increased appetite among the clover blossoms and has grown heavy and slow-moving. Now, with the coming of mid-September, apples and corn and yarrow-tops have become less plentiful, and the nights are cool.

The woodchuck moves with slower gait, and emerges less and less frequently for feeding-trips. Layers of fat have accumulated around his chest and shoulders, and there is thick fat in the axils of his legs. He has extended his summer burrow to a length of nearly thirty feet, and has fashioned a deep nest-chamber at the end of it, far below the level of the frost. He has carried in, usually, a little hay. He is ready for the Long Sleep.

8 When the temperature of the September days falls below 50 degrees or so, the woodchuck becomes too drowsy to come forth from his burrow in the chilly dusk to forage. He remains in the deep nest-chamber, lethargic, hardly moving. Gradually, with the passing of hours or days, his coarse-furred body curls into a semi-circle, like a foetus, nose-tip touching tail. The small legs are tucked in, the hand-like clawed forefeet folded. The woodchuck has become a compact ball. Presently the temperature of his body begins to fall.

9 In normal life the woodchuck's temperature, though fluctuant, averages about 97 degrees. Now, as he lies tight-curled in a ball with the winter sleep stealing over him, this body heat drops ten degrees, twenty degrees, thirty. Finally, by the time the snow is on the ground and the woodchuck's winter dormancy has become complete, his temperature is only 38 or 40. With the falling of the body heat there is a slowing of his heartbeat and his respiration. In normal life he breathes thirty or forty times each minute; when he is excited, as many as a hundred times. Now he breathes slower and slower — ten times a minute, five times a minute, once a minute, and at last only ten or twelve times in an hour. His heartbeat is a twentieth of normal. He has entered fully into the oblivion of hibernation.

10 The Long Sleep lasts, on an average, about six months. For half a year the woodchuck remains unmoving, hardly breathing. His pituitary gland is inactive; his blood is so sluggishly circulated that there is an unequal distribution in the chilled body; his sensory awareness has wholly ceased. It is almost true to say that he has altered from a warm-blooded to a cold-blooded animal.

11 Then, in the middle of March, he wakes. The waking is not a slow and gradual thing, as was the drifting into sleep, but takes place quickly, often in an hour. The body temperature ascends to normal, or rather higher for a while; glandular functions instantly

resume; the respiration quickens and steadies at a normal rate. The woodchuck has become himself again, save only that he is a little thinner, and is ready at once to fare forth into the pale spring sunlight and look for grass and berries.

12   Such is the performance each fall and winter, with varying detail, of bats and worms and bears, and a hundred other kinds of creature. It is a marvel less spectacular than the migration flight of hummingbirds or the flash of shooting stars, but is not much less remarkable.

Questions About "Definition"

1. Mark in your text the synonyms that Devoe uses to explain what the word "hibernation" means. Does he make the meaning of the word clear to you?

2. What does the information Devoe gives you about the woodchuck contribute to your understanding of the meaning of the term hibernation?

3. Write in your own words a formal definition of hibernation.

Questions on Diction and Writing Techniques

1. Underline in your text those words that are new to you, but whose meaning you inferred from their context. Define them in your own words. Compare your definitions with those in your dictionary. Look up in your dictionary any other words that are new to you. Use the words in both groups in sentences.

2. Instead of the diction in (a) paragraph 1, sentence 2; (b) paragraph 7, sentence 3; and (c) paragraph 9, sentence 6, Devoe might have written the sentences with these words:

    A walker there can see only the few animals ready for the winter, and can hear few sounds.

    Now, in September, food has become less plentiful, and the nights are cool.

    Now he breathes slower and slower.

Which versions do you prefer? Why? Write two or three short, simple sentences. Then, enlarge them using the techniques that Devoe uses, or any other appropriate ones.

3. Explain whether, because of the meaning it conveys, "cradle-days" (par. 2) is an apt expression.

4. Is the diction in this essay formal or informal? Make a list of and then characterize the words that determined your answer.

5. What does the simile in paragraph 8 contribute to your understanding of the sentence in which it appears?

6. In the context of this essay, are "spectacular" and "remarkable" (par. 12) vague?

7. After sentence 3 of paragraph 1, Devoe writes "But." He does this to signal that he is about to make a contrast. What is the contrast? Write a sentence or a paragraph in which you use the word with a similar purpose.

8. Devoe helps achieve coherence in paragraph 2 by means of pronoun reference. What is the pronoun, and what is the noun to which it refers? Identify the pronoun, and its referent, in each of two other paragraphs where he uses the same technique to accomplish the same result.

9. How does Devoe make clear to you what he means by the ending of the first sentence of paragraph 4: "and they are various"?

10. Is the main idea of paragraph 5 expressed or implied? If it is expressed, say where; if implied, write it in your own words.

For Discussion, Reading, and Writing

1. To what depth does the woodchuck burrow?

2. How long does its stay underground last?

3. How long does it take for the woodchuck to awake?

4. Divide the essay into single paragraphs or groups of para-
    graphs. Be prepared to discuss in class, on the basis of your
    division, the essay's organization and the progression of its
    ideas. Also, be prepared to comment on the extent to which
    Devoe's explanation amplifies the meaning of hibernation that
    you find in your dictionary.

Division and Classification

IMAGINE, if you will, that the manager of a supermarket were to leave about pell-mell as they arrived from warehouses the numerous items his store offers for sale. Contemplation of the confusion that would result may help you to appreciate how useful is the purposeful arrangement of retail stores' goods, which we take for granted, in creating order out of what otherwise would be disarray.

A supermarket divides its commodities into groups: meat, delicatessen, frozen foods, and so forth. Within a major group it arranges goods in lesser categories; meat, for example, in sections of beef, veal, lamb, and chicken. Conversely, the store groups preparations of the curd of milk under the heading of cheese and classifies cheese, milk, cream, and butter as dairy products. These methods of arrangement are called division and classification.

Division and classification are a means of establishing order among things having some common characteristic. Division is the separation of something into groups or of a group into subgroups. Examples of this process are the separation of all living creatures into plants and animals and the further separation of animals into mammals, fish, birds, and so forth. Classification is the placement of units in a group or of groups in a more inclusive category. Examples of this process are the grouping of the whale, the cow, and the chimpanzee in the class of mammals; the grouping of the trout, the salmon, and the herring in the class of fish; and the further grouping of mammals and fish in the category of animal.

Division and classification are a filing system of a kind whose objective is to explain relationships and to make information comprehensible, handy, and easy to communicate. They have in common that they relate general classes and subclasses. They are so closely associated — being, in a sense, opposite sides of the same coin — that they are often considered together under the single heading of classification.

A system of filing will depend on the classifier. A politician might classify constituents as liberal and conservative to discover how to gear an election campaign. A police chief might classify the areas in a town or city as law-abiding and law-breaking to find out how best to patrol them. A school administrator might classify the population of a district as preschool or school age in order to prepare a school budget. Whatever the purpose, the categories used must have different and mutually exclusive characteristics, as in this amusing passage from *Essays of Elia* by Charles Lamb:

> The human species, according to the best theory I can form of it, is composed of two distinct races, *the men who borrow*, and *the men who lend.* To these original diversities may be reduced all those impertinent classifications of Gothic and Celtic tribes, white men, black men, red men. All the dwellers upon earth, "Parthians, and Medes, and Elamites," flock hither, and do naturally fall in with one or another of these primary distinctions.

In the paragraph that follows, the writer, having defined his term, groups clichés in significant classes to make a semblance of order of their diversity and to show how varied in kind they are:

> There are many varieties of clichés. Some are foreign phrases (*coupe de grâce*; *et tu, Brute*). Some are homely sayings or are based on proverbs ("You can't make an omelet without breaking eggs," *blissful ignorance*). Some are quotations ("To be or not to be, etc.";

"Unwepted, unhonored, and unsung"). Some are allusions to myth or history (*Gordian knot, Achilles' heel*). Some are alliterative or rhyming phrases (*first and foremost, high and dry*). Some are paradoxes (*in less than no time, conspicuous by its absence*). Some are legalisms (*null and void, each and every*). Some are playful euphemisms (*a fate worse than death, better half*). Some are figurative phrases (*leave no stone unturned, hit the nail on the head*). And some are meaningless small change (*in the last analysis, by the same token*) [Theodore M. Bernstein, *The Careful Writer*].

Classification resembles comparison and contrast insofar as it makes an implicit or, as in this paragraph, an explicit comparison between entities:

There are three kinds of book owners. The first has all the standard sets and best sellers — unread, untouched. (This deluded individual owns woodpulp and ink, not books.) The second has a great many books — a few of them read through, most of them dipped into, but all of them as clean and shiny as the day they were bought. (This person would probably like to make books his own, but is restrained by a false respect for their physical appearance.) The third has a few books or many — every one of them dog-eared and dilapidated, shaken and loosened by continual use, marked and scribbled in from front to back. (This man owns books.) [Mortimer J. Adler, "How to Mark a Book"].

Classification is a kind of analysis that facilitates explanation by permitting the discussion, in turn, of each part (subclass) of the whole (major class), as the writer of this introductory paragraph promises to do in the body of his essay:

We all listen to music according to our separate capacities. But for the sake of analysis, the whole listening process may become clearer if we break it up into its component parts, so to speak. For lack of a better terminology, one might name these: (1) the sensuous plane, (2) the expressive plane, (3) the sheerly musical plane. The only advantage to be gained from mechanically splitting up the listening process into these hypothetical planes is the clearer view to be had of the way in which we listen [Aaron Copland, *What to Listen for in Music*].

How classification can be utilized as a pattern of organization may be seen from its use by Vance Bourjaily in two essays on the same subject. In "You Can Tell a Hunter by What He Hunts," his purpose is to explain "that the term *hunter* covers a considerable variety of men, seeking a considerable variety of values." To do this he arranges hunters into groups—duck hunters, quail hunters, deer hunters, and so on—that include the variety of people who hunt and that demonstrate the varying pleasures hunters derive from the sport.

In "In Defense of Hunting," Bourjaily's purpose is to respond to those who advocate laws designed to restrict hunting. In that essay, he uses classification to help him fit responses to the various kinds of detractors of hunting:

> I can distinguish three kinds of attacker, and each deserves a different answer. There are the moralists, who must be answered with an invitation to examine themselves. There are the sentimentalists, who must be answered with straightforward information. The third are simply the politicians, who may be answered with contempt.

Here Bourjaily orders his material and announces to the reader the plan of organization of what is to follow.

DISCIPLINING CHILDREN
John Holt

John Holt, formerly a teacher, first achieved recognition as an innovator in education with **How Children Fail** (1964).

1   A child, in growing up, may meet and learn from three different kinds of disciplines. The first and most important is what we

might call the Discipline of Nature or of Reality. When he is trying to do something real, if he does the wrong thing or doesn't do the right one, he doesn't get the result he wants. If he doesn't pile one block right on top of another, or tries to build on a slanting surface, his tower falls down. If he hits the wrong key, he hears the wrong note. If he doesn't hit the nail squarely on the head, it bends, and he has to pull it out and start with another. If he doesn't measure properly what he is trying to build, it won't open, close, fit, stand up, fly, float, whistle, or do whatever he wants it to do. If he closes his eyes when he swings, he doesn't hit the ball. A child meets this kind of discipline every time he tries to *do* something, which is why it is so important in school to give children more chances to do things, instead of just reading or listening to someone talk (or pretending to). This discipline is a great teacher. The learner never has to wait long for his answer; it usually comes quickly, often instantly. Also it is clear, and very often points toward the needed correction; from what happened he can not only see that what he did was wrong, but also why, and what he needs to do instead. Finally, and most important, the giver of the answer, call it Nature, is impersonal, impartial, and indifferent. She does not give opinions, or make judgments; she cannot be wheedled, bullied, or fooled; she does not get angry or disappointed; she does not praise or blame; she does not remember past failures or hold grudges; with her one always gets a fresh start, this time is the one that counts.

2   The next discipline we might call the Discipline of Culture, of Society, of What People Really Do. Man is a social, a cultural animal. Children sense around them this culture, this network of agreements, customs, habits, and rules binding the adults together. They want to understand it and be a part of it. They watch very carefully what people around them are doing and want to do the same. They want to do right, unless they become convinced they can't do right. Thus children rarely misbehave seriously in church, but sit as quietly as they can. The example of all those grownups is contagious. Some mysterious ritual is going on, and children, who like rituals, want to be part of it. In the same way, the little children that I see at concerts or operas, though they may fidget a little, or perhaps take a nap now and then, rarely make any disturbance. With all those grownups sitting there, neither moving nor talking, it is the most natural thing in the world to imitate them. Children

who live among adults who are habitually courteous to each other, and to them, will soon learn to be courteous. Children who live surrounded by people who speak a certain way will speak that way, however much we may try to tell them that speaking that way is bad or wrong.

₃   The third discipline is the one most people mean when they speak of discipline—the Discipline of Superior Force, of sergeant to private, of "you do what I tell you or I'll make you wish you had." There is bound to be some of this in a child's life. Living as we do surrounded by things that can hurt children, or that children can hurt, we cannot avoid it. We can't afford to let a small child find out from experience the danger of playing in a busy street, or of fooling with the pots on the top of a stove, or of eating up the pills in the medicine cabinet. So, along with other precautions, we say to him, "Don't play in the street, or touch things on the stove, or go into the medicine cabinet, or I'll punish you." Between him and the danger too great for him to imagine we put a lesser danger, but one he can imagine and maybe therefore want to avoid. He can have no idea of what it would be like to be hit by a car, but he can imagine being shouted at, or spanked, or sent to his room. He avoids these substitutes for the greater danger until he can understand it and avoid it for its own sake. But we ought to use this discipline only when it is necessary to protect the life, health, safety, or well-being of people or other living creatures, or to prevent destruction of things that people care about. We ought not to assume too long, as we usually do, that a child cannot understand the real nature of the danger from which we want to protect him. The sooner he avoids the danger, not to escape our punishment, but as a matter of good sense, the better. He can learn that faster than we think. In Mexico, for example, where people drive their cars with a good deal of spirit, I saw many children no older than five or four walking unattended on the streets. They understood about cars, they knew what to do. A child whose life is full of the threat and fear of punishment is locked into babyhood. There is no way for him to grow up, to learn to take responsibility for his life and acts. Most important of all, we should not assume that having to yield to the threat of our superior force is good for the child's character. It is never good for *anyone's* character. To bow to superior force makes us feel impotent and cowardly for not having had the strength or courage to resist. Worse, it makes us resentful and vengeful. We can hardly wait to make someone pay for our humiliation, yield to us as we were once made to yield. No, if we cannot always avoid using the Discipline of Superior Force, we should at least use it as seldom as we can.

Questions About "Division and Classification"

1. Before you read this essay what did discipline mean to you?
2. Where does Holt announce his pattern of organization for this essay?
3. What does Holt's classification contribute to your understanding of discipline?

Questions on Diction and Writing Techniques

1. Mark in your text those words that are new to you, but whose meaning you inferred from their context. Define them in your own words. Compare your definitions with those in your dictionary. Look up in your dictionary any other words that are new to you. Use the words in both groups in sentences.
2. What is Holt's purpose in writing "also" and "finally" (par. 1); "thus" and "in the same way" (par. 2); "therefore," "but," and "for example" (par. 3)?
3. To what, in paragraph 2, does "they" refer?
4. Find in paragraph 1 two instances of Holt's making a generalization supported by examples.
5. What is Holt's purpose in paragraph 1 in writing a short, six-word sentence? Find another instance in this essay of his use of a short sentence for a similar reason.

For Discussion, Reading, and Writing

1. What, according to Holt, is the most important kind of discipline for a child? Why?

2. Why is Nature important as "the giver of the answer"?

3. Write a short essay in which you use classification to help you to organize any collection of related experiences, for example, people you know, places you've been to, teachers you've had.

THE VARIED SPECIES SEEN AFLOAT
Bert Wilson

Bert Wilson is a newspaperman, publicist, tournament bridge player, and free-lance essayist.

---

1   As a veteran of a score of Caribbean cruises, I have found most people aboard ship to be very predictable. They fit into categories—with some crossovers and combinations—and most of these groups can be summed up in single words, including: eater, drinker, sunner, shopper, swimmer, exerciser, dancer, rester, reader, tourer, bridger, gambler.

2   There is still another type, one that pops up late on every cruise. I call its members bilge people, since they apparently emerge from the bowels of the ship on the last day or so, and until then have been unaccounted for and unknown to the regulars on board.

3   Aside from the bilge people, whom you cannot observe long enough to put into any other slot, the members of the various categories fit into their regular routine as soon as the ship slips from the harbor. To them, a cruise is not a well-rounded vacation combining the rewards of an ocean voyage and island visits but a continuation of their favorite way of life back home.

₄   At the risk of arousing the ire of many travelers, let us list these seagoing types and their characteristics.

₅   Eaters — They seem intent on cramming an entire year's caloric intake into one week, or whatever the duration of the cruise. The presailing ritual includes a bon voyage party with hors d'oeuvre and sandwich trays. Then it's quickly into line to arrange for either first- or second-sitting meals and waiting anxiously for the opening dinner gong.

₆   The eater orders something from every course on the menu, and then some. Since two entrees are available, why not ask for both? Your untouched rolls and butter go down with the eater's, and most of the relish tray mysteriously disappears. On the way out, the eater fills pockets with mints, nuts and fruits to top off the cheese and crackers that complemented dessert.

₇   Drinkers — Food, except perhaps an occasional peanut or potato chip, does not interest this group. The drinkers head for the nearest bar as soon as the ship gets far enough away from shore to start service, and they spend the entire trip on a bar stool.

₈   They form a tight little group that moves from bar to bar, finally closing the late-at-night spot in the wee hours. They seem oblivious to the rest of the vessel and its many activities. Their activity is absorbing booze or beer, laughing and joking while doing it. They venture ashore only if the ship's bars are closed.

₉   Resters — They are always tired, take naps, turn in early and rise late. When the ship is in port, they slump in easy chairs, contemplating the scenery. They take elevators instead of using the stairs between decks and often order food and drink brought to their cabins instead of going to the dining room. Extreme cases may also be among the mysterious category of bilge people — because they may not become visible until they stagger out on deck or into the public rooms on the last day of the cruise.

₁₀   Readers — Ask the average cruise passenger where the ship's library is and you will get a blank stare. But the readers know. They bring books with them and seek out more. At each port they grab all the newspapers to find out what is happening in the world they have left behind. Some readers are resters, too, lying back comfortably and passing by the entire voyage with volume after volume.

₁₁   Tourers — Ships' tour organizers adore this type, who line up to take trips regardless of cost or itinerary. Some passengers explore on their own, but tourers go in bunches aboard buses, boats, blimps. While still complaining about a ripoff on the last tour, they embark on another. Their only regret: simultaneous tours. Which to take?

12   **Bridgers**—Hooked on the game, they play incessantly, day and night—rubber, party, duplicate—for fun and for stakes. If they cannot find a fourth, they will forcibly draft some weak-willed passenger and either give a quick lesson or instruct the novice just to say "pass" each time it is the turn to bid. If it's a Goren cruise, the bridgers will isolate themselves from the rest of the passengers, play day and night and talk bridge hands. On their return home, when asked what islands they liked, they will recite: "I held the ace and two little spades, four hearts to the king-10, and my partner . . ."

13   **Gamblers**—The gambler sticks to ships with casinos and slot machines. He also might try to hustle fellow passengers into a high-stakes game of poker or gin rummy. If the island has a casino, he will make a beeline there. His objective might be to make enough to pay for the vacation, or to lose as much again as the vacation costs.

14   While I like to consider myself a well-rounded person, not easily typed, I suppose my logical category would be exerciser. Each day I don my running shoes and jog around the deck, often to the dismay of folks dressing for the first-sitting dinner. Regular visits to the ship's gyms culminate in pedaling the exercycle, straining to 25 situps, tugging the oars of the rowing machine, pulling the weights and shaking to the electric vibrator around my waist.

15   I haunt the Ping-Pong tables, taking on all comers and relieving my frustration that tennis is not really a shipboard practicality. While I avoid actually getting into the swimming pool, I use the tops of the entry ladder as parallel bars, flexing my insignificant muscles and pushing myself up and down with legs extended. Finally, I eschew the elevators, preferring to whirl up and down the staircases and often grasping the rails and swinging monkey fashion for the final half-dozen steps. All this activity seems to hold down my weight gain on a cruise to a paltry three pounds.

16   As for the bilge people, those sad, confused-looking passengers who, perhaps, have lain seasick in their bunks for the entire cruise, what of them? Are their shipboard habits inexplicable? Do they frequent private facilities on the lowest deck, an area un-

known to the majority of passengers? Or are they stowaways, emerging from enforced labor in the galleys? I'm sorry I have no scientific answer. But on the last day of every cruise, my wife and I see them, and either point to them knowingly, or whisper discreetly, so they cannot hear: "Bilge."

Questions About "Division and Classification"

1. Wilson might have classified the people aboard ship according to age, sex, occupation, or attire, or in some other way. Why did he group them as he did?

2. Is his system of classification consistent? Explain.

3. How many kinds of seagoing types does he list?

Questions on Diction and Writing Techniques

1. Underline in your text those words that are new to you, but whose meaning you inferred from their context. Define them in your own words. Compare your definitions with those in your dictionary. Look up in your dictionary any other words that are new to you. Use the words in both groups in sentences.

2. There is a word in paragraph 3 that signals a contrast. What is that word?

3. How does Wilson achieve coherence within and between paragraphs 7 and 8?

4. What method of definition (see pages 276–282) does he use in paragraph 2 to explain what he means by "bilge people"?

5. The paragraphs in this essay may be grouped 1–3, 4–13, 14–16. What is the function of each group?

6. What is the thesis of this essay? Is it expressed or implied? If expressed, say where. If implied, state it in your own words.

For Discussion, Reading, and Writing

1. Fill the blanks in this passage from memory to make it intelligible:

   Aside from the _____ people, _____, whom you cannot observe long enough to _____ into any other slot, the _____ of the various categories fit into their regular _____ as soon as the _____ slips from the harbor. To them, a _____ is not a well-rounded _____ combining the rewards of an ocean voyage and _____ visits but a continuation of their _____ way of life back _____.

   Compare your words with those in paragraph 3.

2. Was the behavior of the people you traveled with or met on any vacation you took or at any resort you went to "a continuation of their favorite way of life back home"? If so, write a short essay about them, using classification as your main pattern of organization.

3. In the travel sections of newspapers (especially on weekends), and in magazines, there are advertisements for cruises, for other kinds of vacation trips—by sea, air, and on the ground—and for vacation resorts. Study some of these ads and, using some of Wilson's categories or your own, write a short essay about the types of people the ads are intended to appeal to.

THE PLUG-IN DRUG
Marie Winn

Marie Winn is the author of many books for parents and children
and of articles for several popular journals.

There is no doubt that children read fewer books when television is available to them. A child is more likely to turn on the television set when he has nothing to do than to pick up a book to
read. (In a survey of over 500 fourth- and fifth-graders, all subjects
showed a preference for *watching* over reading contents of any
kind.) This is partly if not entirely because reading requires greater
mental activity and it is human nature to opt for an entertainment
that requires less effort rather than more.

Children candidly reveal this tendency when speaking of their
television viewing:

"I mean television, you don't have to worry about getting really
bored because it's happening and you don't have to do any work to
see it, to have it happen. But you have to work to read, and that's
no fun. I mean, it's fun when it's a good book, but how can you tell
if the book will be good? Anyhow, I'd rather see it as a television
program," allows the twelve-year-old daughter of a college English
teacher.

Parents confirm the trend. The mother of boys aged 12 and 10
and a girl aged 9 reports:

"My children have trouble finding books they like in the library. They seem to have some sort of resistance to books, even
though my husband and I are avid readers. I think if they didn't
have television available they'd calmly spend more time looking for
something good in the library. They'd *have* to, to avoid boredom.
But now they don't really *look* in the library, whenever I take them.

They don't zero in on anything. It's not the ultimate entertainment for them, reading. There's always something better and easier to do. So they don't have to look hard at the library. They just zip through quickly and hardly ever find more than one or two books that interest them enough to take out."

Those children who have difficulty with reading are even more likely to combat boredom by turning to television than successful readers. Television plays a profoundly negative role in such children's intellectual development, since it is only by reading a great deal that they can hope to overcome their reading problems. This point is frequently raised by teachers and reading specialists when discussing the effects of television viewing on children's reading. Television watching does not prevent normal children from acquiring reading skills (although it may cause them to read less), but it does seem to compound the problems of children with reading disabilities because it offers them a pleasurable nonverbal alternative and thus reduces their willingness to work at reading in order to find vicarious pleasures.

That it is the availability of television that reduces the amount of reading children do rather than some other factor is easily demonstrated. In the absence of a television set—when the set is temporarily broken, or when the family has eliminated television entirely —a universal increase in reading, both by parents and by children, is reported. When the less taxing mental activity is unavailable, children turn to reading for entertainment, more willing to put up with the "work" involved.

Questions About "Division and Classification"

1. What are the distinguishing characteristics of the children Winn writes about?

2. Is her system of division appropriate to her expository purpose? Explain.

3. Would her explanation have been as complete if she had not used division and classification as one of her patterns of organization? Explain.

Questions on Diction and Writing Techniques

1. Does Winn clearly state her thesis? Explain.

2. Making specific reference to the text, comment on whether she sufficiently explains to you the main point of her essay.

3. What expository purpose is served in this essay by interviews? What do they contribute to the effectiveness of Winn's explanation?

4. Compare this essay with "Ousting the Stranger from the House" (pages 229–232). Which essay more convincingly explains its author's attitude toward the effect(s) of TV? Explain.

For Discussion, Reading, and Writing

1. Why, according to Winn, do children opt for watching TV?

2. Using your own experience or your observation of the behavior of others, support or challenge with specific relevant details Winn's view of the effect of TV on how much children (or adults) read.

3. Is it your experience that you read more in the absence of a TV set? Explain.

4. Using division and classification as your main pattern of organization, write a short essay explaining some TV viewers, TV programs, TV commercials, or attitudes toward TV.

THE RIGHT STUFF
Tom Wolfe

Tom Wolfe, American journalist, is an exponent of "the new
journalism," a style of nonfiction marked by energetic,
colorful, factual writing.

1   A young man might go into military flight training believing
that he was entering some sort of technical school in which he was
simply going to acquire a certain set of skills. Instead, he found
himself all at once enclosed in a fraternity. And in this fraternity,
even though it was military, men were not rated by their outward
rank as ensigns, lieutenants, commanders, or whatever. No, herein
the world was divided into those who had it and those who did
not. This quality, this *it*, was never named, however, nor was it
talked about in any way.

2   As to just what this ineffable quality was . . . well, it obviously
involved bravery. But it was not bravery in the simple sense of being willing to risk your life. The idea seemed to be that any fool
could do that, if that was all that was required, just as any fool
could throw away his life in the process. No, the idea here (in the
all-enclosing fraternity) seemed to be that a man should have the
ability to go up in a hurtling piece of machinery and put his hide on
the line and then have the moxie, the reflexes, the experience, the
coolness, to pull it back in the last yawning moment—and then to
go up again *the next day*, and the next day, and every next day, even
if the series should prove infinite—and, ultimately, in its best expression, do so in a cause that means something to thousands, to a
people, a nation, to humanity, to God. Nor was there *a test* to
show whether or not a pilot had this righteous quality. There was,
instead, a seemingly infinite series of tests. A career in flying was

like climbing one of those ancient Babylonian pyramids made up of a dizzy progression of steps and ledges, a ziggurat, a pyramid extraordinarily high and steep; and the idea was to prove at every foot of the way up that pyramid that you were one of the elected and anointed ones who had *the right stuff* and could move higher and higher and even – ultimately, God willing, one day – that you might be able to join that special few at the very top, that elite who had the capacity to bring tears to men's eyes, the very Brotherhood of the Right Stuff itself.

3 None of this was to be mentioned, and yet it was acted out in a way that a young man could not fail to understand. When a new flight (i e , a class) of trainees arrived at Pensacola, they were brought into an auditorium for a little lecture. An officer would tell them: "Take a look at the man on either side of you." Quite a few actually swiveled their heads this way and that, in the interest of appearing diligent. Then the officer would say: "One of the three of you is not going to make it!" – meaning, not get his wings. That was the opening theme, the *motif* of primary training. We already know that one-third of you do not have the right stuff – it only remains to find out who.

4 Furthermore, that was the way it turned out. At every level in one's progress up that staggeringly high pyramid, the world was once more divided into those men who had the right stuff to continue the climb and those who had to be *left behind* in the most obvious way. Some were eliminated in the course of the opening classroom work, as either not smart enough or not hardworking enough, and were left behind. Then came the basic flight instruction, in single-engine, propeller-driven trainers, and a few more – even though the military tried to make this stage easy – were washed out and left behind. Then came more demanding levels, one after the other, formation flying, instrument flying, jet training, all-weather flying, gunnery, and at each level more were washed out and left behind. By this point easily a third of the original candidates had been, indeed, eliminated . . . from the ranks of those who might prove to have the right stuff. . . .

5 The military did not have very merciful instincts. Rather than packing up these poor souls and sending them home, the Navy, like the Air Force and the Marines, would try to make use of them in some other role, such as flight controller. So the washout has to

keep taking classes with the rest of his group, even though he can no longer touch an airplane. He sits there in the classes staring at sheets of paper with cataracts of sheer human mortification over his eyes while the rest steal looks at him . . . this man reduced to an ant, this untouchable, this poor sonofabitch. And in what test had he been found wanting? Why, it seemed to be nothing less than *manhood* itself. Naturally, this was never mentioned, either. Yet there it was. *Manliness, manhood, manly courage* . . . there was something ancient, primordial, irresistible about the challenge of this stuff, no matter what a sophisticated and rational age one might think he lived in.

6   Perhaps because it could not be talked about, the subject began to take on superstitious and even mystical outlines. A man either had it or he didn't! There was no such thing as having *most* of it. Moreover, it could blow at any seam. One day a man would be ascending the pyramid at a terrific clip, and the next—bingo!—he would reach his own limits in the most unexpected way. Conrad and Schirra met an Air Force pilot who had had a great pal at Tyndall Air Force Base in Florida. This man had been the budding ace of the training class; he had flown the hottest fighter-style trainer, the T-38, like a dream; and then he began the routine step of being checked out in the T-33. The T-33 was not nearly as hot an aircraft as the T-38; it was essentially the old P-80 jet fighter. It had an exceedingly small cockpit. The pilot could barely move his shoulders. It was the sort of airplane of which everybody said, "You don't get into it, you *wear* it." Once inside a T-33 cockpit this man, this budding ace, developed claustrophobia of the most paralyzing sort. He tried everything to overcome it. He even went to a psychiatrist, which was a serious mistake for a military officer if his superiors learned of it. But nothing worked. He was shifted over to flying jet transports, such as the C-135. Very demanding and necessary aircraft they were, too, and he was still spoken of as an excellent pilot. But as everyone knew—and, again, it was never explained in so many words—only those who were assigned to fighter squadrons, the "fighter jocks," as they called each other with a self-satisfied irony, remained in the true fraternity. Those assigned to transports were not humiliated like washouts—*somebody* had to fly those planes —nevertheless, they, too, had been *left behind* for lack of the right stuff.

7   Or a man could go for a routine physical one fine day, feeling like a million dollars, and be grounded for *fallen arches*. It happened! —just like that! (And try raising them.) Or for breaking his wrist and losing only *part* of its mobility. Or for a minor deterioration of eyesight, or for any of hundreds of reasons that would make no difference to a man in an ordinary occupation. As a result all fighter jocks began looking upon doctors as their natural enemies. Going to see a flight surgeon was a no-gain proposition; a pilot could only hold his own or lose in the doctor's office. To be grounded for a medical reason was no humiliation, looked at objectively. But it was a humiliation, nonetheless!—for it meant you no longer had that indefinable, unutterable, integral stuff. (It could blow at *any* seam.)

8   All the hot young fighter jocks began trying to test the limits themselves in a superstitious way. They were like believing Presbyterians of a century before who used to probe their own experience to see if they were truly among *the elect*. When a fighter pilot was in training, whether in the Navy or the Air Force, his superiors were continually spelling out strict rules for him, about the use of the aircraft and conduct in the sky. They repeatedly forbade so-called hotdog stunts, such as outside loops, buzzing, flat-hatting, hedgehopping and flying under bridges. But somehow one got the message that the man who truly *had* it could ignore those rules—not that he should make a point of it, but that he *could*—and that after all there was only one way to find out—and that in some strange unofficial way, peeking through his fingers, his instructor halfway expected him to challenge all the limits. They would give a lecture about how a pilot should never fly without a good solid breakfast—eggs, bacon, toast, and so forth—because if he tried to fly with his blood-sugar level too low, it could impair his alertness. Naturally, the next day every hot dog in the unit would get up and have a breakfast consisting of one cup of black coffee and take off and go up into a vertical climb until the weight of the ship exactly canceled out the upward pull of the engine and his air speed was zero, and he would hang there for one thick adrenal instant—and then fall like a rock, until one of three things happened: he keeled over nose first and regained his aerodynamics and all was well, he went into a spin and fought his way out of it, or he went into a spin and had to eject or crunch it, which was always supremely possible.

9   Likewise, "hassling"—mock dogfighting—was strictly forbidden, and so naturally young fighter jocks could hardly wait to go up in, say, a pair of F-100s and start the duel by making a pass at each other at 800 miles an hour, the winner being the pilot who could slip in behind the other one and get locked in on his tail ("wax his tail"), and it was not uncommon for some eager jock to try too tight an outside turn and have his engine flame out, whereupon, unable to restart it, he has to eject . . . and he shakes his fist at the victor as he floats down by parachute and his half-a-million-dollar aircraft goes *kaboom!* on the palmetto grass or the desert floor, and he starts thinking about how he can get together with the other guy back at the base in time for the two of them to get their stories straight before the investigation: "I don't know what happened, sir. I was pulling up after a target run, and it just flamed out on me." Hassling was forbidden, and hassling that led to the destruction of an aircraft was a serious court-martial offense, and the man's superiors knew that the engine hadn't *just flamed out,* but every unofficial impulse on the base seemed to be saying: "Hell, we wouldn't give you a nickel for a pilot who hasn't done some crazy rat-racing like that. It's all part of the right stuff."

10   The other side of this impulse showed up in the reluctance of the young jocks to admit it when they had maneuvered themselves into a bad corner they couldn't get out of. There were two reasons why a fighter pilot hated to declare an emergency. First, it triggered a complex and very public chain of events at the field: all other incoming flights were held up, including many of one's comrades who were probably low on fuel; the fire trucks came trundling out to the runway like yellow toys (as seen from way up there), the better to illustrate one's hapless state; and the bureaucracy began to crank up the paper monster for the investigation that always followed. And second, to declare an emergency, one first had to reach that conclusion in his own mind, which to the young pilot was the same as saying: "A minute ago I still *had* it—now I need your help!" To have a bunch of young fighter pilots up in the air thinking this way used to drive flight controllers crazy. They would see a ship beginning to drift off the radar, and they couldn't rouse the pilot on the microphone for anything other than a few meaningless mumbles, and they would know he was probably out there with engine failure at a low altitude, trying to reignite by lowering his auxiliary

generator rig, which had a little propeller that was supposed to spin in the slipstream like a child's pinwheel.

11   "Whiskey Kilo Two Eight, do you want to declare an emergency?"

12   *This* would rouse him!—to say: "Negative, negative, Whiskey Kilo Two Eight is not declaring an emergency."

13   Kaboom. Believers in the right stuff would rather crash and burn.

Questions About "Division and Classification"

1. By what standard does Wolfe divide the men in military flight training?

2. Does Wolfe make clear to you the qualities of the flight trainees in each category? Explain.

3. Comment on whether Wolfe's pattern of organization in this essay effectively explains the attributes needed to succeed as a fighter pilot.

4. Why didn't Wolfe divide the trainees according to rank or any other standard?

Questions on Diction and Writing Techniques

1. Mark in your text those words that are new to you, but whose meaning you inferred from their context. Define them in your own words. Compare your definitions with those in your dictionary. Look up in your dictionary any other words that are new to you. Use the words in both groups in sentences.

2. Find two examples of Wolfe's use of slang. Are they appropriate in this essay? Explain.

3. What is the simile that Wolfe uses to explain "this ineffable quality" (paragraph 2)? Find an instance in this essay of his use of another simile for a similar purpose.

4. Why does Wolfe explain the meaning of "flight" (par. 3), "hot dog stunts" (par. 8), and "hassling" (par. 9)?

5. What does Wolfe signal with "furthermore" (par. 4); "yet" (par. 5); "moreover" (par. 6); "or" (par. 7); "but" (par. 8); "like-wise" (par. 9)? Find two or more additional instances where Wolfe uses these or other transitional words to help achieve coherence.

6. What words does Wolfe choose to achieve chronological order in paragraph 4?

For Discussion, Reading, and Writing

1. Which of these statements, according to Wolfe, are true (T), which false (F)?

   A. _____ A young man going into military flight training found himself enclosed in a fraternity.

   B. _____ The trainee was given a test to find out whether he had the right stuff.

   C. _____ When fighter pilots were in training their superiors spelled out rules which "the man who truly *had* it" ignored.

   D. _____ Hassling was strictly forbidden.

   E. _____ A fighter hated to declare an emergency because it would look bad on his record.

   F. _____ The world was divided into those who could fly and those who could not.

   G. _____ The idea seemed to be that any fool could risk his life.

   H. _____ Going to see a flight surgeon was a no-gain proposition.

2. Using division and classification as your main pattern of organization, write a short essay about (a) teachers you have known, (b) people in your home town or neighborhood, (c) your fellow students, or (d) any other people you are familiar with.

Process

A process is a sequence of actions or operations. Process, the pattern of organization, is a method of exposition whose function is to analyze such a sequence and to convey a clear understanding of it to the reader.

There are two kinds of process analysis. One is an explanation that tells *how to do something* — how to bake a cake, how to change a tire, how to plant corn, how to fish for trout. The paragraph on page 214 telling how to use a handsaw is an example of this kind. The writer's purpose is instructive: to make the consecutive steps so clear that the reader will know how to use the tool. The second is an explanation of *how something is (or was) done* — how you selected your college, how an electric motor works, how General Grant took Richmond, how you dissected a frog. They are alike insofar as both kinds explain the successive and interdependent steps that lead to an end. To make clear to the reader how that end is reached is the purpose of the writer who uses process as a pattern of organization.

The writer of "Menial Jobs Taught Me a Lot" (analyzed on pages 31–35) uses process in his third paragraph (italics added):

. . . *The first thing each morning,* I had to drive a truck to a supply depot to pick up odds and ends of building materials. *Then,* having driven back to the construction site, I had to unload them where they were needed. *After that,* I had to haul materials from one or another location on the site to others. *That done, and for most of the rest of the day,* I had to unload by hand from trailers and to stack in orderly piles tons and tons of bulky materials such as rough lumber, roofing shingles, and kegs of nails. *At the end of the day,* I was obliged to clean up rubbish from the outside and inside of buildings under construction, load it on my truck and *then* unload it at a refuse dump on the site.

In using this method of exposition he has two purposes: (1) to explain how something was done – how he did the work of a laborer on a construction project, and (2) to make clear, through this example, why his jobs "soon become boring." In his essay, process is one of three patterns of organization. The others are illustration (see pages 236–240) and comparison and contrast (see pages 258–262). All are used for the common purpose of clarifying the thesis and supporting its generalization.

Here are some things to keep in mind when you write a process analysis:

1. *Process must not be confused with narration.* Process relates a sequence of events, so it is in a way like narration (see pages 168–172). But narration generally is concerned with the story itself; whereas the purpose of process analysis is expository: to set forth information and ideas.

2. *Be sure you know your subject well.* To obtain the information you need for your explanation, draw on as many of the writer's sources of material (discussed in Part Three) as your topic requires.

3. *Organize your material systematically.* The safest procedure by far is to present its parts in sequence, making sure that no part of a series needed for clarity is omitted.

4. *Explain each step simply and in sufficient detail.* How much detail is needed will depend on who your readers are. You should be aware of how much information they already have

about your subject. You run the risk of boring a knowledgeable reader if you say too much, of leaving confused an ignorant one if you say too little. The general rule is to tell your readers whatever they may reasonably want to know in order to understand clearly how to do something or how something is or was done.

5. *Use appropriate language.* Define terms that may require special knowledge or whose meaning your readers may not get from the context. Your writing should not be obscure or confusing. Your audience is entitled to an explanation that is easy to understand.

6. *Be sure the time sequence is clear.* To achieve clarity and coherence in process analysis it is often helpful to stress the time sequence. Use temporal diction: *first,* do this; *then,* do that; *finally,* do thus and so. Notice with what care, in the italicized words in the paragraph quoted on page 324, the writer emphasizes the sequence of actions.

The use of these suggestions is demonstrated in this exemplary passage from Vilhjalmur Stefansson's *My Life With the Eskimo:*

The whole principle of successfully stalking a seal is just in realizing from the first that he is bound to see you and that your only hope is in pretending that you also are a seal. If you act and look so as to convince him from the first that you are a brother seal, he will regard you with unconcern. To simulate a seal well enough to deceive a seal is not difficult, for, to begin with, we know from experience that his eye-sight is poor. You can walk up without taking any special precautions until, under ordinary conditions of light, you are within two hundred and fifty or three hundred yards. Then you have to begin to be more careful. You move ahead while he is asleep, and when he wakes up you stop motionless. You can safely proceed on all fours until within something less than two hundred yards, but after that you will have to play seal more faithfully. Your method of locomotion will then have to

From *My Life with the Eskimo* by Vilhjalmur Stefansson (New York: Macmillan, 1913), pp. 108–111. Reprinted by permission of McIntosh and Otis, Inc.

be that of the seal, which does not differ very materially from that of a snake, and which therefore has its disadvantages at a season of the year when the surface of the ice is covered with puddles of water anywhere from an inch to twenty inches in depth, as it is in spring and early summer. You must not only crawl ahead, seal-fashion, but you must be careful to always present a side view of your body to the seal, for a man coming head-on does not look particularly like a seal.

Until you are within a hundred yards or so the seal is not likely to notice you, but somewhere between the hundred yard and the seventy-five yard mark his attention will suddenly be attracted to you, and instead of going to sleep at the end of his ordinary short period of wakefulness, he will remain awake and stare at you stead-ily. The seal knows, exactly as well as the seal hunter knows, that no seal in this world will sleep continuously for as much as four minutes at a time. If you lie still that long, he will know you are no seal, and up will go his tail and down he will slide into the water in the twinkling of an eye. When the seal, therefore, has been watch-ing you carefully for twenty or thirty seconds, you must raise your head twelve or fifteen inches above the ice, look around seal-fashion, so that your eyes will sweep the whole circle of the hori-zon, and drop your head again upon the ice. By the time he has seen you repeat this process two or three times in the space of five or six minutes he will be convinced that you are a seal, and all his worries will be gone. From then on you can proceed more rapidly, crawling ahead while he sleeps and stopping while he remains awake, never doing anything unbecoming a seal. In this way you can crawl within five or ten yards of him if you like, and as a matter of fact I have known of expert seal hunters who under emergencies would go after a seal without any ordinary weapon and crawl so near him that they could seize him by a flipper, pull him away from his hole, and club or stab him. My Eskimo companions generally used to crawl within about fifteen or twenty yards; but I have found under ordinary circumstances that fifty yards is close enough for a man with a rifle. The animal lies on a slippery incline beside his hole, so that the shot that kills him must kill him instantly. It must shatter the brain or break the spinal cord of the neck; the slightest quiver of a muscle will send him sliding into the water and all your work will have been to no purpose.

THE JEANING OF AMERICA—
AND THE WORLD

Carin C. Quinn

Carin C. Quinn, a free-lance writer, did graduate work
in immigration and folklore.

1   This is the story of a sturdy American symbol which has now
spread throughout most of the world. The symbol is not the dollar.
It is not even Coca-Cola. It is a simple pair of pants called blue
jeans, and what the pants symbolize is what Alexis de Tocqueville
called "a manly and legitimate passion for equality. . . ." Blue jeans
are favored equally by bureaucrats and cowboys, bankers and dead-
beats; fashion designers and beer drinkers. They draw no distinc-
tions and recognize no classes; they are merely American. Yet they
are sought after almost everywhere in the world—including Russia,
where authorities recently broke up a teen-aged gang that was selling them on the black market for two hundred dollars a pair. They
have been around for a long time, and it seems likely that they will
outlive even the necktie.

2   This ubiquitous American symbol was the invention of a
Bavarian-born Jew. His name was Levi Strauss.

3   He was born in Bad Ocheim, Germany, in 1829, and during
the European political turmoil of 1848 decided to take his chances
in New York, to which his two brothers already had emigrated.
Upon arrival, Levi soon found that his two brothers had exaggerated their tales of an easy life in the land of the main chance. They
were landowners, they had told him; instead, he found them pushing needles, thread, pots, pans, ribbons, yarn, scissors, and buttons
to housewives. For two years he was a lowly peddler, hauling some
180 pounds of sundries door-to-door to eke out a marginal living.

From *American Heritage*, April–May 1978, pp. 16–18. © 1978 by American Heritage Publishing Co., Inc. Reprinted by permission from *American Heritage* (April/
May 1978).

When a married sister in San Francisco offered to pay his way West in 1850, he jumped at the opportunity, taking with him bolts of canvas he hoped to sell for tenting.

4   It was the wrong kind of canvas for that purpose, but while talking with a miner down from the mother lode, he learned that pants—sturdy pants that would stand up to the rigors of the diggings—were almost impossible to find. Opportunity beckoned. On the spot, Strauss measured the man's girth and inseam with a piece of string and, for six dollars in gold dust, had them tailored into a pair of stiff but rugged pants. The miner was delighted with the result, word got around about "those pants of Levi's," and Strauss was in business. The company has been in business ever since.

5   When Strauss ran out of canvas, he wrote his two brothers to send more. He received instead a tough, brown cotton cloth made in Nimes, France—called *serge de Nimes* and swiftly shortened to "denim" (the word "jeans" derives from *Gênes*, the French word for Genoa, where a similar cloth was produced). Almost from the first, Strauss had his cloth dyed the distinctive indigo that gave blue jeans their name, but it was not until the 1870s that he added the copper rivets which have long since become a company trademark. The rivets were the idea of a Virginia City, Nevada, tailor, Jacob W. Davis, who added them to pacify a mean-tempered miner called Alkali Ike. Alkali, the story goes, complained that the pockets of his jeans always tore when he stuffed them with ore samples and demanded that Davis do something about it. As a kind of joke, Davis took the pants to a blacksmith and had the pockets riveted; once again, the idea worked so well that word got around; in 1873 Strauss appropriated and patented the gimmick—and hired Davis as a regional manager.

6   By this time, Strauss had taken both his brothers and two brothers-in-law into the company and was ready for his third San Francisco store. Over the ensuing years the company prospered locally, and by the time of his death in 1902, Strauss had become a man of prominence in California. For three decades thereafter the business remained profitable though small, with sales largely confined to the working people of the West—cowboys, lumberjacks, railroad workers, and the like. Levi's jeans were first introduced to the East, apparently, during the dude-ranch craze of the 1930s, when vacationing Easterners returned and spread the word about

the wonderful pants with rivets. Another boost came in World War II, when blue jeans were declared an essential commodity and were sold only to people engaged in defense work. From a company with fifteen salespeople, two plants, and almost no business east of the Mississippi in 1946, the organization grew in thirty years to include a sales force of more than twenty-two thousand, with fifty plants and offices in thirty-five countries. Each year, more than 250,000,000 items of Levi's clothing are sold — including more than 83,000,000 pairs of riveted blue jeans. They have become, through marketing, word of mouth, and demonstrable reliability, the common pants of America. They can be purchased pre-washed, pre-faded, and pre-shrunk for the suitably proletarian look. They adapt themselves to any sort of idiosyncratic use; women slit them at the inseams and convert them into long skirts, men chop them off above the knees and turn them into something to be worn while challenging the surf. Decorations and ornamentations abound.

7   The pants have become a tradition, and along the way have acquired a history of their own — so much so that the company has opened a museum in San Francisco. There was, for example, the turn-of-the-century trainman who replaced a faulty coupling with a pair of jeans; the Wyoming man who used his jeans as a towrope to haul his car out of a ditch; the Californian who found several pairs in an abandoned mine, wore them, then discovered they were sixty-three years old and still as good as new and turned them over to the Smithsonian as a tribute to their toughness. And then there is the particularly terrifying story of the careless construction worker who dangled fifty-two stories above the street until rescued, his sole support the Levi's belt loop through which his rope was hooked.

Questions About "Process"

1. Does Quinn explain clearly the steps by which Levi's invention became "the common pants of America" (par. 6)? Explain, making specific reference to the text.

2. To what extent does this essay increase your knowledge of how blue jeans came to be popular?

3. Does Quinn appear to know her subject well? What is her major source of material?

Questions on Diction and Writing Techniques

1. Quinn uses "it" in sentences 3 and 4 of paragraph 1 to help achieve coherence in the paragraph. Find another example of her use of a pronoun for the same reason in that paragraph and elsewhere in the essay (see pages 34–35).

2. Define the following words and write sentences using each of them appropriately: ubiquitous (par. 2), sundries (par. 3), mother lode (par. 4), gimmick (par. 5), idiosyncratic (par. 6).

3. What is Quinn's purpose in writing the short sentence, "Opportunity beckoned" (par. 4)?

4. By what means does the writer try to convince you that blue jeans "adapt themselves to any sort of idiosyncratic use" (par. 6)?

5. What is the writer's purpose in using "for example" in paragraph 7?

6. Explain the organization of this essay by stating the function of single paragraphs or groups of paragraphs.

For Discussion, Reading, and Writing

1. "The Jeaning of America—and the World" is mainly about:

   A. how a simple pair of pants called blue jeans became a sturdy American symbol which has spread throughout most of the world.

   B. the ingenuity of Levi Strauss.

   C. the adaptability of blue jeans to any sort of idiosyncratic use.

   D. the phenomenal success of the company that Levi Strauss founded.

   E. the future of blue jeans in America—and the world.

2. Why, according to Quinn, is "a simple pair of pants called blue jeans" (par. 1) a symbol of America? Why a symbol of equality? Do you agree with her judgment? Why or why not?

3. Write a paragraph explaining how to wash, repair, patch, or cut off the legs of blue jeans.

FREEWRITING

Peter Elbow

Peter Elbow has taught at a number of colleges and has directed writing programs in universities and community groups. In this excerpt from **Writing Without Teachers** (1973), he explains a technique he recommends to improve one's ability to write.

1   The most effective way I know to improve your writing is to do freewriting exercises regularly. At least three times a week. They are sometimes called "automatic writing," "babbling," or "jabbering" exercises. The idea is simply to write for ten minutes (later on, perhaps fifteen or twenty). Don't stop for anything. Go quickly without rushing. Never stop to look back, to cross something out, to wonder how to spell something, to wonder what word or thought to use, or to think about what you are doing. If you can't think of a word or a spelling, just use a squiggle or else write, "I can't think of it." Just put down something. The easiest thing is just to put down whatever is in your mind. If you get stuck it's fine to write "I can't think what to say, I can't think what to say" as many times as you want; or repeat the last word you wrote over and over again; or anything else. The only requirement is that you *never* stop.

2   What happens to a freewriting exercise is important. It must be a piece of writing which, even if someone reads it, doesn't send

From *Writing Without Teachers* by Peter Elbow. Copyright © 1973 by Oxford University Press, Inc. Reprinted by permission.

any ripples back to you. It is like writing something and putting it in a bottle in the sea. The teacherless class helps your writing by providing maximum feedback. Freewritings help you by providing no feedback at all. When I assign one, I invite the writer to let me read it. But also tell him to keep it if he prefers. I read it quickly and make no comments at all and I do not speak with him about it. The main thing is that a freewriting must never be evaluated in any way; in fact there must be no discussion or comment at all.

₃   Here is an example of a fairly coherent exercise (sometimes they are incoherent, which is fine):

> I think I'll write what's on my mind, but the only thing on my mind right now is what to write for ten minutes. I've never done this before and I'm not prepared in any way—the sky is cloudy today, how's that? now I'm afraid I won't be able to think of what to write when I get to the end of the sentence—well, here I am at the end of the sentence—here I am again, again, again, again, at least I'm still writing—Now I ask is there some reason to be happy that I'm still writing—ah yes! Here comes the question again—What am I getting out of this? What point is there in it? It's almost obscene to always ask it but I seem to question everything that way and I was gonna say something else pertaining to that but I got so busy writing down the first part that I forgot what I was leading into. This is kind of fun oh don't stop writing—cars and trucks speeding by somewhere out the window, pens clittering across peoples' papers. The sky is still cloudy—is it symbolic that I should be mentioning it? Huh? I dunno. Maybe I should try colors, blue, red, dirty words—wait a minute—no can't do that, orange, yellow, arm tired, green pink, violet magenta lavender red brown black green—now that I can't think of any more colors—just about done—relief? maybe.

Questions About "Process"

1. What is Elbow's purpose in writing this piece?

2. Does Elbow use any technical terms that you might not be expected to understand?

3. What does "'They are sometimes called 'automatic writing,' 'babbling,' or 'jabbering' exercises" (par. 1) contribute to your understanding of the meaning of "freewriting exercise"?

4. Would you have difficulty following Elbow's instructions? Why or why not?

5. Does the inclusion of an example of freewriting help Elbow achieve his purpose? Explain.

Questions on Diction and Writing Techniques

1. Is Elbow's use of commands—"don't stop," "go quickly"— appropriate? Explain.

2. What is Elbow's purpose in writing the last sentence of paragraph 1?

3. Is this diction meaningful to you: "doesn't send any ripples back to you. It is like writing something and putting it in a bottle in the sea" (par. 2)? Why or why not?

4. How much of the success of Elbow's explanation can you attribute to its being based on personal experience?

5. What is Elbow's thesis (see pages 5-9)? Does his essay convince you to accept it as valid? Explain.

For Discussion, Reading, and Writing

1. Which of these statements, according to Elbow, are true (T), which false (F)?

   A. _____ The most effective way to improve your writing is to do freewriting exercises once in a while.

   B. _____ The point of freewriting is to rush through it as quickly as possible.

   C. _____ If you can't think of a word, just use a squiggle.

   D. _____ The only requirement of freewriting is that you never stop.

   E. _____ Lack of coherence in freewriting is fine.

2. Follow Elbow's instructions. Freewrite for ten minutes. Be prepared to comment in class about your experience.

3. Write a short essay, based on your personal experience, about how to

   Buy a used car

   Plan a party

   Apply for a summer job

   Prepare a meal

   Make a laboratory experiment

BREAD AND FACTORIES
John Hess

John Hess, coauthor of **The Taste of America**, is a syndicated columnist.

---

1   Civilization was built on grain. Western civilization used it mainly in the form of bread made of flour, water, a little leaven (yeast), and salt. For the basic loaf, anything else was an adulteration, and the perpetrator was subject to being pilloried in the marketplace.

2   When bread was well made, the staff of life asked little of the earth. All agriculture was of course organic, and manures and rotation restored the soil. The millstones were turned by people, then by beasts, then by water or wind. The ovens were heated by such fuel as came to hand.

3   Until the late industrial age, it was common knowledge that bread, like wine, varied in taste and quality with the soil and condi-

tions in which the wheat was grown. Platina, a 15th-century Vatican epicure, wrote that the best bread was made from wheat that grew on hillsides (and indeed the most delicious bread that I ever ate was in a Greek mountain village where the wheat was still sown by hand, nourished with donkey manure, cut by scythes, flailed, and stone-ground). In the mid-19th century, Frederick Law Olmsted observed that the closer he got to the new lands of the frontier, the better the bread tasted. Sylvester Graham, the prophet of whole grain, wrote

> They who have never eaten bread made of wheat recently produced by a pure virgin soil, have but a very imperfect notion of the deliciousness of good bread; such as is often to be met with in the comfortable log houses in our western country.

4   By 1837, the large millers of the Atlantic Coast were speeding up their mills and shipping tight-packed flour in barrels to all ports. Mary Hooker Cornelius in *The Young Housekeeper's Friend*, published in 1846, wrote:

> Newly ground flour which has never been packed is very superior to barrel flour, so that the people in Western New York, that land of finest wheat, say that the New England people do not know what good flour is.

5   Mrs. Cornelius was already observing the gradual abandonment of wheat-growing in the older regions along the coast. The industry settled in the Great Plains and gradually expanded into vast, single-crop, mechanized spreads. As the rich soil thinned, increasing amounts of fertilizer and herbicide and pesticide, all synthesized from natural gas and petroleum, had to be applied each year. The result is an enormous crop, a source of national wealth and power, but also a poor-tasting flour.

6   Already in Graham's time, the mills were bolting out of the wheat all of the bran and much of the germ, which would gum up and scorch if the millstones turned fast. In the next 40 years, steel shears and rollers completed the transformation of flour from a golden, fat, and nourishing food to a lifeless chalk dust. Yeast could barely live on it, so bakers added sugar. From decade to decade, cookbooks added more and more sugar to replace the rich flavor of

true flour, creating the addiction to sweetness that now afflicts the American palate. Yeast itself was often replaced by faster chemical leavens, which brought about a national scandal at the turn of the century, involving charges that the public was being poisoned and that officials were being corrupted to let it happen.

7   Great new strides were achieved in this century. Flour mills were concentrated in a few major grain centers. There they ground the wheat, employing a score of chemicals to keep it from spoiling, packaged it, and shipped it long distances to market.

8   The neighborhood baker went the way of the town mill. A dwindling number of bread factories dominated the market with heavy advertising, delivering the product in huge vans. Fuel was cheap. The new factory loaf was "improved" to its present condition of wrapped, sliced Styrofoam, dosed with fungicide to prevent mold and with polysorbates to keep it from drying. (The TV commercial for one packaged mix cries "Super-moist!" as if that were a virtue.) Permanent shelf life was achieved.

9   The most advanced bakeries now resemble oil refineries. Flour, water, a score of additives, and huge amounts of yeast, sugar, and water are mixed into a broth that ferments for an hour. More flour is then added, and the dough is extruded into pans, allowed to rise for an hour, then moved through a tunnel oven. The loaves emerge after 18 minutes, to be cooled, sliced, and wrapped.

10   They call this bread.

11   A century of complaint about the impoverishment of the staff of life has led the industry to "enrich" it by adding a few of the nutrients it has removed—only a few—and none of the rich array of earthy flavor and body that our forebears loved.

12   Clinicians recently discovered what the ancients well knew, that roughage was an important element of diet. ITT Continental Baking Company met this need with a loaf that promised added fiber. The government has insisted that the company identify the ingredient more plainly. It is sawdust. We have come to that.

Questions About "Process"

1. What is Hess's purpose in writing this essay?

2. How well does Hess know his subject? Explain, making specific reference to the text. What is the source(s) of his material?

3. Does Hess tell you simply and in sufficient detail the steps whereby bread became reduced in taste and quality?

4. Mark in your text the words by means of which he makes clear the time sequence of bread's adulteration over the years.

Questions on Diction and Writing Techniques

1. Mark in your text those words that, though new to you, you understood from their context. Define them in your own words. Compare your definitions with those in your dictionary. Look up in your dictionary any other words that are new to you. Use the words in both groups in sentences.

2. Instead of "bread factories" (par. 8), Hess might have chosen "bakeries." Why did he use the words he did?

3. How does Hess support the statement that he makes in the first sentence of paragraph 3?

4. A cause-and-effect relationship is expressed in paragraph 5. What is the cause? What is the effect?

5. With what does Hess compare today's most advanced bakeries? Why does he do this?

6. Paragraph 10 consists of a single four-word sentence. What is its effect on you? Find elsewhere in this essay another short sentence that Hess uses with the same purpose.

For Discussion, Reading, and Writing

1. Into what, according to Hess, did the mills transform flour in the second half of the nineteenth century?

2. What, according to him, are the great new strides in making bread in this century?

3. How does one contemporary baking company meet the need for roughage?

4. Write, in about one hundred words, an answer to the question, "What did the writer explain in this essay?"

WORLD'S SMARTEST TROUT
Geoffrey Norman

Geoffrey Norman is outdoors editor of **Esquire** magazine.

1   Charles Fox has spent thirty years of his life trying to save one small part of the world instead of all of it. And he has succeeded. His world is trout fishing and he has saved the Letort, though he would deny it.

2   The Letort is not even a river. It is called Letort Spring Run and it flows through Carlisle, Pennsylvania, in the southern third of that state. It is probably not accurate to say that the Letort "flows" anywhere. "Seeps" is more descriptive of what the stream does. But it is fertile. The limestone bed makes for highly alkaline water, which supports abundant insect life, which in turn supports a good population of trout. The cycle works that way as long as everything is left alone.

3   But that wasn't the case when Fox first bought property on the Letort in 1945. In those days nature was generally held in low regard. Fish and game departments, infected by their own brand of hubris, believed that trout simply couldn't make it alone and that the only way to ensure continued trout fishing was to raise fish scientifically in hatcheries before putting them in the rivers and streams. "Put and take" it was called, and some fishermen took to following the hatchery trucks on their rounds. They would help unload the fish, then quickly assemble their rods and catch as many of the bewildered hatchery trout as the law would allow. For a man like Fox, who had written books on trout fishing and who loved the dry fly almost indecently, it was too much to bear.

4   "I wanted to see if we could get back to natural reproduction in the Letort, but the fish bureaucrats just laughed at me. They

thought it was impossible and they weren't even willing to try. So I decided to do it by myself. There weren't very many property owners along the river then. I went around to all of them and proposed that we work as a group. We couldn't get any laws passed by the state, so we had to use what was on the books. We decided to use the trespass laws. We put signs up saying that it was all right to fish on the property as long as you obeyed certain regulations. If you didn't, then you would be trespassing. Then we listed the regulations: barbless hooks, no trout under ten inches, limit of four trout a day. Every year we made it a little tougher. The fish had to be bigger and you couldn't keep as many. Pretty soon we were up to fourteen-inch trout and you could only keep two.

5   "But we were also getting some incidents. We didn't have anybody in uniform patrolling the stream. State wardens only enforced the legal limits. So if you saw somebody taking more fish than we said you could, you had to get his name to report him. And he wasn't about to give you his name. You would have to wrestle him down to the ground and take his wallet away from him. What we really wanted was some help from the state."

6   But the state was not about to help Fox and his little group of property owners. When he began his project, he worried that the state would not agree to stop stocking trout in the Letort. "I was wrong on that one. When we first started posting our own regulations, one of the men from Fish and Game came to me and told me that if we went through with it, by God, he wasn't going to put another trout in the stream. He told me that we'd have to come crawling to him before he'd stock again. He actually told me, 'You're going to come crawling to me.' Can you imagine that?"

7   Reclaiming the stream was not easy. There was more to it than making the limits tougher and keeping the hatchery trucks out. "To sustain natural reproduction," Fox says, "a stream needs four things: food, cover, brood stock, and gravel. We had the first three but we didn't have any gravel."

8   So Fox began putting gravel into the stream. Trout spawn in the gravel, first making a bed by fanning the bottom with their fins. Once the eggs have been deposited and fertilized, the hens fan gravel over them for protection. The Letort's gravel had been silted over and washed downstream by the time Fox arrived on the scene.

9   Over the years, Fox has put more than one hundred tons of gravel into the Letort. With it, he has built a spawning area just below his house, and during November and December, when the big brown trout settle on these beds to spawn, people come out from town to stand along the banks and watch.

10   The fish are there every morning, and Fox is down there with them, either to watch or to fish. You can find the stream easily enough when you are in the area, and when you find it, expect to be frustrated. The Letort trout are not easily fooled. They have seen it all. I caught a fish of a pound or so one day, and the next afternoon when I went back to the same spot, I asked a young boy if he was having any luck. "No. But there was a fellow caught one here yesterday," he said. One fish from the Letort, and I was already a local legend.

11   The fish are tough and demanding, so after you have put them down with everything you try, and you have lost a fly or two on bad casts, put the rod away and walk the river. Admire the fish and the wildlife and the man-made spawning beds near the pumping station. Eventually Charles Fox will come by on some errand or another—he tends the stream every day.

12   You won't have any trouble with conversation. And you might even learn something. I always do.

Questions About "Process"

1. Did Norman make clear to you the steps that Charles Fox took to save the Letort? Explain, making specific reference to the text.

2. If you lived on a river like the Letort when Fox first bought his property, and if you had the means, could you, with the information in this essay, restore the river so that the trout could reproduce naturally in it? Explain.

Questions on Diction and Writing Techniques

1. Mark in your text those words that are new to you, but whose meaning you inferred from their context. Define them in your

own words. Compare your definitions with those in your dictionary. Look up in your dictionary any other words that are new to you. Use the words in both groups in sentences.

2. Norman's subject is ecology. Be prepared to discuss in class whether he restricted his subject sufficiently for him to be able to explain his topic to you in a short essay.

3. What does "But" (par. 3) signal to you?

4. Norman states that the Letort trout are not easily fooled. How does he explain and support this general statement?

5. Summarize this essay in a paragraph or two of not over one hundred words.

For Discussion, Reading, and Writing

1. What is "put and take"?

2. What four things does a stream need to sustain natural reproduction?

3. Be prepared to discuss in class, with apt examples, what might be the cumulative effect if each person concerned about humankind's spoiling the environment were to try to save one part of the world instead of all of it.

4. Choose a subject that you know well and might want to write about (such as one of those in the left-hand column below). Then, with the purpose of writing about how something is or was done, restrict your subject (as in the right-hand column) so that you can do justice to it in a short essay.

Cars	How a Salesman at XYZ Motors Sold Me a Used Car
Food	How I Shop for Delicatessen at a Supermarket
Nature	How a Friend Grows Potted Plants Indoors
Athletics	How Mr. Smith Coaches Left-handed Batters on Our College Baseball Team
Students	How My Roommate Gets Up in the Morning

Write the essay.

Causal Analysis

WHEN your car doesn't start on a cold morning, you wonder why, reasoning from the fact of its failure to start to a possible cause or causes: empty gas tank, frozen fuel line, run-down battery, or defective coil. You might also consider possible effects of your car's failure: being late for an appointment, missing a class, losing your job. In both instances, you would be making a causal analysis —establishing and explaining the relationship between cause and effect and between effect and cause.

We use this method of reasoning daily to get answers to everyday questions:

Why didn't Mary phone yesterday?

Why is John late?

Why does my head ache this morning?

Why is the price of food so high?

Why must I study today?

We use it to answer weightier questions:

What makes tides?

What caused World War II?

Why is logic a useful discipline?

Why did Columbus sail the Atlantic?

Why is there an energy crisis?

There are three kinds of cause: necessary, contributory, and sufficient.

A *necessary* cause *must be present* for the effect to occur but by itself cannot produce the effect. Oxygen, for example, is necessary to produce fire but by itself cannot produce fire. Other factors are needed: combustible material and ignition.

A *contributory* cause *may lead* to an effect but cannot produce it by itself. For instance: Jogging contributes to Maria's good health, but a balanced diet, daily calisthenics, and eight hours sleep a night are also important. As long as she continues to exercise regularly and eat and sleep well, Maria might give up jogging yet maintain her good health. Another example:

> In its effect on family relationships, in its facilitation of parental withdrawal from an active role in the socialization of their children, and its replacement of family rituals and special events, television has played an important role in the disintegration of the American family. But of course it has not been the only contributing factor, perhaps not even the most important one. The steadily rising divorce rate, the increase in the number of working mothers, the decline of the extended family, the breakdown of neighborhoods and communities, the growing isolation of the nuclear family — all have seriously affected the family [Marie Winn, *The Plug-In Drug: TV and the American Family*].

A *sufficient* cause *by itself* can produce an effect. A speeding bullet is sufficient to kill a deer. A bullet is not a necessary cause of a deer's death; the animal might die from other causes such as old age or starvation. Here is another example of a sufficient cause:

Malaria was for centuries a baffling plague. It was observed that persons who went out at night often developed the malady. So, on the best *post hoc* reasoning, night air was assumed to be the cause of malaria, and elaborate precautions were taken to shut it out of sleeping quarters. Some scientists, however, were skeptical of this theory. A long series of experiments eventually proved that malaria was caused by the bite of the *anopheles* mosquito. Night air entered the picture only because mosquitoes prefer to attack in the dark [Stuart Chase, *Guides to Straight Thinking*].

Since the bite of the anopheles mosquito, unlike night air, can by itself produce malaria, it is a sufficient cause.

An example of a common error that beginning writers make in causal analysis is a statement such as this:

Crime in America is caused by poverty.

Although poverty may be a contributory cause, it is not a sufficient cause. Contrast that oversimplified assertion with the more cautious

One of the causes of crime in America is poverty.

and with this judicious statement:

Most crime in America is born in environments saturated in poverty and its consequences: illness, ignorance, idleness, ugly surroundings, hopelessness. Crime incubates in places where thousands have no jobs, and those who do have the poorest jobs; where houses are old, dirty and dangerous; where people have no rights [Ramsey Clark, *Crime in America*].

Clark, in his causal analysis, is careful to qualify "crime" by saying "*most* crime" and to claim that crime is the effect not of poverty alone but of "poverty *and its consequences.*" He then specifies what these consequences are. He also makes clear that poverty is a *remote* cause, one that is distant from an effect; and that "illness, ignorance, idleness, ugly surroundings, hopelessness" are a *proximate* cause, one that is close to the effect. The diagram shows this relationship.

REMOTE CAUSE

Poverty

↓

PROXIMATE CAUSE

Illness, ignorance,
idleness, ugly surroundings,
hopelessness

↓

EFFECT

Crime

When you use causal analysis, you must avoid oversimplification and keep in mind that an effect may be the consequence of two or more causes or a chain of causes, as in this example:

> The chain of events which brought the children into the hospital began in the 1950s when the AEC started a long series of nuclear explosions at its Nevada test site in the conviction that ". . . these explosives created no immediate or long-range hazard to human health outside the proving ground." But among the radioactive particles of the fallout clouds that occasionally escaped into the surrounding territory was the isotope iodine-131. As these clouds passed over the Utah pastures, iodine-131 was deposited on the grass; being widely spread, it caused no alarming readings on out-door radiation meters. But dairy cows grazed these fields. As a result, iodine-131, generated in the mushroom cloud, drifted to Utah farms, was foraged by cows, passed to children in milk, and was gathered in high concentration in the children's thyroid glands. Here in a period of a few weeks the iodine-131 released its radiation. If sufficiently intense, such radiation passing through the thyroid cells may set off subtle changes which, though quiescent and hidden for years, eventually give rise to disease [Barry Commoner, *Science and Survival*].

Observe that a writer may use causal analysis both as a means of explaining and as a way of imposing order on material – that is, as a pattern of organization. You can see this function of causal analysis in part of a paragraph from Will Durant's *Caesar and Christ*. First comes the topic sentence:

> The political causes of decay were rooted in one fact—that increasing despotism destroyed the citizen's civic sense and dried up statesmanship at the source.

Then comes the development:

> Powerless to express his political will except by violence, the Roman lost interest in government and became absorbed in his business, his amusements, his legion, or his individual salvation. Patriotism and the pagan religion had been bound together, and now decayed. The Senate, losing ever more of its power and prestige after Pertinax, relapsed into indolence, subservience, or venality; and the last barrier fell that might have saved the state from militarism and anarchy. Local governments . . . no longer attracted first-rate men.

We might diagram the organization of this paragraph thus:

REMOTE CAUSE

Despotism

↓

PROXIMATE CAUSE

Destruction of civic
sense and statesmanship

↓

EFFECTS

1. The Romans lost interest in government.
2. Patriotism decayed.
3. The Senate weakened.
4. Local governments no longer attracted first-rate men.

Here are some points to keep in mind when you use causal analysis:

1. *Consider the available data and supporting evidence.* Like a detective seeking to solve a crime, the writer looking for causal relationships must decide on lines of inquiry and kinds of useful information. All material gathered should be analyzed with care before you assign causes.

2. *Re-examine your material for possible alternative causes and effects.* Don't let your preconceptions divert you from this task, which is necessary for success in causal analysis. Even in the case of the relationship between cigarette smoking and lung cancer, where preponderant evidence points to a correlation between the two, other causes may be contributory or sufficient causes—gypsum particles, coal dust, radiation, polluted air, carcinogens still unknown.

3. *Offer evidence to support what might otherwise be merely an assertion of a causal relationship.* Where appropriate, use facts and figures to convince your readers of the validity of your causal analysis. Statistics and the testimony of experts will often more readily convince them to accept your analysis than will your unsupported assertion that A was the cause of B or that D was the effect of C.

TEENAGERS AND BOOZE
Carl T. Rowan

Carl T. Rowan, recipient of awards for distinguished journalism,
is a well-known newspaperman and commentator on the
American scene.

1   America's young people have found a potent, sometimes addictive, and legal drug. It's called alcohol.

2   Drinking is nothing new for teen-agers. In fact, it's a kind of ritual of youth. In recent years, however, a great many youngsters from all walks of life have turned to drugs like marijuana, heroin and barbiturates. Reports coming in now from schools and national studies tell us that there's a change occurring. The newest way for kids to turn on is an old way—with alcohol.

3   Listen to these words of a high school senior in Brooklyn, as told to a reporter from *Newsweek* magazine: "A lot of us used to smoke pot, but we gave that up a year or two ago. Now my friends and I drink a lot . . . and in my book, a high is a high."

4   Why are youngsters rediscovering booze? One reason is pressure from other kids to be one of the gang. Another is the ever-present urge to act grown-up. For some, it eases the burden of problems at home or at school. And it's cheaper. You can buy a couple of six-packs of beer for the price of three joints of pot.

5   Perhaps the main reason is that parents don't seem to mind. They tolerate drinking—sometimes almost seem to encourage it. In part this may be due to the fact that parents themselves drink; in part it's because they're relieved to find that their children are "*only*" drinking, and are not involved with pot, LSD or other drugs.

6   What these parents may not realize is that alcohol is also a drug, and a potentially dangerous one. Furthermore, few are aware

just how young the drinkers are these days. The National Council
on Alcoholism reports that in 1972 the age of the youngest alcohol-
ics brought to its attention dropped from fourteen to twelve. Other
studies have found that three fourths of senior-high students have
used alcohol—an increase of 90 per cent in three years. And 56 per
cent of junior-high students have tried alcohol.

7   The Medical Council on Alcoholism warns: The potential
teen-age drinking problem should give far more cause for alarm than
drug addiction. Many schools have reacted to teen-age drinking.
They've started alcohol-education programs. But a lot of experts
feel that teen-agers are not going to stop drinking until adults do.

Questions About "Causal Analysis"

1. Where does Rowan announce the subject of his causal analysis?

2. Does Rowan amply analyze the teenage drinking problem? Explain. Can you think of a cause that he fails to mention?

3. Which of the causes that Rowan enumerates is itself an effect?

4. How does Rowan support his statement about "how young the
   drinkers are these days" (par. 6)?

Questions on Diction and Writing Techniques

1. What is Rowan's purpose in writing the short sentence, "It's
   called alcohol" (par. 1)? Find another instance in this essay of
   his using a short sentence for the same reason.

2. Why does Rowan choose to write "in fact" in paragraph 2?

3. What purpose is served by "however" in paragraph 2? What do
   "furthermore" (par. 6) and "but" (par. 7) contribute to the paragraphs in which they appear?

4. Rowan might have written the last sentence of paragraph 2 like
   this: "The newest way for kids to turn on, with alcohol, is an
   old way." Why did he write the sentence as he did?

5. Why does Rowan quote from the interview of the high school senior from Brooklyn?

6. There is a circumlocution—a roundabout expression—in the first part of the last sentence of paragraph 5. Revise that portion of the sentence to eliminate unnecessary words.

For Discussion, Reading, and Writing

1. Drinking, according to Rowan, is "a kind of ritual of youth" (par. 2). Do you agree? Why or why not?

2. Using causal analysis as your main pattern of organization, explain in a short essay why you do or do not drink alcoholic beverages.

3. Using interviews as one of your sources of material, write a short essay in which you explain why some of the people you know drink.

4. In a short essay, show by causal analysis how any person you know well has affected some aspect of your life for better or worse.

STRAIGHT-A ILLITERACY
James P. Degnan

James P. Degnan, professor of English at the University of Santa Clara in California, uses personal experience and observation as his sources of material for this essay about a widespread kind of illiteracy.

1   Despite all the current fuss and bother about the extraordinary number of ordinary illiterates who overpopulate our schools, small

From *Harper's* magazine, September 1976, pp. 37–38. Reprinted by permission of the author.

attention has been given to another kind of illiterate, an illiterate whose plight is, in many ways, more important, because he is more influential. This illiterate may, as often as not, be a university president, but he is typically a Ph.D., a successful professor and textbook author. The person to whom I refer is the straight-A illiterate, and the following is written in an attempt to give him equal time with his widely publicized counterpart.

2   The scene is my office, and I am at work, doing what must be done if one is to assist in the cure of a disease that, over the years, I have come to call straight-A illiteracy. I am interrogating, I am cross-examining, I am prying and probing for the meaning of a student's paper. The student is a college senior with a straight A average, an extremely bright, highly articulate student who has just been awarded a coveted fellowship to one of the nation's outstanding graduate schools. He and I have been at this, have been going over his paper sentence by sentence, word by word, for an hour. "The choice of exogenous variables in relation to multi-colinearity," I hear myself reading from his paper, "is contingent upon the derivations of certain multiple correlation coefficients." I pause to catch my breath. "Now that statement," I address the student—whom I shall call, allegorically, Mr. Bright—"that statement, Mr. Bright, what on earth does it mean?" Mr. Bright, his brow furrowed, tries mightily. Finally, with both of us combining our linguistic and imaginative resources, finally, after what seems another hour, we decode it. We decide exactly what it is that Mr. Bright is trying to say, what he really *wants* to say, which is: "Supply determines demand."

3   Over the past decade or so, I have known many students like him, many college seniors suffering from Bright's disease. It attacks the best minds, and gradually destroys the critical faculties, making it impossible for the sufferer to detect gibberish in his own writing or in that of others. During the years of higher education it grows worse, reaching its terminal stage, typically, when its victim receives his Ph.D. Obviously, the victim of Bright's disease is no ordinary illiterate. He would never turn in a paper with misspellings or errors in punctuation; he would never use a double negative or the word "irregardless." Nevertheless, he is illiterate, in the worst way: he is incapable of saying, in writing, simply and clearly, what he means. The ordinary illiterate—perhaps providentially protected from college and graduate school—might say: "Them people down

at the shop better stock up on what our customers need, or we ain't gonna be in business long." Not our man. Taking his cue from years of higher education, years of reading the textbooks and professional journals that are the major sources of his affliction, he writes: "The focus of concentration must rest upon objectives centered around the knowledge of customer areas so that a sophisticated awareness of those areas can serve as an entrepreneurial filter to screen what is relevant from what is irrelevant to future commitments." For writing such gibberish he is awarded straight As on his papers (both samples quoted above were taken from papers that received As), and the opportunity to move, inexorably, toward his fellowship and eventual Ph.D.

4   As I have suggested, the major cause of such illiteracy is the stuff—the textbooks and professional journals—the straight-A illiterate is forced to read during his years of higher education. He learns to write gibberish by reading it, and by being taught to admire it as profundity. If he is majoring in sociology, he must grapple with such journals as the *American Sociological Review*, journals bulging with barbarous jargon, such as "ego-integrative action orientation" and "orientation toward improvement of the gratificational-deprivation balance of the actor" (the latter of which monstrous phrases represents, to quote Malcolm Cowley, the sociologist's way of saying "the pleasure principle"). In such journals, Mr. Cowley reminds us, two things are never described as being "alike." They are "homologous" or "isomorphic." Nor are things simply "different." They are "allotropic." In such journals writers never "divide anything." They "dichotomize" or "bifurcate" things.

Questions About "Causal Analysis"

1. What is Degnan's purpose in this essay?

2. What, according to Degnan, is the major cause of straight-A illiteracy?

3. Does Degnan convince you of a clear-cut relationship between cause and effect?

4. Does he fulfill his announced purpose? Explain.

5. Explain how the organization of the material helps accomplish Degnan's causal analysis.

Questions on Diction and Writing Techniques

1. Why is it necessary for the writer to define the "straight-A illiterate" (par. 1)?

2. What methods does he use in his definition? (See pages 276–282.)

3. Write in a sentence how Degnan defines the "straight-A illiterate."

4. Define the following words and write sentences using each of them appropriately: allegorically (par. 2), gibberish (par. 3), providentially (par. 3), inexorably (par. 3).

5. Why, according to Degnan, is "the victim of Bright's disease . . . no ordinary illiterate" (par. 3)? How does he explain this idea?

6. What is the function of "Not our man" (par. 3)?

7. How does Degnan explain what he means by "barbarous jargon" (par. 4)?

8. Does Degnan's choice of "stuff" (par. 4) reveal his attitude toward his subject? Explain.

For Discussion, Reading, and Writing

1. Contrast the first paragraph with the second paragraph. Which do you prefer? Why?

> I returned, and saw under the sun, that the race is not to the swift, nor the battle to the strong, neither yet bread to the wise, nor yet riches to men of understanding, nor yet favor to men of skill; but time and chance happeneth to them all [Ecclesiastes 9:11].

> Objective consideration of contemporary phenomena compels the conclusion that success or failure in competitive activities exhibits no tendency to be commensurate with innate capacity, but that a considerable element of the unpredictable must invariably be taken into account [George Orwell, "Politics and the English Language"].

2. According to Degnan, the straight-A illiterate "may, as often as not, be a . . . textbook author" (par. 1). Bring to class an example or two of straight-A illiteracy that you have encountered in your textbooks.

3. Find a paragraph exemplifying "straight-A illiteracy" in a journal such as *American Sociological Review* or elsewhere. What is the effect on you of such writing? Rewrite the paragraph in acceptable language.

4. Making sure to clearly establish connections between causes and effects and to distinguish between necessary, contributory, and sufficient causes, write a short essay on a subject, properly restricted, such as

Inflation

Violence on TV

Poverty and Crime

What Makes Airplanes Fly

What College Has Done for Me

FROM UNHAPPY PATIENT TO ANGRY LITIGANT
Louise Lander

Louise Lander, an attorney with extensive experience with health and the law, is the author of **Defective Medicine: Risk, Anger, and the Malpractice Crisis**.

1   The medical press was triumphant; on June 1, 1976, after over a year of nothing but disaster to report on the malpractice

front, a victory had finally been scored on the side of the medical profession. A doctor sued for malpractice had had the guts to sue his patient back, and a jury in Chicago had found the patient, her husband, and her lawyers liable for "willful and wanton involvement in litigation without reasonable cause" and the lawyers also liable for legal malpractice.

2   One of the exuberant articles recording that landmark event was written by the doctor-plaintiff himself, a radiologist named Dr. Leonard Berlin, who took to the pages of the magazine *Medical Economics* to tell his story to his fellow physicians. That story does vindicate Dr. Berlin in the sense of making his medical and legal innocence convincing. But, more to the point, his story inadvertently reveals what motivates patients to take the extraordinary step of hauling their doctors into court.

3   Mrs. Harriet Nathan injured the little finger of her right hand while playing tennis and went to the emergency room of a suburban Chicago hospital, where Dr. Berlin had an office in the radiology department. He supervised the taking of a series of X rays, diagnosed the injury as a dislocated joint, and sent her on to see an orthopedic surgeon named Dr. William Meltzer. Dr. Meltzer's treatment, which apparently followed generally accepted orthopedic procedures, nonetheless failed to completely relieve the pain and deformity of the injured finger.

4   Five months after the injury, Dr. Berlin relates in his article, he was telephoned by Mrs. Nathan's husband, Gilbert, who told him that "his wife's finger was deformed and still painful, and that they were both angry at Dr. Meltzer. The orthopedist, Gilbert said, had not taken Harriet's injury seriously, and had been rude and abrupt. Gilbert intimated that they might bring a malpractice suit against Meltzer, and that if they did, they'd 'have to involve' me, too."

5   What Mr. Nathan said over the telephone reflects precisely those elements of a doctor-patient encounter that are indispensable to a patient's decision to bring a malpractice suit. Actual medical malpractice — professional performance that demonstrably falls below professional standards — is not indispensable. Some sort of injury or unhappy outcome *is* indispensable; here no one disputed that Mrs. Nathan's hand was permanently deformed, and we may assume that it gave her pain and made certain activities difficult or

impossible. But the injury, the objective sign that something went wrong, is not sufficient; injury by itself does not translate into the intense hostility that a lawsuit expresses. That objective sign must be joined with the subjective state of being angry—here, the Nathans' natural reaction to their perception that Dr. Meltzer "had not taken Harriet's injury seriously, and had been rude and abrupt."

6 The anger is usually provoked by a doctor, although increasingly hospitals are finding themselves defending lawsuits that reflect anger at their employees. And the rules of the legal game may dictate a lawyer's tactical decision to sue others beyond the original object of the patient's anger, as Dr. Berlin discovered when he was drawn into the net cast by the Nathans' anger at his colleague.

7 We should therefore grant what many doctors, for their own purposes, loudly insist on: that there is a difference between actual malpractice and a malpractice suit or claim. The injured patient, as he attempts to cope with pain, disappointment, and economic loss, rarely has the means of knowing at the outset whether negligence, fluke, or some unalterable body process is responsible for his misery. Conversely, there can be malpractice in the sense of medical negligence without its causing injury. A doctor, for example, may stupidly make an erroneous diagnosis, but the treatment he prescribes for what he thinks is wrong may turn out to be substantially the same as the treatment for what is really wrong.

8 While malpractice as a legal concept declares both injury and negligence to be equally indispensable, malpractice claims as a social disruption declare the supremacy of injury. There are, moreover, a few statistical indications that the number of injuries is enormously larger than the number of malpractice claims, a disproportion that confirms the notion that although a medical injury is necessary to a malpractice claim, it is not by itself sufficient to trigger one.

9 A federally sponsored interview study conducted in 1972, for example, found that over 40 percent of the sample had had some "negative medical care experience"; of those, over 85 percent believed that some kind of medical failure had been involved, but only 8 percent had even considered seeking legal advice.

10 Another statistical tidbit implies that what a medical or hospital observer perceives as an injury differs from what a patient perceives as an injury worth filing a claim about. A risk-management program of an unnamed hospital association generated about

700,000 reports of unusual incidents (such as equipment failures, anesthesia deaths, slips and falls) over a 20-year period. During the same period, only 15,000 malpractice claims were filed, and 85 percent of these involved incidents that were *not* reported.

11   What distinguishes injuries that do not become malpractice claims from injuries that do, and what even colors the patient's perception of what constitutes an injury, is the subjective element of patient anger; without anger, an act as hostile as a lawsuit, particularly against as well-established an authority figure as a physician, is impossible to contemplate. Thus, while for legal purposes medical malpractice represents the intersection of patient injury and physician negligence, for social purposes a malpractice claim represents the intersection of patient injury and patient anger.

Questions About "Causal Analysis"

1. According to Lander, is "actual malpractice" a necessary cause for a patient to sue a doctor for malpractice? Explain.

2. Is injury of some sort a sufficient cause for a suit for medical malpractice? Explain.

3. Is the anger of a patient provoked by a doctor a necessary, contributory, or sufficient cause for malpractice? Explain.

4. In the chain of causality that ends with a malpractice suit, what is the proximate cause, what the remote cause?

Questions on Diction and Writing Techniques

1. Mark in your text those words that are new to you, but whose meaning you inferred from their context. Define them in your own words. Compare your definitions with those in your dictionary. Look up in your dictionary any other words that are new to you. Use the words in both groups in sentences.

2. Match each italicized word in Column A with its synonym in Column B.

Column A	Column B
had the *guts*	unreserved
wanton involvement	suggested
exuberant articles	understanding
Gilbert *intimated*	unjustifiable
the patient's *perception*	courage

3. What is the function of "But" in paragraph 2? Find another paragraph in this essay where that word serves the same purpose. Find two or more other examples of Lander's use of transition words.

4. Instead of the second sentence of paragraph 3, Lander might have written: "He supervised the taking of a series of X rays. He diagnosed the injury as a dislocated joint. He sent her to see an orthopedic surgeon named William Meltzer." Which version do you prefer? Why?

For Discussion, Reading, and Writing

1. Which of these statements, according to Lander, are true (T), which false (F):

   A. _____ The medical press was triumphant because a radiologist, Dr. Leonard Berlin, had the guts to sue his own patient.

   B. _____ Dr. Berlin claimed in his lawsuit that the patient, Mrs. Nathan, had a deformed and painful finger because she had not followed his advice.

   C. _____ Mr. and Mrs. Nathan were angry because Dr. Meltzer, to whom Dr. Berlin referred her, had not taken her injury seriously.

   D. _____ Actual medical malpractice is not indispensable to a patient's decision to bring a malpractice suit.

   E. _____ Injury by itself can translate into the intense hostility that a lawsuit expresses.

   F. _____ The anger of patients that is translated into malpractice suits is usually provoked by overcrowded hospitals.

   G. _____ A malpractice claim represents the intersection of patient injury and patient anger.

2. In the book from which this piece is taken, Lander writes, "The surgeon is concerned with thingness—to the state of the wound, not the state of the person." Do you agree? If the statement is in accord with your judgment of medical doctors, write a paragraph or two of causal analysis explaining why, in your view, the statement is valid.

3. Explain in a short essay the effect on you of any person you now know or once knew well.

DISCOVERY OF A FATHER
Sherwood Anderson

Sherwood Anderson (1876–1941) was an American novelist and short-story writer.

1   You hear it said that fathers want their sons to be what they feel they cannot themselves be, but I tell you it also works the other way. A boy wants something very special from his father. I know that as a small boy I wanted my father to be a certain thing he was not. I wanted him to be a proud, silent, dignified father. When I was with other boys and he passed along the street, I wanted to feel a flow of pride: "There he is. That is my father."

2   But he wasn't such a one. He couldn't be. It seemed to me then that he was always showing off. Let's say someone in our town had got up a show. They were always doing it. The druggist would be in it, the shoe-store clerk, the horse doctor, and a lot of women and girls. My father would manage to get the chief comedy part. It was, let's say, a Civil War play and he was a comic Irish soldier. He had to do the most absurd things. They thought he was funny, but I didn't.

₃   I thought he was terrible. I didn't see how mother could stand it. She even laughed with the others. Maybe I would have laughed if it hadn't been my father.

₄   Or there was a parade, the Fourth of July or Decoration Day. He'd be in that, too, right at the front of it, as Grand Marshal or something, on a white horse hired from a livery stable.

₅   He couldn't ride for shucks. He fell off the horse and everyone hooted with laughter, but he didn't care. He even seemed to like it. I remember once when he had done something ridiculous, and right out on Main Street, too. I was with some other boys and they were laughing and shouting at him and he was shouting back and having as good a time as they were. I ran down an alley back of some stores and there in the Presbyterian Church sheds I had a good long cry.

₆   Or I would be in bed at night and father would come home a little lit up and bring some men with him. He was a man who was never alone. Before he went broke, running a harness shop, there were always a lot of men loafing in the shop. He went broke, of course, because he gave too much credit. He couldn't refuse it and I thought he was a fool. I had got to hating him.

₇   There'd be men I didn't think would want to be fooling around with him. There might even be the superintendent of our schools and a quiet man who ran the hardware store. Once I remember there was a white-haired man who was a cashier of the bank. It was a wonder to me they'd want to be seen with such a windbag. That's what I thought he was. I know now what it was that attracted them. It was because life in our town, as in all small towns, was at times pretty dull and he livened it up. He made them laugh. He could tell stories. He'd even get them to singing.

₈   If they didn't come to our house they'd go off, say at night, to where there was a grassy place by a creek. They'd cook food there and drink beer and sit about listening to his stories.

₉   He was always telling stories about himself. He'd say this or that wonderful thing had happened to him. It might be something that made him look like a fool. He didn't care.

₁₀   If an Irishman came to our house, right away father would say he was Irish. He'd tell what county in Ireland he was born in. He'd tell things that happened there when he was a boy. He'd make it seem so real that, if I hadn't known he was born in southern Ohio, I'd have believed him myself.

11 If it was a Scotchman the same thing happened. He'd get a burr into his speech. Or he was a German or a Swede. He'd be anything the other man was. I think they all knew he was lying, but they seemed to like him just the same. As a boy that was what I couldn't understand.

12 And there was mother. How could she stand it? I wanted to ask but never did. She was not the kind you asked such questions.

13 I'd be upstairs in my bed, in my room above the porch, and father would be telling some of his tales. A lot of father's stories were about the Civil War. To hear him tell it he'd been in about every battle. He'd known Grant, Sherman, Sheridan and I don't know how many others. He'd been particularly intimate with General Grant so that when Grant went East, to take charge of all the armies, he took father along.

14 "I was an orderly at headquarters and Sim Grant said to me, 'Irve,' he said, 'I'm going to take you along with me.'"

15 It seems he and Grant used to slip off sometimes and have a quiet drink together. That's what my father said. He'd tell about the day Lee surrendered and how, when the great moment came, they couldn't find Grant.

16 "You know," my father said, "about General Grant's book, his memoirs. You've read of how he said he had a headache and how, when he got word that Lee was ready to call it quits, he was suddenly and miraculously cured.

17 "Huh," said father. "He was in the woods with me.

18 "I was in there with my back against a tree. I was pretty well corned. I had got hold of a bottle of pretty good stuff.

19 "They were looking for Grant. He had got off his horse and come into the woods. He found me. He was covered with mud.

20 "I had the bottle in my hand. What'd I care? The war was over. I knew we had them licked."

21 My father said that he was the one who told Grant about Lee. An orderly riding by had told him, because the orderly knew how thick he was with Grant. Grant was embarrassed.

22 "But, Irve, look at me. I'm all covered with mud," he said to father.

₂₃ And then, my father said, he and Grant decided to have a drink together. They took a couple of shots and then, because he didn't want Grant to show up potted before the immaculate Lee, he smashed the bottle against the tree.

₂₄ "Sim Grant's dead now and I wouldn't want it to get out on him," my father said.

₂₅ That's just one of the kind of things he'd tell. Of course the men knew he was lying, but they seemed to like it just the same.

₂₆ When we got broke, down and out, do you think he ever brought anything home? Not he. If there wasn't anything to eat in the house, he'd go off visiting around at farmhouses. They all wanted him. Sometimes he'd stay away for weeks, mother working to keep us fed, and then home he'd come bringing, let's say, a ham. He'd got it from some farmer friend. He'd slap it on the table in the kitchen. "You bet I'm going to see that my kids have something to eat," he'd say, and mother would just stand smiling at him. She'd never say a word about all the weeks and months he'd been away, not leaving us a cent for food. Once I heard her speaking to a woman in our street. Maybe the woman had dared to sympathize with her. "Oh," she said, "it's all right. He isn't ever dull like most of the men in this street. Life is never dull when my man is about."

₂₇ But often I was filled with bitterness, and sometimes I wished he wasn't my father. I'd even invent another man as my father. To protect my mother I'd make up stories of a secret marriage that for some strange reason never got known. As though some man, say the president of a railroad company or maybe a Congressman, had married my mother, thinking his wife was dead and then it turned out she wasn't.

₂₈ So they had to hush it up but I got born just the same. I wasn't really the son of my father. Somewhere in the world there was a very dignified, quite wonderful man who was really my father. I even made myself half believe these fancies.

₂₉ And then there came a certain night. He'd been off somewhere for two or three weeks. He found me alone in the house, reading by the kitchen table.

₃₀ It had been raining and he was very wet. He sat and looked at me for a long time, not saying a word. I was startled, for there was on his face the saddest look I had ever seen. He sat for a time, his clothes dripping. Then he got up.

31 "Come on with me," he said.

32 I got up and went with him out of the house. I was filled with wonder but I wasn't afraid. We went along a dirt road that led down into a valley, about a mile out of town, where there was a pond. We walked in silence. The man who was always talking had stopped his talking.

33 I didn't know what was up and had the queer feeling that I was with a stranger. I don't know whether my father intended it so. I don't think he did.

34 The pond was quite large. It was still raining hard and there were flashes of lightning followed by thunder. We were on a grassy bank at the pond's edge when my father spoke, and in the darkness and rain his voice sounded strange.

35 "Take off your clothes," he said. Still filled with wonder, I began to undress. There was a flash of lightning and I saw that he was already naked.

36 Naked, we went into the pond. Taking my hand he pulled me in. It may be that I was too frightened, too full of a feeling of strangeness, to speak. Before that night my father had never seemed to pay any attention to me.

37 "And what is he up to now?" I kept asking myself. I did not swim very well, but he put my hand on his shoulder and struck out into the darkness.

38 He was a man with big shoulders, a powerful swimmer. In the darkness I could feel the movement of his muscles. We swam to the far edge of the pond and then back to where we had left our clothes. The rain continued and the wind blew. Sometimes my father swam on his back and when he did he took my hand in his large powerful one and moved it over so that it rested always on his shoulder. Sometimes there would be a flash of lightning and I could see his face quite clearly.

39 It was as it was earlier, in the kitchen, a face filled with sadness. There would be the momentary glimpse of his face and then again the darkness, the wind and the rain. In me there was a feeling I had never known before.

40 It was a feeling of closeness. It was something strange. It was as though there were only we two in the world. It was as though I had been jerked suddenly out of myself, out of my world of the schoolboy, out of a world in which I was ashamed of my father.

41   He had become blood of my blood; he the strong swimmer and I the boy clinging to him in the darkness. We swam in silence and in silence we dressed in our wet clothes, and went home.

42   There was a lamp lighted in the kitchen and when we came in, the water dripping from us, there was my mother. She smiled at us. I remember that she called us "boys."

43   "What have you boys been up to?" she asked, but my father did not answer. As he had begun the evening's experience with me in silence, so he ended it. He turned and looked at me. Then he went, I thought, with a new and strange dignity out of the room.

44   I climbed the stairs to my own room, undressed in the darkness and got into bed. I couldn't sleep and did not want to sleep. For the first time I knew that I was the son of my father. He was a story teller as I was to be. It may be that I even laughed a little softly there in the darkness. If I did, I laughed knowing that I would never again be wanting another father.

Questions About "Causal Analysis"

1. Does Anderson's causal analysis make clear to you why his father was not the kind of person he wanted him to be? Explain, making specific reference to the text.

2. Anderson says that he often was filled with bitterness. Is this an effect, or cause, or both? Explain.

3. Explain in detail the cause of Anderson's ultimate feeling of closeness to his father.

Questions on Diction and Writing Techniques

1. Mark in your text those words that are new to you, but whose meaning you inferred from their context. Define them in your own words. Compare your definitions with those in your dictionary. Look up in your dictionary any other words that are new to you. Use the words in both groups in sentences.

2. Anderson uses words like "shucks." Find four or five more ex-

amples of colloquial words and slang. Are such words appropriate? Why or why not? Among these words is "windbag." What does Anderson's choice of this and similar words tell you about his attitude toward his father in the first two thirds of the essay?

3. What is the point of view in this essay? Is it that of Anderson as a small boy, as a grownup, or as a combination of both? Support your answer with specific reference to the text.

4. What does "But" (paragraph 2) signal to you? Find another example of Anderson's use of the word for a similar reason.

5. Anderson organizes his material in two main groups. Which are the paragraphs in each? How does he signal to you that a change in his description of his father is coming?

6. Anderson uses patterns of organization other than cause and effect. Name them and point out examples of each.

7. Making ample reference to the text, comment on Anderson's use of narration and of description to achieve his expository purpose.

For Discussion, Reading, and Writing

1. Does Anderson, in this essay, seem close to you or distant? Why?

2. Did you at any point have difficulty in reading or understanding Anderson's writing? If so, why?

3. In a paragraph of not over one hundred words, write a summary of this essay.

4. Does any statement that Anderson makes about his father, or any incident he reports, parallel your experience with a parent or guardian? If so, write a paragraph or two on the subject, using causal analysis to explain any generalization you make about him or her.

5. Write a letter (one that you might want to mail) to a parent, teacher, friend, lover, or anyone else, in which you explain what effect his or her behavior has had on you.

Argumentation

ARGUMENTATION, as the term is generally used, is that type of composition in which writers seek to convince others to agree with their point of view or to agree and to take a recommended action. It uses the expository techniques we have been considering and thus is somewhat like exposition. The purpose of argumentation, however, differs from that of exposition. The purpose of exposition is to explain merely. The purpose of argumentation is to explain in order to assure agreement, or to effect a change in point of view, or to influence an action.

You probably know more about argumentation than you realize. If you have ever written to a parent or guardian asking for an increase in your allowance, to a police department urging it to cancel a parking ticket, to the admissions officer of a school requesting the speedy acceptance of your application for admission, to the personnel office of a business applying for a job, or to a lover hoping to patch up a quarrel—you have written argumentation. In other words, you proposed, giving reasons based on relevant facts and ideas, that someone accept your views on a given subject. Such a proposal, in argumentation, is termed a proposition—a statement for or against something that can be shown to be true or false.

Among the meanings of the term "argument" is disagreement, as in "The short-tempered Jack Jones had a violent argument with his landlord." However, the word is used here in another sense: the expression of opinions for or against some point, as in "Attorney Mary Smith presented a convincing argument in favor of the dismissal of the charges against her client."

An argument cannot be about a fact—a statement about what is known and can be verified. That Abe Lincoln was the sixteenth president of the United States; that the headquarters of the United Nations is in New York City; that the chemical composition of water is H_2O; that sailboats are propelled by wind; that bronze is an alloy consisting essentially of copper and tin—these are certifiable statements about what is known. They leave nothing to argue about.

Nor can an argument be about matters of taste. Your preference for strawberry rather than vanilla ice cream; for chino trousers rather than blue jeans; for hiking rather than mountain climbing—these, insofar as they indicate merely what you happen to like, do not permit the presentation of reasons for or against them.

Here are a few suggestions to help you write a convincing argumentative essay:

1. *Get your facts.* If your readers are to believe what you say, you must know what you're writing about. Study your subject and marshal all the information about it that you can. Except when you rely heavily on personal experience and observation, cite established facts wherever possible and when appropriate introduce the testimony of recognized authorities to support your propositions. Your college library, with its general and specialized books of reference, probably has all the data you need. Among the many other useful sources of information are agencies of the United States Government and the United States Government Printing Office, various departments of state and city governments, chambers of commerce, and innumerable business and professional associations.

2. *Formulate your position.* After you have assembled your material, restrict your subject to what you can argue strongly

with the information on hand and within the limits of the
length of your essay. Then decide what your position, pro
or con, on your proposition will be. (See Part One, pages
2–6, for a discussion of restricting broad subjects.)

3. *State your proposition clearly.* The proposition "General
Grant was a greater man than General Lee" is vague because it sets up no criteria for measuring greatness. "Grant
was a greater general than Lee" would be an improvement
because there are standards by which skills as the commander of a large military force may be measured. Better
still would be "Grant was a greater strategist than Lee" because it sets up military strategy as a criterion and also
thereby limits the proposition. Unless you define your
terms carefully (see "Definition," pages 276–282), you cannot arrange the evidence needed to prove the truth of your
proposition.

4. *Be aware of your audience.* Ask yourself: Who am I trying to
convince? What are their views, their biases, their likely
responses?

5. *Write the introduction.* In a short introductory paragraph,
announce your subject and the position you are taking on
it, as in this example:

Today's inflation cannot be controlled by voluntary means. The
only way to curb it is with wage and price controls.

Notice that this introductory paragraph sets up the organization of the rest of the essay. The first part of the body of
the essay might show why voluntary controls are ineffective; the second part might tell why wage and price controls
would be effective. Announcing the division of a subject in
an introductory paragraph is a sound tactic and helps the
writer to organize the parts of the argument.

6. *Build an argument.* Argue your position on a proposition by
advancing individual points in support of it—that is, by presenting the reasons for your judgment. These should be
stated as minor propositions to which the rule of clarity ap-

plies. Let's consider possible minor propositions in support of this proposition: Final grades in college should be abolished:

(a) Final grades encourage students to learn by rote.
(b) Grades lead to harmful competition among students.
(c) Low grades discourage some students.
(d) There are adequate substitutes for final grades: (1) pass-fail system of grading; and (2) teachers' written comments on students' performance.

Each minor proposition would have to be supported with proof consisting of sound, relevant evidence.

7. *Test your argument.* The simplest way to test your position on a proposition is to evaluate its opposite. It is thus useful, while planning the first draft of your essay, to list points in opposition to the minor propositions you intend to advance, matching them point by point. In the case of the minor propositions just listed, this is how you might arrange your material:

Pro	*Con*
(a) Final grades encourage students to learn by rote.	Many students need prodding. Final exams serve this purpose.
(b) Grades lead to harmful competition among students.	In our society, competition is inevitable and useful.
(c) Low grades discourage some students.	Those students would probably be discouraged anyway.
(d) There are adequate substitutes for final grades: (1) pass-fail system of grading; and (2) teachers' written comments on students' performance.	These are poor substitutes; they are not precise enough. Both might be a disadvantage to students competing for the sometimes limited openings in graduate schools.

An evaluation of points opposed to your own will also help you appraise your own.

8. *Be honest and fair to opposing views.* If your credibility is questioned by your readers, you will find it more difficult than you otherwise might to get them to believe anything you

say. You will find it less difficult if you treat opposing views fairly. Your readers are more likely to find you honest and trustworthy if you consider dispassionately and in sufficient detail positions opposed to your own. This is where making a list of points in opposition to yours will come in handy.

9. *Restate your position.* Especially in argumentation, your essay will profit from a concluding paragraph that summarizes and emphasizes what you have said in the body of the essay in support of your thesis.

Regardless of how many of these suggestions the limitation of a short essay permits you to adopt, there is one bit of advice you would do well always to keep in mind: The burden of proof is on you. An *assertion*—a statement without support or reason—will fail to convince your audience that your position is valid. Presume that your readers will be both alert and skeptical. Don't overestimate their credulity. It is *your* job to convince *them* by giving support or reasons for every statement you make.

HOW TO KEEP AIR CLEAN
Sydney J. Harris

Sydney J. Harris is an award-winning journalist and author of the syndicated column "Strictly Personal."

1   Some months ago, while doing research on the general subject of pollution, I learned how dumb I had been all my life about something as common and familiar—and essential—as air.

2   In my ignorance, I had always thought that "fresh air" was infinitely available to us. I had imagined that the dirty air around us

somehow escaped into the stratosphere, and that new air kept coming in—much as it does when we open a window after a party.

3   This, of course, is not true, and you would imagine that a grown man with a decent education would know this as a matter of course. What *is* true is that we live in a kind of spaceship called the earth, and only a limited amount of air is *forever* available to us.

4   The "walls" of our spaceship enclose what is called the "troposphere," which extends about seven miles up. This is all the air that is available to us. We must use it over and over again for infinity, just as if we were in a sealed room for the lifetime of the earth.

5   No fresh air comes in, and no polluted air escapes. Moreover, no dirt or poisons are ever "destroyed"—they remain in the air, in different forms, or settle on the earth as "particulates." And the more we burn, the more we replace good air with bad.

6   Once contaminated, this thin layer of air surrounding the earth cannot be cleansed again. We can clean materials, we can even clean water, but we cannot clean the air. There is nowhere else for the dirt and poisons to go—we cannot open a window in the troposphere and clear out the stale and noxious atmosphere we are creating.

7   Perhaps every child in sixth grade and above knows this; but I doubt that one adult in a hundred is aware of this basic physical fact. Most of us imagine, as I did, that winds sweep away the gases and debris in the air, taking them far out into the solar system and replacing them with new air.

8   The United States alone is discharging *130 million tons of pollutants a year* into the atmosphere, from factories, heating systems, incinerators, automobiles and airplanes, power plants and public buildings. What is frightening is not so much the death and illness, corrosion and decay they are responsible for—as the fact that this is an *irreversible process*. The air will never be cleaner than it is now.

9   And this is why *prevention*—immediate, drastic and far-reaching—is our only hope for the future. We cannot undo what we have done. We cannot restore the atmosphere to the purity it had before the Industrial Revolution. But we can, and must, halt the contamination before our spaceship suffocates from its own foul discharges.

Questions About "Argumentation"

1. What is Harris' proposal?

2. What is his main argument? Does he have any other(s)? Explain.

3. Does Harris' argument convince you to accept his proposition as valid? Explain.

Questions on Diction and Writing Techniques

1. Does Harris make clear to you what he had in mind about the infinite availability of fresh air? If so, how? Where, elsewhere in this essay, does he explain an idea in a similar manner?

2. What does "moreover" (par. 5) signal to you?

3. What is Harris' purpose in writing "but" in paragraph 7? Find another instance of his choice of this word for a similar reason.

4. How much of this essay is exposition?

For Discussion, Reading, and Writing

1. What, according to Harris, is frightening about the discharge of impurities into the air?

2. What, according to Harris, is our only hope for the future?

3. "Spaceship" is an often-used metaphor for Earth. Why, in view of the information in this essay, is it apt?

4. Write a paragraph or two in which you argue for the prevention or curtailment in your home town of any one kind of discharge that now pollutes the air there.

5. Write a letter (one that you perhaps would like to mail) to any newspaper (including that on your campus), in which you argue for or against a view expressed in one of its editorials.

EITHER/OR
C. P. Snow

C. P. Snow (1905–1980), English physicist and author, had a varied career that included holding several important positions in the British government and writing novels.

1   Scientists *know* certain things in a fashion more immediate and more certain than those who don't know what science is. Unless we are abnormally weak or abnormally wicked men, this knowledge is bound to shape our actions. Most of us are timid, but to an extent, knowledge gives us guts. Perhaps it can give us guts strong enough for the jobs in hand.

2   Let me take the most obvious example. All physical scientists *know* that it is astonishingly easy to make plutonium. We know this, not as a journalistic fact at second hand, but as a fact in our own experience. We can work out the number of scientific and engineering personnel it needs for a nation-state to equip itself with fission and fusion bombs. We *know* that for a dozen or more states, it would take perhaps only five years, perhaps less. Even the best informed of us always exaggerate these periods.

3   This we know with the certainty of—what shall I call it—engineering truth. We also, most of us, are familiar with statistics and the nature of odds. We know, with the certainty of established truth, that if enough of these weapons are made by enough different states, some of them are going to blow up—through accident or folly or madness. But the numbers do not matter; what does matter is the nature of statistical fact.

4   All this *we know*. We know it in a more direct sense than any politician can know it, because it comes from our direct experience. It is part of our minds. Are we going to let it happen?

₅   All this we *know*. It throws upon scientists a direct and formal responsibility. It is not enough to say scientists have a responsibility as citizens. They have a much greater one than that, and one different in kind. For scientists have a moral imperative to say what they know. It is going to make them unpopular in their own nation-states. It may do worse than make them unpopular. That doesn't matter. Or at least, it does matter to you and me, but it must not count in the face of the risks.

₆   For we genuinely know the risks. We are faced with an either / or and we haven't much time. The *either* is acceptance of a restriction of nuclear armaments. This is going to begin, just as a token, with an agreement on the stopping of nuclear tests. The United States is not going to get the 99.9 percent "security" that [it] has been asking for. This is unobtainable, though there are other bargains that the United States could probably obtain. I am not going to conceal from you that this course involves certain risks. They are quite obvious, and no honest man is going to blink at them. That is the *either*. The *or* is not a risk but a certainty. It is this: There is no agreement on tests. The nuclear arms race between the United States and the Soviet Union not only continues but accelerates. Other countries join in. Within, at the most, six years, China and six other states have a stock of nuclear bombs. Within, at the most, 10 years, some of those bombs are going off. I am saying this as responsibly as I can. *That* is the certainty. On the one side, therefore, we have a finite risk. On the other side, we have a certainty of disaster. Between a wish and a certainty, a sane man does not hesitate.

₇   It is the plain duty of scientists to explain the either / or. It is a duty which seems to me to live in the moral nature of the scientific activity itself.

Questions About "Argumentation"

1. What is the idea whose acceptance Snow proposes in this essay?

2. What argument(s) does he offer in support of the idea?

3. There is a kind of faulty argument called the either-or fallacy, so

called because it assumes only two options although there may be more. Does Snow commit this error? Explain.

4. How many times does Snow write *"know"*? What is his argumentative purpose in repeating the word?

5. "Between a wish and a certainty, a *sane man* [italics added] does not hesitate" (par. 6). Is this an example of name-calling? (See "Getting Personal: *Ad Hominem,*" pages 287–288.) Explain.

Questions on Diction and Writing Techniques

1. Mark in your text those words that are new to you, but whose meaning you inferred from their context. Define them in your own words. Compare your definitions with those in your dictionary. Look up in your dictionary any other words that are new to you. Use the words in both groups in sentences.

2. What transitional words does Snow choose to help achieve coherence within his paragraph?

For Discussion, Reading, and Writing

1. Which of these statements, according to Snow, are true (T), which false (F)?

   A. _____ Scientists are more truthful than journalists.

   B. _____ A scientist's knowledge is more dependable than that of politicians.

   C. _____ Scientists should concern themselves with facts and nothing else.

   D. _____ There is no certainty that if the nuclear arms race continues some nuclear bombs will go off.

   E. _____ Some scientists recommend bomb shelters as a solution to the nuclear bomb problem.

2. Write a paragraph or two in which you argue for or against any point Snow makes.

3. Increasingly, major U.S. corporations are placing advertisements in national and local newspapers (often on the Op-Ed page) and in magazines, taking stands on public issues. Find one such ad that interests you and write a short essay for or against the point of view it expresses.

"I WANTS TO GO TO THE PROSE"
Suzanne Britt Jordan

Suzanne Britt Jordan teaches English at North Carolina State University at Raleigh.

---

1   I'm tired—and have been for quite a while. In fact, I think I can pinpoint the exact minute at which I first felt the weariness begin. I had been teaching for three years at a community college. I had, for quite a while, overlooked ignorance, dismissed arrogance, championed fairness, emphasized motivation, boosted egos and tolerated laziness. I was, in short, the classic modern educator.

2   One day a student, Marylou Simmons, dropped by my office. She had not completed a single assignment and had missed perhaps 50 per cent of her classes. Her writing, what little I saw of it, was illogical, grammatically incorrect and sloppy. "Can I help you, Marylou?" I said cheerily, ever the understanding and forgiving teacher. Her lip began to tremble; her eyes grew teary. It seemed she had been having trouble with her boyfriend. "I'm sorry, but what can *I* do?" I asked. Suddenly all business, Marylou said, "Since I've been so unhappy, I thought you might want to just give me a D or an Incomplete on the course." She smiled encouragingly, even confi-

dently. That's when the weariness set in, the moment at which I turned into a flaming conservative in matters educational. Whatever Marylou's troubles, I suddenly saw that I was not the cause, nor was I about to be the solution.

₃ When I read about declining SAT scores, the "functional illiteracy" of our students, the namby-pamby courses, the army of child psychologists, reading aides, educational liaisons, starry-eyed administrators and bungling fools who people our school systems, my heart sinks. Public schools abide mediocre students; put 18-year-olds, who can't decide what to wear in the morning, into independent study programs; excuse every absence under the sun, and counsel, counsel, counsel. A youngster in my own school system got into a knife fight and was expelled—for one week. I noticed in the paper that bus drivers regularly see riders smoking marijuana and drinking wine on the bus at, for God's sake, 8 in the morning. I could go on, but the public knows well enough the effects of a system of education gone awry.

₄ Consider for a moment what caused the mess. A few years ago people began demanding their rights. Fair enough. They wanted equal education under the law. I'm for it. Social consciousness was born. Right on. Now, enter the big wrong turn, the one that sent our schools into never-never land. We suddenly, naïvely, believed that by offering equal opportunities we could (1) make everybody happy, (2) make everybody well-adjusted, (3) forgive everybody who failed, and (4) expect gratitude to boot. When students were surly, uncooperative, whiny and apathetic, educators decided they themselves didn't know how to teach. So they made it easier on the poor, disadvantaged victims of broken homes, the misfits, the unloved. Well and good. But the catch to such lofty theories is evident. Poverty, ignorance and just plain orneriness will always abound. We look for every reason in the world for the declining test scores of our children, except for stupidity and laziness.

₅ I'm perfectly aware that I sound like an old curmudgeon and it frightens me more than it offends you. But I have accepted what educators can't seem to face. The function of schools, their first and primary obligation, is not to probe tender psyches, to feed and clothe the homeless, nor to be the papa and mama a kid never had. The job is to teach.

The teacher's job is to know his subject, inside out, backward, forward and every which way. Nothing unnerves a student more than to have a teacher who doesn't know his or her stuff. Incompetence they cannot abide. Neither can I.

7   Before educators lost their way and tried to diversify by getting into the business of molding human beings, a teacher was, ideally, someone who knew a certain body of information and conveyed it. Period. Remember crochety old Miss Dinwiddie, who could recite 40 lines of the "Aeneid" at a clip? Picture Mr. Wassleheimer, who could give a zero to a cheating student without pausing in his lecture on frog dissection. Every student knew that it wasn't wise to mess around with a teacher who had the subject down cold. They were the teachers we once despised and later admired.

8   I want them back, those fearsome, awe-inspiring experts. I want them back because they knew what a school was for and didn't waste any time getting on with the task at hand. They were hard, even at times unjust, but when they were through, we knew those multiplication tables blindfolded with both trembling hands tied behind our backs.

9   Before the schoolmasters and the administrators change, they will have to shake off the guilt, the simpering, apologetic smiles and the Freudian theories. Which is crueler? Flunking a kid who has flunked or passing a kid who has flunked? Which teaches more about the realities of life? Which, in fact, shows more respect for the child as a human being?

10   Just today I talked to a big blond bruiser of a football player who wants to learn the basics of grammar. I didn't tell him it was too late. You see, he was a very, very good football player, so good that he never failed a course in high school. He had written on a weekly theme, "I wants to go to the prose and come fames." He may become a pro, may even become famous, but he will probably never read a good book, write a coherent letter or read a story to his children. I will, however, flunk him if he does not learn the material in the course. My job means too much to me to sacrifice my standards and turn soft. Suppose that every time my student played football badly, the coach said it was "just a game." Suppose the coach allowed him to drink booze, stay up all night, eat poorly and play sloppily. My student would be summarily dismissed from the team or the team would lose the game. So it goes with academic courses.

11   The young people are interested, I think, in taking their knocks, just as adults must take theirs. Students deserve a fair chance, and, failing to take advantage of that chance, a straightforward dismissal. It has been said that government must guarantee equal opportunity, not equal results. I like that. Through the theoretical fog that has clouded our perceptions and blanketed our minds, we know what is equitable and right. Mother put it another way. She always said, "Life is real; life is earnest." Incidentally, she taught me Latin and never gave me air in a jug. I had to breathe on my own. So do we all.

Questions About "Argumentation"

1. What statement does Jordan affirm in this essay?

2. Is the anecdote of Marylou Simmons valid as an argument in favor of Jordan's position? Explain. Is paragraph 10?

3. To better understand what Jordan is saying in this essay, write a summary of it in a paragraph of 100 words or less. Explain in a paragraph whether Jordan convinces you of the validity of her position.

Questions on Diction and Writing Techniques

1. Mark in your text those words that are new to you, but whose meaning you inferred from their context. Define them in your own words. Compare your definitions with those in your dictionary. Look up in your dictionary any other words that are new to you. Use the words in both groups in sentences.

2. Does Jordan make clear to you what she means by "the classic modern educator"? Explain.

3. Underline the sentence in paragraph 1 that exemplifies Jordan's use of coordination. What is the advantage of combining similar grammatical elements in a series as Jordan does in that sentence?

4. Underline the three three-word sentences in this essay. What is their effect?

5. Find four sentence fragments in this essay. Rewrite each to make it a complete sentence. Which versions do you prefer? Why?

For Discussion, Reading, and Writing

1. When did the weariness Jordan talks about set in?

2. What was "the big wrong turn" (par. 4)?

3. What is it, according to Jordan, that educators nowadays can't seem to face?

4. The main idea of this essay is (circle one):

   A. When giving a student a grade, teachers should take into account his or her personal problems.

   B. Public schools abide mediocre students.

   C. The job of teachers is to teach.

   D. Flunking a kid who has flunked is not cruel.

   E. Government must guarantee equal opportunity, not equal results.

5. Write a paragraph arguing for or against any idea Jordan expresses in this essay.

6. State in a declarative sentence what you consider to be the characteristic(s) of an ideal teacher. Write a paragraph or two to convince someone to agree with your opinion.

WHO KILLED BENNY PARET?
Norman Cousins

Norman Cousins was for many years the editor of **Saturday Review**. This essay appeared there on May 5, 1962, soon after the notorious Emile Griffith–Benny Paret welterweight championship prize fight.

1   Sometime about 1935 or 1936 I had an interview with Mike Jacobs, the prize-fight promoter. I was a fledgling newspaper reporter at that time; my beat was education, but during the vacation season I found myself on varied assignments, all the way from ship news to sports reporting. In this way I found myself sitting opposite the most powerful figure in the boxing world.

2   There was nothing spectacular in Mr. Jacobs's manner or appearance; but when he spoke about prize fights, he was no longer a bland little man but a colossus who sounded the way Napoleon must have sounded when he reviewed a battle. You knew you were listening to Number One. His saying something made it true.

3   We discussed what to him was the only important element in successful promoting—how to please the crowd. So far as he was concerned, there was no mystery in it. You put killers in the ring and the people filled your arena. You hire boxing artists—men who are adroit at feinting, parrying, weaving, jabbing, and dancing, but who don't pack dynamite in their fists—and you wind up counting your empty seats. So you searched for the killers and sluggers and maulers—fellows who could hit with the force of a baseball bat.

4   I asked Mr. Jacobs if he was speaking literally when he said people came out to see the killer.

5   "They don't come out to see a tea party," he said evenly. "They come out to see the knockout. They come out to see a man hurt. If they think anything else, they're kidding themselves."

6   Recently a young man by the name of Benny Paret was killed in the ring. The killing was seen by millions; it was on television. In the twelfth round he was hit hard in the head several times, went down, was counted out, and never came out of the coma.

7   The Paret fight produced a flurry of investigations. Governor Rockefeller was shocked by what happened and appointed a committee to assess the responsibility. The New York State Boxing Commission decided to find out what was wrong. The District Attorney's office expressed its concern. One question that was solemnly studied in all three probes concerned the action of the referee. Did he act in time to stop the fight? Another question had to do with the role of the examining doctors who certified the physical fitness of the fighters before the bout. Still another question involved Mr. Paret's manager; did he rush his boy into the fight without adequate time to recuperate from the previous one?

8   In short, the investigators looked into every possible cause except the real one. Benny Paret was killed because the human fist delivers enough impact, when directed against the head, to produce a massive hemorrhage in the brain. The human brain is the most delicate and complex mechanism in all creation. It has a lacework of millions of highly fragile nerve connections. Nature attempts to protect this exquisitely intricate machinery by encasing it in a hard shell. Fortunately, the shell is thick enough to withstand a great deal of pounding. Nature, however, can protect man against everything except man himself. Not every blow to the head will kill a man—but there is always the risk of concussion and damage to the brain. A prize fighter may be able to survive even repeated brain concussions and go on fighting, but the damage to his brain may be permanent.

9   In any event, it is futile to investigate the referee's role and seek to determine whether he should have intervened to stop the fight earlier. This is not where the primary responsibility lies. The primary responsibility lies with the people who pay to see a man hurt. The referee who stops a fight too soon from the crowd's viewpoint can expect to be booed. The crowd wants the knockout; it wants to see a man stretched out on the canvas. This is the supreme moment in boxing. It is nonsense to talk about prize fighting as a test of boxing skills. No crowd was ever brought to its feet screaming and cheering at the sight of two men beautifully dodging

and weaving out of each other's jabs. The time the crowd comes alive is when a man is hit hard over the heart or the head, when his mouthpiece flies out, when blood squirts out of his nose or eyes, when he wobbles under the attack and his pursuer continues to smash at him with poleax impact.

10   Don't blame it on the referee. Don't even blame it on the fight managers. Put the blame where it belongs—on the prevailing mores that regard prize fighting as a perfectly proper enterprise and vehicle of entertainment. No one doubts that many people enjoy prize fighting and will miss it if it should be thrown out. And that is precisely the point.

Questions About "Argumentation"

1. What is Cousins' purpose in this essay?

2. What conclusion does he reach about the death of Benny Paret?

3. Does he sufficiently explain his view of the cause of Paret's death to convince you to accept it as valid? Explain.

Questions on Diction and Writing Techniques

1. What is the derivation of "colossus" (par. 2)? How is the word related to "colossal," "Colosseum," and "coliseum"?

2. What is Cousins' purpose in writing: "pack dynamite in their fists" (par. 3), "hit with the force of a baseball bat" (par. 3), "smash at him with poleax impact" (par. 9)?

3. In paragraph 9 Cousins, using different verbs, might have written "when his mouthpiece *falls* out, when blood *comes* out of his nose or eyes, when he *falters* under the attack." Which version do you prefer? Why?

4. What is the topic sentence of paragraph 9? Is the paragraph unified (see pages 24–27)?

5. Define "mores" (par. 10) and write a sentence using it appropriately.

6. Comment on whether paragraph 10 performs well the function of a concluding paragraph (see pages 30–31).

7. Explain the purpose and the effect of the writer's use of the interview as a source of material.

8. Explain how Cousins' organization contributes to the convincingness of his essay.

For Discussion, Reading, and Writing

1. Fill the blanks in this passage from memory to make it intelligible:

   Don't blame it on the _____. Don't even blame it on the _____ managers. Put the blame where it belongs – on the prevailing mores that regard prize fighting as a perfectly proper enterprise and vehicle of _____. No one doubts that many people enjoy prize fighting and will _____ it if it should be _____ out. And that is precisely the point.

   Compare your words with those in paragraph 10.

2. Would Cousins have explained his subject more convincingly if, in paragraph 6, he had used vivid language as, for example, Mailer did in "The Death of Benny Paret" (pages 85–87)? Why or why not? If your answer is Yes, rewrite the paragraph. Be prepared to discuss, in class, description as a means of affecting the reader's attitude toward a subject.

3. Write an argumentative essay on any subject that interests you, incorporating information gathered in one or more interviews with fellow students, teachers, or any other persons (you may be able to borrow a tape recorder from the audiovisual department of your college).

4. Find in any newspaper under "Help Wanted" an ad that seeks to fill a position that you might qualify for, and might indeed like to have. Write a letter giving convincing reasons why you should be given the job.

Glossary

Active Voice and Passive Voice: A verb may be active—Betsy *blew* the whistle—or passive—The whistle *was blown* by Betsy—depending on whether the subject in a sentence is the actor or the recipient of the act mentioned in the verb.

Allusion: A passing reference to a literary or historical figure or event: "Language must be protected not only by poets but by the saving remnant of people who care—even though, as the flood rises, their role may be nearer *Canute*'s than *Noah*'s." (Douglas Bush, "Polluting Our Language")

Argumentation: See pp. 366–370.

Causal Analysis: See pp. 342–347.

Cause and Effect: See pp. 342–347.

Chronological Order: In a paragraph or essay, the placement of material in temporal sequence.

Circumlocution: A roundabout expression: *due to the fact that* (instead of *because*); *at that point in time* (instead of *then*); *for the simple reason that* (instead of *because*); *in the event that* (instead of *if*).

Cliché: An expression that is stale and ineffective because of overuse: *cool as a cucumber*; *strong as an ox*.

Coherence: The cohesiveness of the sentences in a paragraph and of the paragraphs in an essay. Also, the mechanical means of holding together sentences or paragraphs. It is not to be confused with *unity*, a term that refers to content.

Comparison and Contrast: See pp. 258–262.

Concluding Paragraph: A paragraph that sums up, evaluates, or draws a conclusion from the rest of the essay.

Connotation and Denotation: The *connotation* of a word is its associated or implied meaning, as opposed to its *denotation*, its definition. Beer may be *defined* as an alcoholic beverage brewed by fermentation from cereals. It may *connote* relaxation, good fellowship, well-being, and other feelings and thoughts, depending on one's associations.

Coordination: A technique for connecting similar grammatical elements in a sentence by combining them either into pairs—*Mary* and *Jane* played *ping pong* and *tennis*—or in a series—After graduation, Bill *took a vacation, got a job,* and *went to work.*

Deduction: See *Induction and Deduction.*

Denotation: See *Connotation and Denotation.*

Density, of a sentence: The amount of information or meaning a sentence contains.

Derivation: The origin or history of a word.

Description: See pp. 193–197.

Dialogue: Conversation between two or more persons.

Diary and Journal: Each is a daily or frequently-made record of personal experiences. See pp. 134–137.

Diction: Choice of words.

Distance: A term used figuratively to indicate how personal or impersonal writing is, i.e., how close the writer appears to be to the reader.

Effect: See *Cause and Effect.*

Essay: A short prose composition on a restricted subject.

Exposition: See pp. 213–216.

Extended Definition: See p. 279.

Fable: A brief story told to teach a moral.

Figure of Speech: Expressive use of language, such as *simile* or *metaphor.*

General and Specific Words: General words include all of a group or class—*fruit, firearms, teacher.* Specific words refer to individual things —*apple, pistol, Professor Anna Smith.* See p. 76.

Illustration: See pp. 236–240.

Imagery: The nonliteral, expressive use of language. The term is synonymous with *Figure of Speech.*

Implied Thesis: See *Thesis and Implied Thesis.*

Induction and Deduction: Induction is a method of reasoning that proceeds from facts to a generalization. Deduction is a method of reasoning that moves from the general to the particular.

Inference: The process of deriving a conclusion from known fact. Also, the conclusion so derived.

Informal Essay: An essay whose purpose is not obviously serious.

Introductory Paragraph: The first paragraph of an essay, designed to announce its dominant idea, to attract the reader's attention, or to do both.

Inversion: The transposition from its normal place of an element in a sentence; for example, *He arrived home at two in the morning* (normal order); *At two in the morning he arrived home* (inverted order).

Irony: The use of words to express a meaning opposite to their apparent meaning, as in the statement, "He's a fine guy," made about a scoundrel. This is called *verbal irony* and is distinguished from *irony of situation,* which exists when the result of an effort is the opposite of what was intended or expected: A student of average accomplishment attends an all-night party, takes a final exam, and gets an A+.

Jargon: Obscure and pretentious language, often marked by long and highly abstract words.

Journal: See *Diary and Journal.*

Loose and Periodic Sentences: See p. 56.

Metaphor: A *figure of speech* in which an implied comparison represents that one thing *is* an unlike thing: "It is the East, and Juliet is the sun!" [*Romeo and Juliet*].

Mixed Metaphor: The combination in a sentence of two or more *metaphors* that evoke inconsistent images. Example: When the chips were down, Governor Jones called for a quarterback sneak.

Modification: A technique for increasing the *density* of a sentence by describing or by limiting or particularizing meaning. See pp. 50–52.

Narration: See pp. 168–172.

Paradox: An attention-getting device consisting of a statement that, although seemingly contradictory or absurd, may be true: "It is possible to get an education at a university" [Lincoln Steffens, *Autobiography*].

Paragraph: A unit of composition, generally consisting of two or more sentences, that develops a single idea.

Parallel Construction: The repetition of sentence elements that have the same grammatical function and form: *I came, I saw, I conquered.*

Passive Voice: See *Active and Passive Voice.*

Periodic Sentence: See p. 56.

Persona: The personality one reveals in one's writing.

Personification: The attribution of human qualities to abstractions or things.

Point of View: See p. 172.

Process: See pp. 323–326.

Pronoun Reference: The use of a pronoun or pronouns in a sentence to refer to a noun in a previous sentence or paragraph.

Sensory Diction: Words that refer to the experiences of the sense of hearing (*crunch, hiss, plop, rustle, scream, squeak*), of taste (*acidic, chocolaty, salty, sour, sugary, tart*), of touch (*fiery, freezing, hard, hot, smooth, soft*), of sight (*cloudy, glossy, polished, shiny, smoky, sweaty*), and of smell (*aromatic, moldy, odorous, perfumed, putrid, reeking*).

Sentence: A unit of composition that expresses a complete thought and that generally consists of at least one main clause.

Sentence Fragment: A word or group of words that is not a complete sentence, but nonetheless is punctuated as a sentence: He stayed home from school. *Even though he felt fine.*

Sentence Variety: The combination of successive sentences of different structures, lengths, and word orders, often with the purpose of avoiding monotony in a paragraph.

Simile: A *figure of speech* in which an expressed comparison is made between two unlike things, generally introduced by *as* or *like:* "What a piece of work is man . . . in action how like an angel, in apprehension how like a god" [Shakespeare, *Hamlet*]; "I wandered lonely as a cloud" [Wordsworth].

Slang: Very informal language—*cool cat, no sweat, far out, rip-off, zonked, quack.*

Specific Language: See *General and Specific Language.*

Standard Sentence: See *Loose and Periodic Sentence.*

Subject: What an essay is about. A subject may be broad or restricted. A broad subject, unlike a restricted subject, is one that is too general for a writer to handle in an essay of a given length. See p. 2.

Subordination: A technique for increasing the amount of information that a sentence contains. See p. 52.

Symbol: Something that is itself and also stands for something else: The Stars and Stripes is a *symbol* of the United States.

Thesis and Implied Thesis: A *thesis* is a statement (sometimes called a thesis statement), often in one sentence, that summarizes the main idea of an essay. An *implied thesis* is one that is not expressed in so many words, but is suggested by the contents of an essay.

Tone: The attitude of the writer toward the reader and toward the subject. In a way, it is like tone of voice; we say of a speaker, "Her tone of voice was angry" or "He spoke in a subdued tone." Compare the tone in these sentences: "Would you please move your car out of the way?"; "Get that goddam jalopy the hell out of there!"

Topic: A *subject* sufficiently restricted for a writer to be able to explain it to his or her readers in an *essay* of a given length.

Topic Sentence: The sentence in a paragraph that expresses the main idea of the paragraph.

Transitional Words and Phrases: Words and phrases used to indicate a relationship between consecutive sentences in order to add a thought (*in addition, also, again, furthermore*), to introduce an illustration (*for example, for instance, to illustrate, thus*), to indicate a conclusion or result (*in conclusion, to sum up, as a result, consequently, accordingly*), or to qualify or contrast (*however, but, still, nevertheless, on the other hand*).

Unity: Consistency of material in an essay or paragraph.

Voice: Aside from meaning the form of a verb, as in *active* and *passive voice*, the term means the unique personality that a writer reveals in his or her writing.

Index of

Terms, Authors,

and Titles

Words, 74–85
  abstract and concrete, 78
  ambiguous and vague, 75
  needless, 84
  specific and general, 76–77
  subordinating, 53
  temporal, 25, 33
  transition, 33, 261

  use of imagery, 78–79
  useless, 83, 84
World's Smartest Trout (Norman),
  338–340
Wright, Richard, 112

Yumbo (Ward), 173–174

ABOUT THE AUTHOR

Morton A. Miller, since graduating from Columbia College in 1935, has had a varied career as a World War II combat photographer, a producer of educational films, a playwright, a general contractor, a land developer, and, since 1969, a teacher. Out of his experience with teaching composition in colleges and with writing occasional essays for journals this text has evolved.